MW01519891

The Volcanoes Of Kilauea And Mauna Loa On The Island Of Hawaii: Their Variously Recorded History To The Present Time, Volume 2, Issues 1-4...

William Tufts Brigham

Nabu Public Domain Reprints:

You are holding a reproduction of an original work published before 1923 that is in the public domain in the United States of America, and possibly other countries. You may freely copy and distribute this work as no entity (individual or corporate) has a copyright on the body of the work. This book may contain prior copyright references, and library stamps (as most of these works were scanned from library copies). These have been scanned and retained as part of the historical artifact.

This book may have occasional imperfections such as missing or blurred pages, poor pictures, errant marks, etc. that were either part of the original artifact, or were introduced by the scanning process. We believe this work is culturally important, and despite the imperfections, have elected to bring it back into print as part of our continuing commitment to the preservation of printed works worldwide. We appreciate your understanding of the imperfections in the preservation process, and hope you enjoy this valuable book.

THE VOLCANOES

OF

KILAUEA AND MAUNA LOA

ON THE

ISLAND OF HAWAII

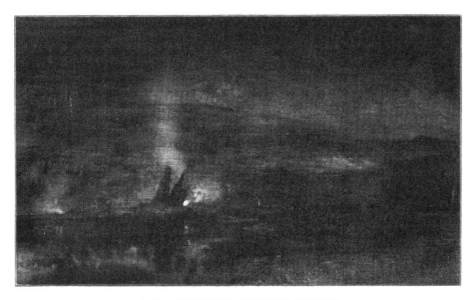

THEIR VARIOUSLY RECORDED HISTORY
TO THE PRESENT TIME

By WILLIAM T. BRIGHAM, A.M., Sc.D. (Columbia).

MEMOIRS OF THE BERNICE PAUAHI BISHOP MUSEUM
Vol. II.   No. 4.

HONOLULU, H. I.
BISHOP MUSEUM PRESS.
1909

THE SCRIPPS INSTITUTION
OF OCEANOGRAPHY
OF THE
UNIVERSITY OF CALIFORNIA
LAJOLLA, CALIF.

GIFT OF
T. WAYLAND VAUGHAN

11469

050
13375

LIBRARY
SCRIPPS INSTITUTION
OF OCEANOGRAPHY
UNIVERSITY OF CALIFORNIA
LA JOLLA, CALIFORNIA

11469

LIST OF PLATES.

Halemaumau, 1880. Furneaux. *Frontispiece.*
XLI. Views of Lava Fall and Its Work.
XLII. Descent into Halemaumau.
XLIII. Three Sentinels and Flow near Little Beggar.
W. T. B.
XLIV. Two Views of Halemaumau.
XLV. Cone in Halemaumau. Pool Below Rim.
XLVI. Drawn Lava from Fall. W. T. B.
XLVII. Mass of Aa, Natural Size. W. T. B.
XLVIII. Cave Stalagmite, Slender Form. W. T. B.
XLIX. Cave Stalagmite, Thick. W. T. B.
L. Pool with Raised Walls. Silva.
LI. Pool of Halemaumau from Below, 1894.
LII. Pool in Halemaumau. 1894.
LIII. South Lake and Island.

LIV. Cone in Halemaumau.
LV. Cone in Halemaumau.
LVI. Cone in Halemaumau.
LVII. The Empty Pit.
LVIII. On the Brink of the Pit.
LIX. General View of Halemaumau.
LX. Dana Lake with Fountains.
LXI. South Lake.
LXII. Floating Islands.
LXIII. A Flow of Aa.
LXIV. Source of Flow of 1880-81.
LXV. A Crack in the Floor of Kilauea. J. J. Williams.
LXVI. Kilauea in 1896. Howard Hitchcock.
LXVII. Mokuaweoweo in 1896. Howard Hitchcock.

Of the photographs, some were taken by J. J. Williams, others are from negatives purchased by him. Those from photographs by the author bear his initials

---

ILLUSTRATIONS.

		PAGE
	Map of Hawaii Showing Lava Flows	3
1.	Old Flow West of Kilauea	4
2.	Limu from Kilauea, 1789	5
3.	Pots on Wailuku near Hilo	6
4.	Mauna Kea from Waiakea, Hilo. Perkins	6
5.	Cinder Cones on Mauna Kea	7
6.	Pool on Mauna Kea, August, 1889	7
7.	Summit of Hualalai from East	8
8.	Pit Crater on Hualalai, 1889	9
9.	Blow-hole on Hualalai, 1889	11
10.	Hualalai from Mauna Loa (9000 ft.)	12
11.	Mauna Loa from Top of Hualalai	13
12.	Breaking Camp, Hualalai, 1889	15
13.	Mauna Loa from Kilauea, 7 A.M.	18
14.	Halemaumau in 1888. Furneaux	20
15.	Pele's Hair from Kilauea	21
16.	Form of Less Fusible Lava	21
17.	Rope Lava	22
18.	Driblet under Lava Fall	22
19.	Sectional Impression of Rope Lava	24
20.	Palagonite from Diamond Head	25
21.	Stony Cellular Lava	25
22.	Lava with Cylindrical Cells	25
23.	Vase Made from Molten Lava	26
24.	Black Volcanic Sand	26
25.	Basaltic Prisms in Wailuku Gorge	27
26.	Halemaumau Smoking	28
27.	Stalactites from Cave near Hilo	30
28.	Stalagmites from a Cave in Kilauea	31
29.	Blow-hole Specimen	32

		PAGE
30.	Fragmentary Lava	34
31.	On the Old Trail to Kilauea	35
32.	Section on Road North of Kilauea	37
33.	Uwekahuna from Volcano House	38
34.	Cracks at Ponahohoa. Ellis	39
35.	Kilauea as Seen by Ellis	40
36.	Ellis' View of Kilauea. Polyn. Researches	41
37.	Dampier's Kilauea in 1825	44
38.	Malden's Plan of Kilauea in 1825	45
39.	Kilauea iki, Showing Lava Streams	47
40.	Kilauea, by Parker & Chase. Dana	48
41.	Wall on North of Kilauea	49
42.	Map of Source of 1840 Eruption	51
43.	Lava Around Trees in Puna. Henshaw	53
44.	Kilauea in 1841. Wilkes	55
45.	Kilauea in 1841. Drayton	56
46.	Diagram in the Coan Letter	58
47.	Lyman's Plan of Kilauea in 1846	59
48.	Lyman's Revised Plan	60
49.	Survey of Mokuaweoweo, 1841. Wilkes	64
50.	The Cathedral from West and Northwest	75
51.	Fountain, Feb. 6 and 7, 1859	76
52.	Fountains Feb. 10, 1859	77
53.	North End of Kilauea	80
54.	Northern Sulphur Bank in 1889	81
55.	Fumarole with Sulphur Crystals	82
56.	Kilauea in 1864. Perry	83
57.	Floor with Spatters	84
58.	Bottom of Previous Fragment	85
59.	Survey of Kilauea, 1865. Brigham	87

(iii)

		PAGE
60.	Kilauea iki	89
61.	Fragment of Flow of 1862	90
62.	Keanakakoi in 1889	91
63.	Craters at Kapoho, Puna	95
64.	Crater Makaopuhi in Puna	96
65.	Kapoho Craters	98
66.	Green Pool, Puna	99
67.	Warm Spring, Puna	100
68.	Earthquake Ruins, 1868	103
69.	Kilauea After Eruption, 1868	107
70.	Lydgate's Survey of Kilauea, 1874	120
71.	Crater of Kilauea	121
72.	Mokuaweoweo. W. W. Hall	122
73.	Lydgate's Mokuaweoweo	123
74.	Kilauea in December, 1874	124
75.	Kilauea in February, 1875	129
76.	Crack in Floor of Kilauea, 1877	131
77.	Sketch of Halemaumau, Jan. 1880	133
78.	An Improved Volcano House. Williams	134
79.	Kilauea in 1880. Furneaux	135
80.	Northward from Southeast Lake	137
81.	Diagram of Elevation	138
82.	Halemaumau from Kau Bank, 1880	140
83.	Lava Spring	141
84.	Bath on Sulphur Bank, 1880. Silva	142
85.	Mokuaweoweo Plan	144
86.	Halemaumau in 1880. Furneaux	147
87.	Diagram, Source of Flow, 1880	148
88.	View of the Source. Furneaux	149
89.	Lava Stream in a forest. Furneaux	150
90.	Waterspout on the flow of 1881. Furneaux	152
91.	Flow of 1881 near Hilo. Furneaux	153
92.	Eruption from Kawaihae Bay. Furneaux	155
93.	Little Beggar in 1889	157
94.	Government Survey of Mokuaweoweo	159
95.	Halemaumau After Eruption of 1886	163
96.	Source of Eruption of 1887. Furneaux	165
97.	Course of Flow of 1887. Furneaux	166
98.	End of Flow of 1887. Furneaux	166
99.	Survey of Halemaumau, July, 1888	170
100.	Spatter Cone in Kilauea, 1889	172
101.	Lava Fall North of Halemaumau	172
		PAGE
102.	Under East Wall of Kilauea	173
103.	Pile of Crusts North of Halemaumau	173
104.	Crack in Bed or Kilauea	174
105.	Floor of Kilauea, 1890	175
106.	About Halemaumau, 1890	176
107.	Halemaumau After the Downfall	177
108.	Cracks on the Brink of the Pit	179
109.	New Portion of Volcano House	180
110.	Halemaumau in October, 1891	181
111.	Dodge's Survey of Halemaumau, 1892	182
112.	Dodge's Survey from V. H. Register	183
113.	Section of Halemaumau, 1892	184
114.	Bishop's Plan of the Lakes	185
115.	Comparative Sections	186
116.	Section of Halemaumau, July, 1894	187
117.	Outline of Island in Lake	189
118.	Dodge's Survey of Halemaumau, '94	190
119.	Dodge's Survey: another copy	191
120.	Friedländer's Mokuaweoweo in 1896	193
121.	Friedländer's Mokuaweoweo by Night	194
122.	Map of Mokuaweoweo, 1896	195
123.	Map of Halemaumau	197
124.	Hitchcock's View of Eruption	199
125.	Eruption of Mokuaweoweo by Day	201
126.	Eruption of Mokuaweoweo by Night	201
127.	Map of Eruption	203
128.	Camp on Mauna Loa, 1905. Pope	204
129.	Halemaumau in December, 1906	205
130.	Western Wall of Mokuaweoweo. Pope	206
131.	Eastern Wall of Mokuaweoweo. Pope	207
132.	Moving Mass of Aa in 1907. Perkins	208
133.	Front of Aa Flow, 1907. Perkins	208
134.	Thurston's Plan of Fire Pool	209
135.	Biart's Plan of Fire Lake	209
136.	Halemaumau, August, 1908. Perkins	210
137.	Surface of Lava by Night. Perkins	211
138.	Surface of Lava by Night. Perkins	211
139.	Halemaumau from Northwest. Perkins	213
140.	Halemaumau Before the Break. Thrum	214
141.	Halemaumau, August, 1909. Reed	215
142.	Section of Fire Pit. Baldwin	217
143.	Lydgate's Survey of Halemaumau	219

INDEX

	PAGE
Aa	4, 16, 77, 96
Alexander, Mauna Loa in 1885	158
Analysis of stalactites	32
Analyses of lavas	33
Ancient walls of Kilauea	49
Anderson, Kilauea in 1909	218
Andrews, Mauna Loa in 1843	63
Augite	23, 29
Baldwin, plan of Kilauea in 1908	217
Baker, Mauna Loa in 1880-81	148, 171
Mauna Loa in 1885	157
Basalt, character of Hawaiian	23
prismatic	24
Bishop, Mauna Loa in 1868	104
plan of Kilauea	184
Black sand	27, 74
Blow-hole on Hualalai	11
Brigham, Hualalai in 1864	9
Hualalai in 1889	13
Kilauea in 1864	80
in 1865	88
in 1880	134
Mauna Loa in 1864	15
Mauna Loa in 1880	19, 143
Byron, Kilauea in 1825	44
Carbonic acid	29
Caves in lava	92, 97, 99
Cathedral cone	75, 88
Centrifugal motion of lava in Kilauea	86
Challenger Expedition, Kilauea in 1875	129
Chase and Parker, Kilauea in 1838	47
Chlorine	29
Chronological history of the eruptions of Kilauea and Mauna Loa	36
Cinder cones of Mauna Kea	5, 27
Clinkstone	24
Coan, Kilauea in 1840	50
in 1842	57
in 1844, 1846	58
in 1847, 1848	61
in 1849-1854	62
in 1855	68
in 1856-1863	74, 75
in 1868	117
in 1869	119
Mauna Loa in 1843	64
in 1849, 1851, 1852	65
in 1855	68
in 1856	71
in 1868	114
in 1875, 1877	127
in 1880	146
Coan, Kilauea in 1881	151
earthquake of 1868	112
tidal wave of 1868	113
landslide of 1868	114
Cross, Kilauea in 1902	200
Dana, Kilauea in 1840	55
Dana Lake	169, 184
Deaths from eruptions	14, 38
from land slide and tidal wave	109, 118
Dibble, eruption of 1789	38
Dodge, surveys of Kilauea	169, 186, 189
Dolerite	23
Dome in Kilauea	60-62, 138, 222
Douglas, Kilauea in 1834	47
Mauna Loa in 1837	63
Earthquakes of 1868	101
of 1887	165, 167
Electric action on lava	33
currents in the lava	93
Elevation of Kilauea dome	60-62, 137
Ellis, Hualalai	9, 12
Kilauea in 1823	40, 41
Emerson, Kilauea in 1886	162
Erosion of lava flows by the sea	4
Ferrous oxide	29
Flames in Kilauea	86, 139
Floating islands in lava	178, 188, 189
Flow of 1801	8, 14
of 1823	40
of 1823	100
of 1840	51
of 1843	64
of 1852	65
of 1855	68
of 1859	75
of 1868	101
of 1880-1881	147
of 1887	165
of 1899	196
of 1907	206
Forms of lava	23-34
Frear, Kilauea in 1894	189
Friedländer, Mauna Loa in 1896	27, 192
Fumaroles	27, 81, 169
Furneaux' paintings	19, 139, 148, 155, 167, 171
Gases from volcanoes	27, 139
Gibson, Kilauea, 1895	130
Goodrich, Kilauea in 1832	46
Green, on vapors from Kilauea	28
Mauna Loa in 1859	78
Mauna Loa in 1873	126
Mauna Loa in 1875	127

PAGE

Green Lake 97
Halemaumau 46, 49, 97
Halema'uma'u 97
Hall, Mauna Loa in 1873 122
Haskell, Mauna Loa 75
Hillebrand, Kilauea in 1868 106
    earthquake of 1868 106-110
    flow of 1868 111
History of eruptions, chronological 36
Hitchcock, C. H., Prof., Mauna Loa and Kilauea
    in 1883 156
Hitchcock, D. H., Mauna Loa in 1881 149
Hitchcock, D. Howard, paintings 73, 186, 192
Hualalai, flow of 1801 .... 8, 14
    ascent by Menzies 8
    ascents by Ellis, Mann and Brigham 9
Hydrochloric acid 29
Hydrogen 28
Ingalls, Mauna Loa in 1899 196
Judd, escape at Kilauea in 1841 57
Kahuku eruption of 1868 .... 111, 114
Keanakakoi 90, 91, 132
Kilauea in 1789 36
    in 1823 .... 40, 100
    in 1824 42
    in 1825 43
    in 1829 46
    in 1832 .... 24, 46
    in 1834, 1838 47
    in 1839 49
    in 1840 50
    in 1841 56
    in 1842 57
    in 1844, 1846 58
    in 1847, 1848 61
    in 1849-1854 62
    in 1855 68
    in 1856-1863 .... 74, 75
    in 1864 80
    in 1865 88
    in 1868 .... 100, 106, 113, 117
    in 1869-1872 119
    in 1873 119-123
    in 1874 123-125
    in 1875 128
    in 1876-1877 130
    in 1878-1879 132
    in 1880 .... 133, 146
    in 1881 155
    in 1882-1884 156
    in 1885 157
    in 1886 162
    in 1887 168
    in 1888 .... 168, 171
    in 1889 174
    in 1890 .... 174, 175
    in 1891 175
    in 1892 184
    in 1893, 1894 185
    in 1895 192
    in 1896 .... 192, 196
    in 1897 196

PAGE

Kilauea in 1898, 1900 199
    in 1901, 1902 200
    in 1903 .... 202, 204
    in 1904, 1905 204
    in 1906 206
    in 1907 209
    in 1908 .... 209, 217
    in 1909 217
Kilauea iki 42, 46, 89, 108, 130
Kinnear's sketch of Halemaumau 133
Kinney and Fuller, flow of 1852 67
Landslide, 1868 .... 102, 109, 114
Lava analyses 33
    of Hawaii, character 23
    forms 23, 34
    fountains of Mauna Loa 77
    spring 141
Limonite 29
Limu, Hawaiian pumice 4, 79, 92, 144
Little Beggar 157
Little Elephant cone 171
Loomis, Kilauea in 1824 42
Lua Pele 61
Lydgate, plans of Kilauea 119, 129, 218
    plan of Mokuaweoweo 123, 145
Lyman, C. S., Kilauea in 1846 .... 58, 61
Lyman, F. S., earthquakes of 1868 101
Magnetite 23
Makaopuhi crater 54, 97
Mann and Brigham, Hualalai in 1863 9
    Kilauea in 1864 80
    Mauna Loa in 1864 15
Mauna Hualalai, see Hualalai.
Mauna Kea 5
Mauna Kohala 5
Mauna Loa, area 161
    ascent by Douglas in 1834 47
    in 1832-1837 63
    in 1841 .... 17, 63
    in 1843 63
    in 1849, 1851, 1852 65
    in 1855 68
    in 1856 71
    in 1859 75
    in 1864 15
    in 1868 101
    in 1868-1872 125
    in 1873 .... 120, 122, 123, 126
    in 1874 .... 123, 124
    in 1875-1877 127
    in 1879 132
    in 1880 .... 19, 133, 143
    in 1880, 1881 147
    in 1885 .... 157, 158
    in 1887 165
    in 1888 168
    in 1890 174
    in 1892 185
    in 1896 192
    in 1899 196
    in 1903 202
    in 1905 204

PAGE

Mauna Loa in 1907 206
Menzies' ascent of Hualalai 8
Merritt, Mauna Loa, 1888 168
Mica 23, 29
Minerals from Hawaiian volcanoes 29
Model of Kilauea 201
Mud-flow, 1868. See Landslide.
Observatory at Kilauea 118
Old Faithful 189
Olivine 23, 29, 54, 84
Pahoehoe 2, 24
Pele's hair 17, 23, 33, 85, 137
     analyses 33
Phonolite 24
Pickering, Kilauea in 1841 56
Pit craters of Hualalai 10
     in Puna 94
Pohaku Hanalei crater 143, 204
Poli o Keawe crater 93
Ponahohoa 40, 140
Pope, Mauna Loa in 1905 204
Prismatic basalt 24
Pukauahi crater 148
Pulu 93
Pumice, see also Limu 23
Puna, legendary lava flows 99
     pit craters 94
Quartz 29
Radium 180
Rate of landslide 102, 114
Rate of lava flows 14, 51, 67, 69, 70,
    72, 73, 75, 76, 105, 116, 149, 151, 153, 167, 206, 207
Ridgeway's plan of Mokuaweoweo 202
River beds changed 4
Rope-lava 23, 24
Salts in lava 14, 29, 54, 69, 117

PAGE

Schaefer, Kilauea in 1874 124
Scoria 27
Scott's sketch of Kilauea 129
Severance, plan of Mokuaweoweo 145
Shepherd, Kilauea in 1839 49
Snow on Mauna Kea 5
     on Mauna Loa 18, 76
Stalactites and stalagmites 29, 93
Steam, volcanic 27, 28, 127
Stewart, Kilauea in 1825 43
     in 1829 46
Stony lavas 24
Strzelecki, Kilauea in 1838 48
Sulphide of iron 29
Sulphur beds 54, 82, 91, 140
Sulphurous acid gas 28
Thurston, Kilauea in 1894 187
     Mauna Loa in 1890 174
Thurston Lake 185
Tidal wave, 1886 .... 103, 113
     of 1872 125
Toler, Kilauea in 1877 130
Traveling fountains 217, 221
Tree moulds of lava 16, 52, 96, 111, 202
Tufa 24
Van Slyke, Kilauea, 1886 164
Vapors from volcanoes 27
Vegetation on Hualalai 10, 12
     on Mauna Loa 19
Volcanic sand 27
Waldron's Ledge 83
Warm springs 14, 98
Whitney, Mauna Loa in 1868 105
Wilkes, Kilauea in 1841 56
     Mauna Loa in 1841 .... 17, 63

HALEMAUMAU   1880   C. FURNEAUX.

Memoirs Bernice Pauahi Bishop Museum II.

KILAUEA AND MAUNA LOA.

Their recorded History to 1909. By WILLIAM T. BRIGHAM, Sc. D.,
Director of the Bernice Pauahi Bishop Museum.

A T the request of the Trustees of this Museum the author of the following account
has returned to his studies of nearly half a century ago when, in company with
the late Horace Mann, he came to these islands to explore the Geology and
Botany of the Group. He is the more ready to continue the record then started because
he has collected much additional information and made many photographs illustrating
the subject that seem worth preserving, and there are errors in his and other publications on the Hawaiian volcanoes that need correction. The result is offered in a form
as free as possible from tentative theorizing; it is mainly a collection of material for
other geologists to use at their discretion in elucidating, as far as it may serve, those
deeper problems often touched but as yet unsolved,—the source of volcanic heat, the
cause of the rise and outflow or ejection of the matter usually classed as volcanic,—on
these Geology has no positive knowledge.

When the results of this early exploration by the author on the geological side
were published in 1868, followed by a later paper on the same theme in 1869,[1] no
thought was entertained of any return to the scenes of these most enjoyable journeyings, but in 1880 an expected eruption of Mauna Loa brought him back with the artist
Mr. Charles Furneaux, and eight years later he returned to make Honolulu his residence. All the time from 1864 to this writing he has kept in touch with the Hawaiian
Islands, and although his active work has turned aside from vulcanology in great
measure, yet his visits to the Halemaumau of Kilauea have now numbered more than
forty during these years. Journeyings through the wonderful volcanic region of
Central France and along the Rhine; to Vesuvius; a sight of Ætna, Stromboli and
the Campi Phlegræi, and a more careful reconnaissance of the Guatemalan volcanoes;
and not least, a journey through the entire volcanic region of the northern island of
New Zealand, have kept alive an interest in volcanic matters which was kindled by a

---

[1] Memoirs of the Boston Society of Natural History, vol. I, pt. 3: Ibid, vol. I, pt. 4. The publication of the full
results of the botanical part was stopped by the lamented death of Mr. Mann, whose Enumeration of Hawaiian Plants,
published in the proceedings of the American Academy of Arts and Sciences, procured him the honor of an election
as Fellow of that Academy. A Flora of the Hawaiian Islands was partly published by the Essex Institute at the
time of his death.

careful survey of Kilauea in 1865. If little new be added to the story, some corrections authorized by greater knowledge, and perhaps a more orderly arrangement of the material in hand, may be a sufficient apology for attempting in this paper to carry on to the present year some of the admirable work of the author's friend, the late James Dwight Dana, whose name is identified with Hawaiian vulcanology. His disquisition on Volcanic Characteristics is easily accessible and need not be repeated here: the petrology may also be omitted, for the knowledge of the intimate structure of rocks is greatly increasing year by year, and many have written thereon. Here the reader may look only for a connected story of the activities of the Hawaiian volcanoes in historic times, with all the accuracy at the writer's command from a long familiarity with the visible phenomena and the written record and a personal acquaintance with most of those whose testimony is quoted.   .

The Island of Hawaii.

To those who are not familiar with the geography of Hawaii a glance at the map will render clearer my explanation. The area, 4015 square miles, is wholly composed of the lavas poured out by the five volcanoes which rise 31,000 feet from the bed of the ocean, and nearly 14,000 from its surface. Not all crude lava, for ages of decomposition and the wear and tear of the elements, with the rapid work of the vegetable transformer have made soil of great fertility and suited to many crops, so that if many of the higher ridges are devastated by the lately molten rock not yet relieved of its savage form, the valleys present all the beauties of a tropical vegetation. Here are the few rivers, especially on the northern or windward side, that the island can boast, and in their course are many and most picturesque waterfalls. If rivers of water are uncommon over three-quarters of the island, rivers of stone are sufficiently apparent to indicate the process by which the island has been formed. In the newer parts the lava streams are everywhere, and in some places they have cut through the forests and made their way to the sea, as will be seen in the course of our studies of the volcano in action. Often the traveler in the uplands comes across a mass of jagged and apparently lawless rock (Fig. 1), impassable for his horse, almost for himself: all our modern resources of explosives could hardly work such disorder, such desolation. As he cannot cross the frozen lava stream just here he may follow it up and at last come to a portion of the flow where the surface is comparatively smooth where he and his horse can walk as on a paved street, a surface the natives call *pahoehoe* (see Pl. XLI), and the name has so completely supplied a want in our vocabulary that, in spite of the

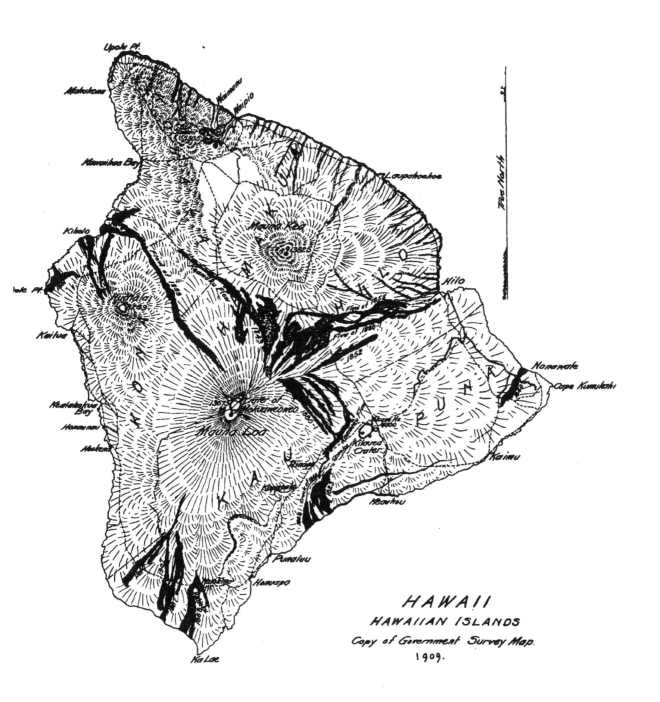

Upolu Pt.

Mahukona

Kawaihae Bay

Kiholo

Keahole Pt.

Kailua

Kealakekua Bay

Honaunau

Mokeni

Kaulana

Waimanu
Waipio

P. Laupahoehoe

Mauna Kea
13825

Hilo

Flow of 1855

Flow of 1880

1852

Hualalai
10269

Grave of
Kalaneopuu

Mauna Loa

Mauna Kea
5000

Kilauea
Crater

Keauhou

Nanawale

Cape Kumukahi

Kaimu

Puna

Kau

Punaluu

Honuapo

Kahuku

Ka Lae

HAWAII
HAWAIIAN ISLANDS
Copy of Government Survey Map.
1909.

The North

objurgations of an English geologist, it has been adopted by all geologists treating of the Hawaiian lavas. Another native word, *a-a*, supplies another want, for nowhere in the English language is there a word expressive of the roughness of the rock mass to which this word is applied (Pl. XLVII); a third, *limu*, meaning moss or seaweed, is well applied to the basaltic pumice which accompanies all the Hawaiian *outbursts* of lava (Fig. 2).

Now the rough scoriæ, a-a and limu, quickly invite vegetation when moisture is present, and do their best to cover the ravages of Pluto with the garments of Ceres, but the smooth lava does no such good work, although pleasanter to walk upon; only when its great slabs, smooth or slightly wrinkled in the cooling process, are cracked, can the vegetable get a footing. We will return to the forms and nature of the lava later with such help as flat pictures can give the reader.

While rivers of water irrigate and support the vegetation in the lower valleys, they, in bringing down soil, of course erode the hills and cut the valleys deeper; a process Dana has well illustrated from the erosion of one of the Pacific islands. The rivers of stone build up and often where the river has cut a channel on

FIG. I.   OLD FLOW WEST OF KILAUEA.

this island, as in the case of the Wailuku at Hilo, we see a contest between the destruction and the renewal. Within historical times the river has more than once been wiped out by the fiery flood, and has patiently set to its work of cutting a new channel (Fig. 3).

It is easy to see that the constant outpour of lava from a group of volcanic vents would not only increase the height of an island but its circumference as well in an even proportion were there not some check to the latter increase. The check in the present case is the erosive power of the sea currents and waves. Hawaii is not protected by a fringing coral reef, for owing to the frequent submarine eruptions as well as to the flows that rush down the mountain sides and push out the shore line, the coral polyp does not generally flourish as around the islands where active volcanic growth has ceased, consequently there is no natural breakwater to the strong action of currents and waves. However hard the surface of a lava stream where it meets the sea, its physical structure is such that the waves find easy access to the bubbles, hollows, caves, so common in its structure, and after presenting water spouts for years perhaps, the almost ceaseless beating of wave succeeding wave demolishes and sweeps away the ruins. It is probable that Hawaii is not growing from accretions of lava along shore more than it is wasting by marine erosion.

FIG. 2. GREEN LIMU FROM KILAUEA, 1789: NATURAL SIZE.

The time is near at hand for a more complete physiographic sketch of the Hawaiian group than has hitherto been possible, but at the present the portion that most interests us is the cluster of mountain peaks which marks the site of the orifices from which the building of the island of Hawaii (where alone are active volcanoes) has been effected. There are five of these mountains prominent on the face of Hawaii. In the northwest Mauna Kohala, or Mt. Kohala, has long been extinct and its slopes to the eastward have been buried beneath the lava streams from its mighty neighbor on the northeast, Mauna Kea (White Mountain). The summit of Kohala shows little sign of volcanic action, is swampy, and the source of much water used for irrigation. Its height is 5489 feet, but little more than that of Kilauea on the southeast.

Mauna Kea (Fig. 4) also has long been extinct and its summit is covered with cinder cones (Fig. 5), most of them with deep craters filled all the year with snow which supplies the summit pool occupying the only crateriform depression on the summit (Fig. 6). Its depth is not known, as the only party which has made the ascent when the pool was frozen over, so far as the author is informed, neglected to ascertain this interesting measure. Usually considered the highest of the Hawaiian volcanoes (13,825 feet), its mass is less, and its real summit lower than that of Mauna Loa (13,675 feet), only the cinder cones give the superior height, and as these are composed of loose cinder

FIG. 3. THE POTS ON THE WAILUKU NEAR HILO.

Perkins.   FIG. 4. MAUNA KEA FROM WAIAKEA, HILO.

FIG. 5. CINDER CONES ON MAUNA KEA.

FIG. 6. THE POOL ON MAUNA KEA IN AUGUST, 1889.

they are slowly settling and in time will dispose of all claims to superior elevation. From the base of the cones on Kea the mass of Loa seems not only grander but higher as well. The sides of Kea are dotted with lateral cones making her appear, like Ætna, a "Mother of Mountains."[1]

As one sails up the western coast of Hawaii it is difficult to see where Mauna Loa ends and Mauna Hualalai begins, but at Kailua its distinct and cone-crowned summit rising to the height of 8275 feet, marks its individuality. This mountain has been quiescent for many years, but unlike Kohala and Kea, of whose former activity not even native legends are known, it has been in eruption within the period when white men have had knowledge of this group. Its history is, however, brief, and the exact date is uncertain on which the last eruption occurred. From both natives and missionaries the author obtained the date of 1801. Others have given 1800 and 1803. Ellis says, "about twenty years ago" in describing his visit in 1823, so it may be considered to have occurred very early in the nineteenth century. A party of naturalists

FIG. 7.   SUMMIT OF HUALALAI FROM EAST.

from Vancouver's expedition, led by Mr. A. Menzies, made the first ascent in January, 1794. The account of this given in the narrative of Vancouver's voyage is meagre, the entry under date of January 26 being:

> The party accompanying Mr. Menzies returned with him on Saturday, after having had a very pleasant excursion, though it had been somewhat fatiguing in consequence of the badness of the paths in the interior country, where in many places the ground broke in under their feet. Their object had been to gain the summit of Mowna Roa [Mauna Loa], which they had not been able to effect in the direction they had attempted it; but they had reached the top of another mountain, which though not so lofty as Mowna-rowna [Mauna Loa] or Mowna kaah [Mauna Kea], is yet very conspicuous, and is called by the natives Worroray [Hualalai]. This mountain rises from the western extremity of the island, and on its summit was a volcanic crater that readily accounted for the formation of that part of the country over which they had found it so dangerous to travel.[3]

Vancouver gives an engraving of a crater on Hualalai, but it has not been identified. Menzies was a botanist and not a geologist, and his journals are preserved in England from which we learn much of the vegetation of this trip, but little or nothing of the geological condition of this volcano.[4]

[2] In 1889 the author made the ascent of Mauna Kea from the Hilo side and found it very easy on horseback. From the Waimea side the ascent is shorter and easier.
[3] A Voyage of Discovery to the North Pacific Ocean and round the World. London, 1798, vol. III, p. 14.
[4] A portion of his journals has been reprinted in Thrum's Annual for 1908.

The Rev. William Ellis made the ascent in 1823, and his account will be quoted later, but as the present writer had more in view the geology of the mountain, he will first give his own account of the ascent made thirty-eight years later, though still during the life of this excellent missionary who read and approved the account that follows.[5]

On Thursday afternoon, July 28, 1864, Mr. Horace Mann and myself, with a native guide left Kaawaloa. Our way led at first through open pastures, then through tracts of tall ferns, and finally we came to the forest, where the soil was

FIG. 8. PIT CRATER ON HUALALAI, 1889.

black and muddy, and the bushes so close as to almost prevent our passage in some places—gigantic raspberries (*Rubus hawaiiensis*) with stems two inches in diameter at the base and more than twenty feet long, hung across our path and often scratched both ourselves and our horses in spite of our precautions. It rained hard so that we were quite wet, and the clouds prevented our seeing much on either side. After some six miles of forest, we came upon a bed of a-a, fresh-looking and rough, and the trees were thinner and smaller. We were now on a dismal plain of pahoehoe and gravelly sand, where in the scotch mist we could see but little out of our path. This was the elevated plain between the mountains, and being at least 5000 feet above the sea the atmosphere was cold as well as damp.

[5] This account was first printed in the Memoirs of the Boston Society of Natural History, vol. I, p. 380.

A leguminous tree (*Sophora chrysophylla*), called by the natives Mamane, was common; the sandal-wood was seen here and there, but of small size, and the ohelo (*Vaccinium penduliflorum*) covered the ground thickly, and was loaded with its large red and purple berries. Twisted lava streams, and masses of scoriæ crossed our path, and so complicated were they that it was almost impossible to trace their course. About sunset we came to the place our guide had selected for our camp, and we soon had a fire at which we dried ourselves and roasted some sweet potatoes, and as the rain had ceased, slept comfortably under some bushes. Our water came from a curious pool in the last place one would think of looking for water, in the midst of a horribly rough bed of scoriæ almost as porous as pumice, and broken into irregular masses of all sizes. The basin holds about twelve gallons of cold, pure water, and has no evident inlet or outlet, yet is never entirely exhausted; we nearly emptied it and the next morning it was full again. It was found accidentally, and three columns of stone are piled up to mark the place, which would be most difficult to find without these signals.

At half-past five in the morning we started for the summit, toward which a good path led for some distance, and we galloped over the hard gravel beds, dodging in a zigzag course the clumps of bushes in our way. The morning was clear, and the birds, which are scarce near the shore, were abundant, and sang merrily. The path ended after three miles, and we had to slowly pick our way over difficult and even dangerous lava-fields. Our horses occasionally broke through, causing some trepidation to the riders, but no accidents occurred; and after passing nearly round the summit, crossing the flow of 1801, and counting ten flows from the top, and many others almost indistinguishable, we reached the base of the highest plateau at eight o'clock, and left our horses in a little valley where strawberries were abundant, and also American potatoes, planted by some native.

A climb up a steep slope some three hundred feet high, and we were in the midst of a series of large pit craters extending over the entire summit. These craters were very much alike, from three to five hundred feet deep, and from seven hundred to a thousand feet in diameter. The walls were of solid grey lava capped very seldom by more recent basalt (although fresh looking lava was piled near by), and were nearly perpendicular. Vegetation extended to the bottom, and the beautiful Silver-sword (*Argyroxiphium sandvicense*) was growing in the clefts far down the sides. The bottom was usually flat and gravelly, but in some cases covered with smooth black lava, and in others rough and broken. Fragments of the walls were often seen at their base, and in one crater they were partly melted into the fresh lava which covered the bottom, proving that the compact lava of this mountain summit is fusible by the melted black basalt.

No signs of steam or sulphurous fumes were visible, but on the edge of one of the deepest craters, on the wall which separated it from another less than two hundred feet distant, was a mound of scoriæ some fifty feet high, composed of drops and slightly agglutinated fragments of all sizes and colors, black, blue, orange, red, golden, apparently ejected in a viscid state, and in the centre of this a blow-hole about twenty-five feet in diameter, and as nearly as we could judge by throwing stones, eighteen hundred feet deep to a ledge, to one side of which we could see a deeper, rather smaller hole.

FIG. 9. BLOW-HOLE ON HUALALAI. FROM A PHOTOGRAPH TAKEN IN 1889.

I was obliged to lie flat on the edge to examine it, the scoriæ were so loose, and the whole cone jarred as we climbed over it.[6] The inside of the blow-hole was of a brown color, smooth as if turned, and grooved horizontally. No vertical striæ could be distinguished, but as these horizontal grooves seem to correspond to the strata of the adjoining crater walls, I suppose that the projecting ridges mark the more solid substance of these strata which would be in their centre, while the scoriæ which separate the beds to some extent, would permit the deeper action of the vapors that have formed the hole. The wearing force must have been chemical rather than mechanical, as the wall of the crater adjoining, which is not more than twenty-five or thirty feet

[6] When I again visited this blow-hole twenty-five years later the top had fallen in, much reducing the height. This was a favorite depository among the ancient natives for foreskins, umbilical cords, etc., and tradition declares that not a few of the idols doomed to destruction were cast into this almost sacred hole as preferable to the usual cremation.

thick, would have given way to any violent explosion. (Fig. 9.) A similar blow-hole was described by Ellis lower down the mountain. He ascended Hualalai in 1823 and found on the side of the mountain a large extinguished crater, about a mile in circumference and apparently four hundred feet deep. The sides were regularly sloped, and at the bottom was a mound with an aperture in its top. By the side of this large crater, divided from it by a narrow ridge of rock, was another, fifty-six feet in circumference, from which volumes of sulphurous smoke continually ascended. No bottom could be seen, and on throwing stones into it they were heard to strike against its sides for eight seconds. There were two other apertures very near this, nine feet in diameter, and apparently two hundred feet deep.[7] This corresponds so nearly with the blow-hole we saw on the summit that it is almost certain that vapors formed or at least enlarged both.

FIG. 10. THE SUMMIT OF HUALALAI SEEN FROM MAUNA LOA (9000 FEET).

From the vegetation of the summit I should not consider Hualalai more than 8500 feet high,[8] although some have placed it at 10,000. It is covered with lateral cones and its summit is flat, with many pit craters. More than one hundred and fifty lateral cones have been counted and it will be seen from the sketch made from the slopes of Mauna Loa the same summer that they vary both in size and in slope.

In the afternoon we camped about a mile from our last night's resting place, between two cones. Our guide shot two of the native geese (*Nesochen sandvicensis*), which were fine eating. The number of these geese has been much underrated. Although they are found only on the highlands of Hawaii and Maui, their number admits of the annual slaughter of several hundred without sensible diminution. They build their nests in the grass and lay two or three eggs, white and about the size of a common goose's egg. They are web-footed, but are never seen in the water; indeed there is no water on the uplands, and their food is principally berries and a common *Sonchus*. The strawberries (*Fragaria chilensis*) were nearly out of season. Trees were comparatively small. The mamane, sandal-wood, *Dodonæa viscosa, Geranium cuneatum,* were

[7] Ellis, Tour of Hawaii, London edition.
[8] Height as obtained many years after this by the Hawaiian Survey is 8275 feet.

the most common, and many compositæ with brilliant yellow blossoms (*Raillardia*, *Dubautia*, etc.) were seen all through the plain.

I made me a bed of bracken (*Pteris aquilina*) as I might in New England on a similar occasion, and with my feet towards a fire of great mamane logs, went to sleep. The night was clear and cold,—so cold that I awoke and moved nearer the fire. It was strangely silent; the stars were shining brightly, and directly in front of me was the grand Mauna Loa. At half-past three the moon rose over the slopes of Mauna Kea and I fell asleep again. In the morning at sunrise the thermometer marked 46° Fahr. As the sun rose, the lava-flow of 1859 was visible through its whole length from near

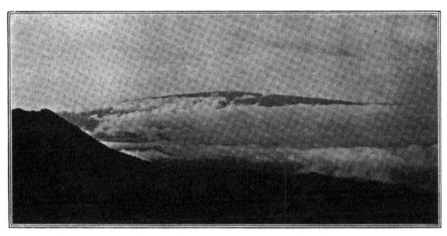

FIG. 11. MAUNA LOA FROM TOP OF HUALALAI.

the summit of Mauna Loa to the sea near Kawaihae, shining like a river of silver, owing to its glossy black surface. Could it have been more beautiful when a river of fire? All the plain between the mountains, which covers many square miles, is intersected by lava-flows from all three mountains, and is wholly rocky and uneven, with caves and beds of a-a. The vegetation is scanty, but enough to support large flocks of goats. A road was attempted by Government some years ago under the direction of Dr. Judd, from Kailua on the western coast of Hawaii to Hilo, but only fifteen miles of this road (which was not intended for wheeled vehicles) were built. Caves are the only sources of water here, the surface being too porous to retain pools or streams; but in the caves the water from the frequent rains drips from the roof and is collected in calabashes.

Since this ascent I have been again to the summit of this mountain (in 1889) and found little change to note. The wild goats had disappeared and packs of wild dogs, little less dangerous than wolves to a solitary footman, had taken their range. Acres of an introduced purple thistle of a most luxuriant growth were found on our path some distance below the summit.

The only recorded eruption from this mountain took place in 1801, and was certainly not the one seen by Turnbull as has been stated; his record is, "On the evening of February 1, 1803, we stood along the shore [of Hawaii] to the eastward, taking the advantage of a land breeze. In this course we had a very full view of some eruptions from the volcanoes in the centre of the island of Owhyhee."[9]

The account of Ellis, taken from the lips of an Englishman and of natives, is as follows:

> Stone walls, trees, and houses all gave way before it, even large masses of rocks of hard ancient lava, when surrounded by the fiery stream, soon split into small fragments, and, falling into the burning mass, appeared to melt again, as borne by it down the mountain's side. Offerings were presented, and many hogs thrown alive into the stream to appease the anger of the gods, by whom they supposed it was directed, and to stay its devastating course. All seemed unavailing, until one day the king Kamehameha, went attended by a large retinue of chiefs and priests, and, as the most valuable offering he could make, cut off part of his own hair, which was always considered sacred, and threw it into the torrent. A day or two after, the lava ceased to flow. The gods, it was thought, were satisfied.

To this eruption is referred the sad story, often told to travelers by the natives, of the death of a mother and her infant. At the beginning of the century the base of Hualalai had many fishermen's hamlets along its shore. At night, while all were sleeping, the eruption began. The stream of lava came thundering down upon the people on the shore, and while nearly all succeeded in escaping, in one hut only the husband was awakened, and in his terror he fled leaving his wife and child. Before she was aroused by the shrieks of her friends, the lava had encircled the hut and escape was no longer possible. The lava set fire to the house, and the woman sprang into a pandanus tree near by, but her refuge was of short avail, and the lava-stream, which was flowing into the sea, consumed, as it passed, the two human sacrifices to Pele.

The remarkable rapidity with which this stream descended indicates great fluidity. It appears to have flowed fifteen miles in two or three hours, much of the way through forests. Its source was a little below the summit, and it issued in two streams, one to the northwest and the other to the northeast. Twenty-three years after this Ellis found a warm spring at Kailua where Glauber's salts were formed by the action of sulphurous vapors on sea water, and warm springs were also found at Kawaihae at tide level. These are now cooled and there are no signs of volcanic activity anywhere on the mountain. This latest effort of Hualalai, besides destroying several small

---

[9] A Voyage round the World in the years 1800–1804 by John Turnbull. London, 1813. P. 144.

villages, and filling up fish ponds, ended by changing the coast line for twenty miles from a bay to a headland several miles beyond the old coast. The streams which in former ages flowed at intervals down its sides do not appear to be of so great volume as those from Mauna Loa, and this may be owing to the great number of vents. Their physical structure, however, is identical with that of those from the other mountains.

Continuing my description of the mountains before attempting the story of their eruptions, I will offer the account of my first ascent of Mauna Loa, made almost immediately after that of Hualalai.

FIG. 12. BREAKING CAMP ON THE INLAND BASE OF HUALALAI, 1889.

On Tuesday, August 2, we left the hospitable house of Rev. J. D. Paris, the missionary at Kaawaloa. The native magistrate, Kupake, had heard of our intended journey and sent us two large dried fish, a most acceptable present, and a large gourd water-bottle. We secured as guide Kaakakawai, an old goat hunter, and we had also three native bearers and a pack mule. For the first six or eight miles our road was the same as when we ascended Hualalai, and, as then, we got wet through in passing the forest, this time by a thunder storm of short duration. We camped at night on the mountain-plain near Judd's road, and in the morning sent back our horses and prepared our raw-hide sandals for climbing over the rough lava, as there is no path for horses up the *smooth* dome of Mauna Loa.[10] We went nearly east until we struck

[10] As will be seen later, fair trails are now known up both sides of Mauna Loa.

the flow of 1859, and then followed that up more than eight miles. The surface was black and shining and quite brittle, and as we walked over it, it sounded like a hard frozen crust of snow. The outer surface to the depth of nearly half an inch was very porous and readily separated from the harder interior. In many places the lava had flowed up hill, dammed up behind by its rapidly hardening crust; and it sometimes attained an elevation of twenty-five or thirty feet without breaking from its pipe. Bubbles of great size, some still perfect, others broken in, were very common, and in some of the caves thus formed ferns were growing in the moist atmosphere. On the surface cracks also we found a *Polypodium*, but lichens were rare. Here and there we came to a deep round hole, and by its side lay the bleaching tree that had been burned off. The clumps of shrubs often approached within twenty feet of the flow, but in other places they had been killed to a distance of fifty feet, probably by gases, as they were not at all charred.

Immense beds of a-a with almost perpendicular sides, crossed our way, sometimes at the edge, sometimes directly across the flow, but always more or less level on top. The roughness of this a-a was greater than any we had met before; and we needed the raw-hide sandals we had prepared for such places, as well as thick buckskin gloves to protect our hands from the sharp needle-like points. Often the deep canal which the fiery river had made for itself, was visible through large breaks in the covering crust, and on approaching a hole of this nature I found myself on the verge of a gulf a hundred feet deep, of unknown length, and, as nearly as I could see, two hundred feet wide. The bottom was rough and cracked, and mainly covered with the fragments from the roof and sides, fallen since the lava had ceased to flow. The crust on which I stood was but a few inches thick, and although I had tested it with my staff before, I thought it safest to lie down and crawl until I had got several rods from the hole, and I did not venture near another.

The roughness of the flow at last turned us aside to the right on to the old pahoehoe which is covered thinly with grass and small bushes along the numerous cracks. Mauna Loa remained clear all day, and the summit did not seem very far off. Indeed at seven o'clock in the evening when we decided to camp for the night, had it not been that we were still within the limit of vegetation, I should have been inclined to push on and reach the summit that night. The whole surface of the mountain is undulating, and as we reached what seemed to be the top, we found a shallow valley and another hill beyond, and so it was all the way. We got the most sheltered place we could find, as we had no tent, and there were not enough bushes to make a hut; Kaakakawai shot a goat, and we ate our supper. The wind was quite cold, and we were not warm enough to sleep well, and while we were awake we saw a most novel sight,—what I may call an inverted sunset. The clouds had risen rapidly until they quite covered the plain and dashed their misty van against the base of the three giants, quite cutting them off from the rest of the world except Haleakala on Maui which towered above the mist. The surface of the clouds was rough and in constant motion, and as the sun sank into it, it seemed to kindle into flames of the most brilliant colors. All the golden canopy we usually see above the setting sun, was below it here, and above, all was clear. The clouds swept up nearly eight thousand feet, but no higher, and we were soon asleep above their limits.

The morning was clear and not very cold, and the view of Hualalai and Kea was very grand. At seven o'clock we had eaten our morning meal, put out our fire, and started on our way. The craters of 1859 were just on our left as we went up, and for two miles the crevices were filled with the *limu* or basaltic pumice, which is green and very light, and with Pele's hair. This fine volcanic glass was blown more than sixty miles during this eruption. At three o'clock two of our kanakas gave out, and we were obliged to leave them, assuming their burdens ourselves. The others were sick, and bound their heads up with leaves, complaining that their heads and stomachs were affected, imputing it all to the wind, which, however, was very light. Mr. Mann and myself felt no inconvenience from the altitude during the journey.

At night we were about half a mile from the terminal crater, and we found a long narrow cave, once the bed of a small lava stream, and still horrid with projecting points. It was five feet wide, two feet high, and of considerable length. We slept in Indian file, or rather tried to sleep; our bed was a magnified rasp, and although we broke off as many of the teeth as we could, more than enough remained. We needed all our blankets to protect us from the severe cold which froze water solid in the cave at our feet, but we had to push a fold beneath every time we turned. I got up before sunrise, and the air seemed intensely cold; I ran to a little hill and saw the sun come up through the clouds, and then crawled into the cave again and breakfasted. We then covered ourselves well with blankets, and walked up to the crater. Mokuaweoweo is the most perfectly formed crater on the Islands although not the largest. The walls almost a thousand feet high, are nearly perpendicular and unbroken for much of the circuit. When the United States Exploring Expedition ascended Mauna Loa in 1841, the bottom was rough, and contained eight or ten cones, some of considerable height; now there were only two cones, about two hundred feet high each, near the eastern wall; the whole bottom had been overflowed with fresh black lava, and as examined with a powerful glass was no rougher than an ordinary lava-stream. We were on the highest wall, 13,675 feet above the sea, and on the opposite side from the Wilkes encampment.   On a small pile of stones was a sandal with the inscribed names, Paris, Alexander, Haskell, 1859.   The sandal looked new and fresh as if just cut from the hide.   I was told that a cow once strayed up here in search of water, and died, and her body was found dried and retaining its shape completely.

The hard compact gray stone of the walls is much cracked and exhibits deep strata as elsewhere.   Scattered along the edges, and in various places over the great summit plain were large irregular masses of a solid reddish clinkstone of a sort much used formerly for stone adzes.   Several immense cracks parallel with the crater walls extended some distance.   These sometimes contained ice; and on breaking the surface,

FIG. 13.   MAUNA LOA FROM KILAUEA AT 7 A.M.

which was some two inches thick, we found a large supply of fine water in the ice, with which we replenished our water-bottles.   No snow was visible, and it is a mistake to suppose these summits within the limits of perpetual snow, as has been stated.   Seldom in the summer is any snow found here except in the caves where it is preserved as in ice-houses.   Snow sometimes falls on both Mauna Loa and Mauna Kea, but, except in winter, it disappears as soon as the sun rises.

At first we did not see any signs of volcanic activity, but at last discovered steam issuing from the northern bank.   Mr. Mann advised a descent into the crater and we attempted it, but after climbing down more than half way gave it up.   Adjoining Mokuaweoweo are two small pit craters on the major axis of the elliptical main crater, and into the southern one a stream of lava has flowed from the main crater.   The summit plain is much fissured, and several small cones both north and south, but on the same general line, mark eruptive agencies. So extensive is this plain that one walks nearly a mile before catching sight of the ocean, consequently no one at the sea level has ever seen the top about the crater, and when fire is seen at the summit, it means that the rising column of lava must attain a height of considerably over a thousand feet to be visible from the shore. At nine o'clock we commenced the descent as our time was limited, and about two in the afternoon a thick misty rain came on, and our guide wished to stop as he could not see the way; we had, however, three compasses, and proceeded without difficulty, although drenched, to the plain, where we found a cave and contrived to light a fire. At nine o'clock the rain ceased, the stars came out brightly, and as the cave still dripped, we rolled ourselves up in our blankets, wet through as we were, and with our feet to the fire slept well all night. In the morning we wrung out our clothes, which dried in the course of two hours as we were walking rapidly in the sun, and about noon rested on the edge of the forest, several miles west of where we had come up, at a spring which, as they always are on this island, was in a very improbable place,—the most elevated part of an open plain. Its position was marked by a pile of stones; no stream ran from it, and it was carefully covered to keep the wild hogs out, whose marks we saw near by among the strawberries and on the trees. Striking into the woods we walked down at a rapid rate, although the muddiness of the path, and the many trees that had fallen across the way, made it very laborious. Added to this, it began to rain as we came into the region of ferns, and we were again wet through. Vegetation on the leeward side of Mauna Loa only extends to the height of six or seven thousand feet, but on the windward slopes to nearly ten thousand.

It is not difficult to obtain the average slope of this mountain, but seen from Kilauea the slopes to the southwest and to the northeast vary perceptibly, but the angle of 7° is the average, and explains the name *Las Mesas* given by the Spanish discoverers of the group, also the "Long Mountain." (See Fig. 13.)

In 1880 I made the ascent of Mauna Loa from the eastern side accompanied only by an excellent guide, but mounted on an admirable mule. We came to the dairy at Ainapo in the afternoon, and after a short halt, pushed on to the limit of vegetation where there was still grass for our animals, and rested for the night. Our view of Kilauea was almost a bird's eye one, and the appearance was of a great city in flames. The crags about Halemaumau seemed the ruins of burning structures, and it was not until sheer weariness closed my eyes that I could look at anything else (Fig. 14). By three o'clock in the morning we were on our upward

way, and early in the morning halted near the brink of the crater a little south of
the Wilkes camp, to which the officers of the American expedition with a large company of native bearers had climbed forty years before with so much trouble. My
object was to see the traces of an eruption in Mokuaweoweo, the summit crater which,
appearing in the spring of that year, had induced me to again visit Hawaii. All the
way up the temperature of the caves had been considerably above that of the outer air,
but on the summit there were only the cold lavas of the May eruption. Much limu

FIG. 14. HALEMAUMAU IN 1888. FURNEAUX.

or basaltic pumice covered the plain for acres, and the wall of the crater was very loose
and insecure where we stood.

We returned by the same trail, if trail there was, it was invisible to me, but my
guide never hesitated, neither did the mule, and we returned safely to Ainapo before dark,
and were at the Volcano House at Kilauea next day in the early forenoon. For some
distance above Ainapo the way led through a dry open forest, with many dead koa trees,
and little sub-vegetation owing to the herds of cattle pastured there; when once beyond
this forest, the vegetation faded rapidly and the surface assumed the roughness of the
ordinary lava stream, and was undulating as on the other side, and only here and there
smooth for a short distance. Cracks often crossed our trail, and sometimes were

FIG. 15. PELE'S HAIR FROM KILAUEA.

FIG. 16. FORM OF LESS FUSIBLE LAVA.

[399]

FIG. 17. ROPE LAVA.

FIG. 18. DRIBLET UNDER LAVA FALL.

[400]

bridged for the mule by lava slabs and fragments, a shaky structure, and I was always glad when they were not too wide for my agile animal to leap. Fortunately we had no fogs, and no symptoms of mountain sickness. I felt, however, that if a storm had overtaken us, we should have had little chance of holding to our trail; a light fall of snow would have concealed it." More important ascents we will record later.

General Character of the Lavas of Hawaii.

I DO not intend to enter fully into the many analyses of the products of the Hawaiian volcanoes, but simply sketch the coarser composition and the external appearance of the lavas, that my reader who is not familiar with these volcanoes may better understand the descriptions that follow of the activities of the volcanoes and the ejected material met with in crater or lava-stream.

Of the two general classes into which geologists have divided lavas, the acid or trachytic,—Trachyte, Obsidian, Pumice, Granite,—and the basic of which Basalt or Dolerite is the type, we have on Hawaii only the latter class. Basalt contains a feld-spar having more lime than soda, augite, sometimes in well defined crystals, chrysolite or olivine in green nodules, often agglomerated, but generally diffused through the mass, and almost invisible to the naked eye. Magnetite is also present, and rarely Mica. Silica, Iron, Soda, and Lime are the final constituents.

When the ordinary lava is thrown into the air as in the tremendous fountains that often accompany the eruptions of Mauna Loa, drops are thrown off, and, caught on the currents of hot air, spin out a glassy filament sometimes exceeding three feet in length. These glassy threads are locally called "Pele's hair" (Fig. 15), and in the crater of Kilauea, as also wherever jets of lava are thrown up, they are constantly forming during the ordinary active condition. When the lava cools rapidly, as in these threads, the structure is glassy: when the cooling is slow the texture is stony: this is well shown in the impression of an actual specimen of rope-lava shown in Fig. 19. The outside is compact, while as we pass to the interior the cells grow larger and the magma is stone-like. The less fusible portion of the lava often separates in a rough form (Fig. 16); the more fusible, like Pele's hair, retains its ductility in a surprising manner until the high temperature of the air in which it is formed is considered. Lengths of three or four feet have been found spun from the fountains of lava on the slopes of Mauna Loa during an eruption. The plasticity of the molten lava is well

---

"A fuller account of this ascent was published in the American Journal of Science in 1888, and this will be inserted later with the accounts of the eruption of that year (1880-81).

shown in Fig. 23, of a curious vase wrought from the molten lava of Halemaumau
with no better tools than round and charred sticks. The cooling surface of the pahoehoe still in motion wrinkles in the ways shown in many of the plates of this memoir,
and the wrinkles often become twisted into fine rope-like forms (Fig. 17), with a very
black and shining surface.

Of the stony lavas there are many varieties, from the compact phonolite or
clinkstone which takes a good polish, and from the hardest varieties of which the old
Hawaiians made their adzes and other stone tools, to the very cellular form shown in
Fig. 21, a hard form often used for building, and the strangely elongated cells of specimens found near the shore east of
Hilo (Fig. 22). The more compact kinds used for building show
almost no cells, while that from
the surface quarries is more or less
cellular, and often well sprinkled
with olivine which impairs its value
as a building stone. Even the fairly
compact rocks are quite permeable
to water, making excellent filters,
and the apparently smooth and
non-porous pahoehoe gives passage to rains as may be seen in

FIG. 19.   IMPRESSION OF A SECTION OF ROPE LAVA.

the mountain caves. Basalt is more apt than other lavas to assume the prismatic form
on cooling, and many contraction specimens can be found in the gorge of the Wailuku
above Hilo (Fig. 25), and more perfectly detached ones are found on Kauai.

We must not forget the ductility shown in the lava falls, examples of which
are shown in many illustrations. In the eruption of 1832 in Kilauea a fall of nearly
200 feet was continuous: a portion of this fall is shown in Plate XLVI. A driblet
from another fall is shown in Fig. 18.

When, by violent explosions as in the eruption of Kilauea in 1789, the lava is
torn to pieces or ground into sand, a material is formed that under the influence of
moisture tends to recombine into a volcanic sandstone called tufa, but this reunion of
particles is usually, if not always, accompanied by a rearrangement of composition
which may be decomposition or metamorphism. Tufa is not common on Hawaii, but
abundant on Oahu, where the coast craters, Diamond Head, Punchbowl and others are
composed of it. In the quarry on Punchbowl a tolerably firm tufa has been employed
for building purposes, but has not proved durable. The sand may be mixed with

FIG. 20. PALAGMITE FROM DIAMOND HEAD.

FIG. 21. STONY CELLULAR LAVA.   FIG. 22. LAVA WITH CYLINDRICAL CELLS.

FIG. 23. VASE MADE FROM MOLTEN LAVA.

FIG. 24. BLACK VOLCANIC SAND.

larger fragments of rock or with fragments of coral reef and shells as in the case of Diamond Head, which exploded through the reef (Fig. 20), forming a coarser conglomerate. The varying color, brown to red, comes from the decomposition of the hydrous ferrous oxide ($Fe_2O_3 + Aq.$). The coarser black sand (Fig. 24) is formed by the forcible contact of molten lava with water, as at Nanawale when the lava stream of 1840 fell into the sea.

Scoria, a term originally applied to the slag or dross of metals, has been rather loosely applied to all the odds and ends of a lava discharge, from a-a to cinders. The

FIG. 25. BASALTIC PRISMS IN WAILUKU GORGE.

finer scoriæ or cinders are the constituents of cinder cones like those on Mauna Kea, which hold together chiefly by the cohesion of the rough surface of the cinders. The black sand (Fig. 24) is found in layers under Honolulu and elsewhere, and is much used in building operations.

The vapors or gases emitted from the craters of the volcanoes when active are never true smoke, but mainly steam. In the crater of Kilauea a distinction must be made between the vapors from Halemaumau and those arising from the outer crater: the latter being the rain products either directly, as after a shower, or from the more lasting surface springs. It is remarkable how permanent some of the steam-holes around Kilauea are. I have observed some of the more prominent ones, as those near

Keanakakoi, for forty-five years and have seen little change."[12] The cloud which often, but not always hangs over the active pit is the steam condensed by the cold winds from Mauna Loa ten thousand feet above it, and as steam has been thought the main factor in the rise of lava in the craters, it should be noticed how small the supply of steam in the active outpour of Kilauea really is. While the heat would of course render the aqueous vapor invisible directly in or over the pit, that very heat drives the steam up into the cold regions, and it would be seen as cloud, or pour down as rain if abundant, but neither effect is always produced at times of greatest activity, and when

FIG. 26. KĪLAUEA WITH SO-CALLED SMOKE FROM HALEMAUMAU.

the pit is empty of molten lava the smoke is often most abundant (Fig. 26). Next to steam sulphurous acid (H_2SO_3) is abundant, and so far as my experience goes is always present: this dry vapor is pungent and in passing through a stream of it one must hold his breath. This gas is often so abundant as to prevent travel around the lee side of the pit, sometimes even of the main crater. Hydrogen, supposed to be the result of the decomposition of water by great heat, is often present and its combustion is seen in the flames that play around the cracks or, as in 1880, rise in considerable

[12] The late Wm. Lowthian Green in his valuable "Vestiges of the Molten Globe," II, p. 75, writes: "It has sometimes been said that the large quantities of *pure aqueous vapor* often noticed in and about Kilauea, shows that it is steam, or the vapor of water, which produces the appearance of 'ebulition' in the lava lakes. We venture to suggest that any vapor of water which had been intimately mixed or 'boiled up' with the white-hot molten lavas of the Kilauea lakes, could never again appear at the surface as pure steam. It would be partially decomposed, and unmistakably tainted with sulphuretted hydrogen. Even the moist air which escapes would be so tainted. There is an evident source for all the pure steam found about Kilauea in the rain and the surface waters that get to the hot rocks: but they must be less hot than incandescent: or else the proportion of water to molten lava must be sufficiently great to reduce the temperature below a full red heat."

volume from blow-holes on the edge of the active pit. Carbonic acid, which is common where volcanoes break through calcareous substrata, as in France and Italy, is rare on Hawaii; so is chlorine and its compound with hydrogen, (HCl) hydrochloric acid: which would seem to show that sea-water does not often break through the island walls to the molten interior.

Minerals are uncommon in and around the Hawaiian volcanoes, but salts formed by the union of escaping gases with the elements in the lava are common as incrustations in the crater caves or under the crust of the floor, such as gypsum, alum, glauber salt, etc. Augite in fine crystals, olivine in nodules of some size, mica in minute hexagonal plates, quartz in small crystals, and rarely *en masse*, are the more common minerals. The gases convert the rocks into soil far more rapidly than the frosts of colder climates. The sulphides of iron, pyrite and marcasite which have been considered the source of the sulphurous vapors abounding in the crater when active, must be almost entirely decomposed for they are seldom found in the cold lava: natives have brought me the former in small specimens thinking it gold, but I have myself only once found it in Kilauea. The ferrous oxides are common, both red and yellow, and were well known to the old Hawaiians as a source of paint for their canoes, and coloring for their kapas. They are often found in the lava streams as lumps or rounded masses as if rolled, seldom as deposits, except in swamps as limonite.

Stalactites and Stalagmites.—There is a curious formation, at times common in the caves that exist beneath the floor of Kilauea crater, and not infrequent in similar caves in dead streams of lava on the mountain slopes. At first glance the small grey rods that hang from the roof, and the curiously modeled droppings beneath these, seem to be of igneous origin, or droppings of melted lava from the roof. An examination *in situ* shows that this is not the case. The roof of these caves averages two feet thick, and where the stalactites occur is unbroken. On removing the tubes with care one finds no visible crack, and there is generally no fresh molten lava on the upper surface. The formative process may be clearly seen as the tubes grow from day to day. Professor Dana, after quoting my account in his "Characteristics of Volcanoes,"[13] could hardly believe the rapidity of the process, but observations repeated more than once during the last forty years only confirm my early description, which I here repeat. I have caught the steel-grey deposit in the drops on the end of the tubes upon my finger and watched its solidification. Usually the tubes are straight cylinders, from one to three-eighths of an inch in diameter, and somtimes more than two feet long. As any sharp earthquake would at once break such long rods from the

[13] Dana, Characteristics of Volcanoes, p. 341.

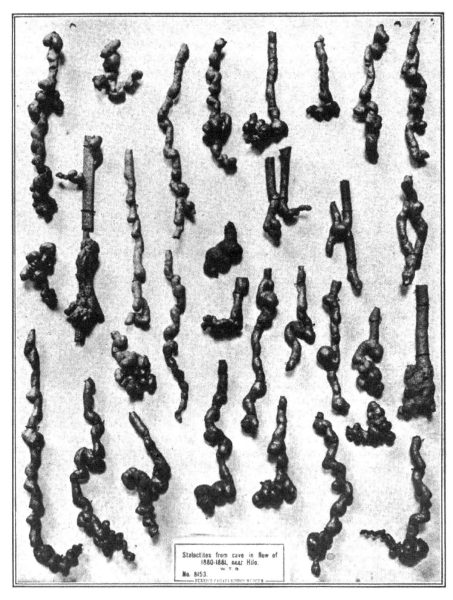

Stalactites from cave in flow of
1880-1881, near Hilo.
W. T. B.
No. 8153.
BERNICE PAUAHI BISHOP MUSEUM

FIG. 27.

[408]

roof they must grow with rapidity to attain such length between the frequent jars. The bore is almost never continuous, and while externally they are smooth (with

a minute crystalline marking), within, a mass of stony cells often nearly occupying the diameter of the tube is presented. As long as these tubes grow downward in the quiet upper region of the cave they hang perpendicularly, but when they reach farther down the currents of air and steam blow the drop with the deposits aside and the tube becomes distorted: it may even return on itself. Many of the resulting forms are shown on the opposite page. This collection was obtained from a low cave in the flow of 1881 near Hilo, and as there were many breaks through the roof the currents of air were strong and irregular. There was no steam, but plenty of moisture when I visited the cave, and there was no active growth. In

FIG. 28. STALAGMITES FROM A CAVE IN KILAUEA.

one cave in Kilauea in 1865 the growth of the stalactite was at about the rate of an inch a week, but owing to the varying amount of water or steam the production is quite irregular. They are sometimes coated with beautiful white crystals of gypsum, some-times tipped with needle-like transparent crystals of the same mineral, where the cave is high. The natives collect them with the upper open joint of a long bambu. The drip on the floor of the cave forms much thicker and more irregular stalagmites, as may be seen in Plates XLVIII and XLIX. Specimens have been found which exceed eight inches in diameter, and these are usually low and flat-topped. The more slender ones sometimes rise to a height of two feet; and so rapidly is the silica deposited, that they seldom increase in diameter, but are true *acrogens*, none of the suspended silica run-ning down the sides. Fig. 28. The process of formation is this: the water from the fre-quent rains, and the condensing steam, act upon the soluble por-tions of the superin-cumbent rock, carrying along the silica and lime to be deposited in the

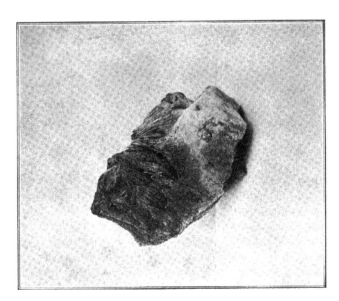

FIG. 29. BLOW-HOLE SPECIMEN.

form of tubes and their incrusting gypsum, and the resulting stone is quite anhydrous, as will be seen from the following analysis of specimens not coated with gypsum:[14]

SiO_3	Al_2O_3	Fe_2O_3	MnO	Ca O	MgO	Na_2O	K_2O
51.9	13.4	15.5	0.8	9.6	4.8	3.0	1.1 = 100.1

Specific gravity, 2.9. The temperature of the caves is usually from 80°–95° Fahr. Other specimens examined by Prof. Dana had a hardness of 5–5.25, and a specific gravity of 1.656.[15] The imitative forms arising from the evaporation of the siliceous solutions in the caves are often quite curious, some resembling bunches of raisins, from a partial collapse of the incrusting bubble. The structure of all is stony and very cellular. The microscopic structure is clearly described by Dana in the volume referred to.

[14] Analyzed by Mr. John C. Jackson in the laboratory of Dr. C. T. Jackson, Boston.
[15] Geology of the United States Exploring Expedition, p. 201.

Before leaving the brief account of the common external forms of lava, it may be of interest to the reader to have before him some of the analyses of the Hawaiian lavas as given in my former essay on the Hawaiian volcanoes, and in more recent publications:

	A	**B**	**C**	**D**	**E**	**F**	**G**	**H**	**I**	**K**
	G=2.7					G=2.97	G=3.01	G=2.80	G=2.75	G=2.66
SiO_2	49.0	49.2	51.19	39.74	50.00	49.20	48.82	48.60	53.81	50.82
TiO_2						1.72	1.16		2.01	undet.
Al_2O_3	13.0	7.8		10.55	6.16	14.90	15.22	25.45	13.48	9.14
Fe_2O_3		13.7				4.51	5.72	17.55	3.02	7.33
FeO	15.0		30.26	22.29	28.72	12.75	9.65	1.20	7.39	7.03
MnO	7.8	13.0				0.28	0.67	tr.	tr.	0.38
CaO	8.9	8.4		2.74	7.40	9.20	10.40	2.20	10.34	11.63
MgO	0.4	5.1	18.16	2.40	2.00	3.90	4.55	0.98	6.46	7.22
Na_2O	4.5	1.8		21.62		1.96	2.10	} 1.38	3.23	1.02
K_2O	2.3	trace			6.00	0.95	0.90		0.64	3.06
P_2O_5						0.42	tr.	tr.		
H_2O		0.5		.33		0.10		1.87	0.57	1.74
	100.9	99.5	99.61	99.67	100.28	99.89	99.19	99.23	100.95	99.37

Of these analyses A was of dark bottle-green lava drops from Halemaumau. Dr. C. T. Jackson.

B. Pele's hair, Kilauea, 1864. Both protoxide and peroxide of iron were present, but owing to the presence of oxide of manganese the proportions were not determined. J. C. Jackson.

C. Pele's hair, Kilauea, 1840. B. Silliman, Jr.

D. Pele's hair, same source and analyst.

E. Pele's hair, light colored. Analyzed by J. Peabody.

F. Recent vitreous basalt, fresh and unaltered. Silvestri.[16]

G. Older basalt, but fresh. Silvestri.

H. Older basalt, much altered. Silvestri.

I. Compact basalt-obsidian. Cohen.[17]

K. Pele's hair. Cohen.

Another form of lava has been found and may be found again, a fragment of which is shown in Fig. 29. In a blow-hole the late Mr. H. Rexford Hitchcock found some specimens which seem to me to have been formed by an electric current acting on a plastic mass containing much iron. The masses are of considerable specific gravity (2.857), and the surface is arranged precisely as iron filings place themselves

[16] Comitato Geologico d'Italia, Bolletino, 1888, xix, 128, 168.
[17] N. Jahrbuch für Mineralogie, etc., 1880, ii, 23.

around the pole of a magnet. Similar specimens were found in Vesuvius, but in Kilauea only this one locality has been discovered, and the specimens referred to are (or were) in the Museum of the Boston Society of Natural History.

Another form of lava is found in narrow seams, and scattered over the ground in places. I am inclined to attribute it to shrinkage cracking.

FIG. 30. FRAGMENTARY LAVA.

FIG. 31. OHIA FOREST ON THE OLD TRAIL TO KILAUEA.

The Recorded History of the Eruptions.

WE may well begin the record of the unusual activities of the Hawaiian volcanoes which are called eruptions, with Kilauea, for of this volcano we have the earliest authentic account. No word of the then shape of the crater; to the Hawaiians, who are our chroniclers, the cup was naught beside its terrible contents,—and these are reported clearly and at considerable length. There is no reason to doubt

1789 the substantial accuracy of the report of the eruption of 1789, although such a paroxysmal eruption has not since been repeated, for the physical proofs are abundant around the crater in the deposits of limu and sand. In 1864 it was thought that these were mainly on the south and west of the crater in desolate regions exposed to the prevailing winds which would carry the vapors and gases constantly, and the ejecta of any explosive eruption, provided the regular winds prevailed, which they probably did not during the explosive eruption of 1789. It is true that vast deposits of black and fine sand still are found to the leeward of the crater, much more than enough to fill the present vast crater, and a still larger portion must have been carried down the mountain side by the rains (often torrential) of more than a century. Around the greater part of the circumference of the crater bushes and trees had covered the ground, but in recent years the building of a carriage road from Hilo has laid bare deposits of this eruption extending far on the northeast side of Kilauea, and the present work on a road around Kilauea iki has given sections of great interest, showing the easily recognized sand and the even more conspicuous limu, fresh and bright in coloring as on the days of its ejection. A pile of fragments of compact rock of light grey color, then the limu often in green fragments larger than a man's fist; then the grey sand in slightly indicated layers, heaped over the pile of rocks as a nucleus extending to the surface where the vegetation has concealed the formation (Fig. 32).

The bones of the perished warriors I have myself seen in the place where they are said to have died, but the relics were limited to a few thigh bones. To fully appreciate the feelings of the Hawaiians at this time we must note the other historical events bearing on the catastrophe we are about to recount. Kamehameha, the young chief at the court of Kalaniopuu, king or moi of Hawaii, noticed by Lieutenant George Vancouver during Cook's visit as a rather savage looking youth, had become moi of Kona, Kohala and Hamakua, and was striving to subdue the rest of the island of Hawaii. In obedience to priestly counsels Kamehameha had built the last of the great stone temples of his ancestral worship, Puokohalà, on the hill overlooking the

Bay of Kawaihae on the west side of the island and in the midst of his kingdom. It was dedicated to his god Kukailimoku (Ku who shakes the islands), and for this pious work the reward promised was the kingship of the entire group. To a religious people such as the old Hawaiians undoubtedly were, the gods were real beings quite able to keep their promises, and yet the feudal duties to their chiefs kept the people in great uncertainty how this result was to be brought about. It seems that the building of the heiau or temple was looked upon by the whole people of Hawaii with interest or terror as they were with Kamehameha or against him in fealty to their own moi.

FIG. 32. SECTION ON ROAD NORTH OF KILAUEA IKI.

Prominent among the opponents of the future conqueror was Keoua, moi of Kau and Puna, and as an attack on his district of Kau had been made by the men of Kamehameha, Keoua was hastily summoned from Hilo where he was trying to raise help against the man who was still considered an usurper. The trail from Hilo to Kau led by the crater of Kilauea, and on a cliff overlooking the volcano was the ancient temple of Oalalauo, dedicated to Pele and her family deities of the volcanic realms, where lived Kamakaakaakua (the eye of god), a noted soothsayer. The record is silent, naturally, as the story was told to missionaries of the new faith, of the offerings no doubt made to the dreaded deities at this place. The trail continued along the northern edge of Kilauea by Uwekahuna, the highest part of the wall, and on southward of the present road to Kapapala. It was the trail by which, in 1864, Mr. Mann and myself approached the volcano in our journey around Hawaii.

Keoua and his army encamped probably on the level ground near the temple Oalalauo. During the night the eruption began by throwing out cinders and even heavy stones, the whole accompanied by the glare of molten lava, thunder and lightning. Fearstruck, the party in the morning did not dare to go on, but spent the day in making offerings to Pele, but as on the next two nights there were similar disturb-

ances they at last set out in three divisions. I now quote the account given by the
Rev. Sheldon Dibble,[18] taken from those who survived this terrible journey:

> The company in advance had not proceeded far, before the ground began to shake and
> rock beneath their feet, and it became quite impossible to stand. Soon a dense cloud of darkness
> was seen to rise out of the crater, and almost at the same instant the thunder began to roar in the
> heavens and the lightning to flash. It continued to ascend and spread abroad until the whole region
> was enveloped, and the light of day was entirely excluded. The darkness was the more terrific,

FIG. 33. UWEKAHUNA FROM VOLCANO HOUSE.

> being made visible by an awful glare from streams of red and blue light variously combined, that
> issued from the pit below, and lit up at intervals by the intense flashes of lightning from above. Soon
> followed an immense volume of sand and cinders which were thrown in high heaven and came down
> in a destructive shower for many miles around. Some few persons of the forward company were
> burned to death by the sand and cinders, and others were seriously injured. All experienced a
> suffocating sensation upon the lungs and hastened on with all possible speed.
>
> The rear body, which was nearest the volcano at the time of the eruption, seemed to suffer
> the least injury, and after the earthquake and shower of sand had passed over, hastened forward to
> escape the dangers which threatened them, and rejoicing in mutual congratulations that they had
> been preserved in the midst of such imminent peril. But what was their surprise and consternation,
> when on coming up with their comrades of the centre party, they discovered them all to have become
> corpses. Some were lying down, and others were sitting upright clasping with dying grasp, their
> wives and children, and joining noses (their form of expressing affection) as in the act of taking a
> final leave. So much like life they looked, that they at first supposed them merely at rest, and it

[18] History of the Sandwich Islands, by Sheldon Dibble. Lahainaluna, 1843, p. 65.

was not until they had come up to them and handled them, that they could detect their mistake. The whole party, including women and children, not one of them survived to relate the catastrophe that had befallen their comrades. The only living being they found was a solitary hog, in company with one of the families that had been so suddenly bereft of life. In those perilous circumstances, the surviving party did not even stay to bewail their fate, but leaving their deceased companions as they found them, hurried on and overtook the company in advance at the place of their encampment.

In a few days from this time the army of Keoua met their enemies and joined in several battles. At length Kameeiamoku went to Keoua in the disguise of a friend, and with much smooth speech and fair promises, prevailed on him to go to Kawaihae

FIG. 34. CRACKS AT PONAHOHOA. FROM PLATE IN ELLIS' TOUR OF HAWAII.

and have an interview with Kamehameha. Keoua and his followers, of whom the narrators of this scene were a part, retreated in the direction they had come. On their return they found their deceased friends as they had left them, entire, and exhibiting no other marks of decay, than a sunken hollowness in their eyes; the rest of their bodies were in a state of entire preservation. They were never buried, and their bones lay bleaching in the sun and rain for many years.

Keoua went on to Kawaihae trusting in the false chiefs, and on landing was treacherously murdered with his companions and their bodies offered as a pleasing sacrifice on the altar of the new temple. It is claimed that this was not done by the orders of Kamehameha. No doubt the popular belief was that Pele was fighting for Kamehameha, and this helped out the promise of the priests.

The description of this eruption at once reminds us of the eruption of Vesuvius in 79 A.D.; the same black, lofty column of smoke spreading out at a great height, lightnings, and the destructive showers of sand such as overwhelmed Pompeii. Could it have marked as in the Italian volcano, a renewal of activity after a long rest, and were the scoriæ the remains of the long-cooled crust at the bottom of the crater? South and west of Kilauea where the sand deposits are quite extensive, the whole ground is cracked with earthquake throes. These rents are sometimes filled with the black sand, and sometimes, especially near Ponahohoa, with lava. It seems probable that

FIG. 35. VIEW OF KILAUEA AS SEEN BY ELLIS.

from these cracks came the steam or vapor so destructive to the army, as those nearer the crater did not suffer from this cause.

The appearance of Kilauea as described by Mr. Ellis, who visited it in 1823 and was the first to publish an account of it, was quite unlike its present condition. In the various editions of Ellis' Tour of Hawaii the illustrations made from his original sketch do not agree, and I have selected that given in the London edition, presumably published under the author's supervision; also a later one made for his Poly-

1823 nesian Researches, published in 1839 (Fig. 36). The crater was evidently in an unfilled state, and was emptying itself, as the action was much diminished when he revisited the scene the next year. It may be allowable to consider 1823 the date of an eruption, although no lava-stream, if we except the traces at Ponahohoa, appeared above ground." The volcano discharged as usual by a lateral rent,

[19] I have since seen the outflow of this eruption as marked on the map of Hawaii.

the side walls of the dome yielding before the pressure of the enclosed lava, and quietly allowing the passage of the molten current to the sea. It was, I confess, a little puzzling to me, when I gave this opinion forty years ago, how the crater could be leaking out to any extent and yet be so active on the surface as Ellis describes it, but I have since seen more of the working of this wonderful place and am no longer puzzled. I have seen the bottom drop out and leave the Halemaumau quite empty, and the process was a silent one with no activity on the surface. I have again seen the surface in the pit fall so rapidly that there could be no doubt that the supply was

FIG. 36. VIEW OF KILAUEA. ELLIS, IN POLYNESIAN RESEARCHES.

tapped, and some interruption intervening; the subsidence not only stopped but the action on the surface became more violent than for a long time. This last seems to have been the case in August, 1823, when he saw what he describes as follows:

Immediately before us yawned an immense gulf, in the form of a crescent, upwards of two miles in length, about a mile across, and apparently eight hundred feet deep. The bottom was filled with lava, and the southwest and northern parts of it were one vast flood of liquid fire in a state of terrific ebullition, rolling to and fro its fiery surge and flaming billows. Fifty-one craters of varied form and size rose like so many conical islands from the surface of the burning lake. Twenty-two constantly emitted columns of gray smoke, or pyramids of brilliant flame, and many of them at the same time vomited from their ignited mouths streams of florid lava which rolled in blazing torrents down their black indented sides into the boiling mass below.

The sides of the gulf before us were perpendicular for about four hundred feet, when there was a wide horizontal ledge of solid black lava of irregular breadth, but extending completely round. Beneath this black ledge the sides sloped to the centre, which was, as nearly as we could judge, three or four hundred feet lower. It was evident that the crater had been recently filled with liquid lava up to this black ledge, and had, by some subterranean canal, emptied itself into the sea, or inundated the low land on the shore. Between nine and ten [in the evening], the dark clouds and heavy fog that since the setting of the sun had hung over the volcano, gradually cleared away. The agitated mass of liquid lava, like a flood of molten metal, raged with tumultuous whirl. The lively flame that danced over its undulating surface tinged with sulphurous blue, or glowing with mineral red, cast a broad glare of dazzling light on the indented sides of the insulated craters whose bellowing mouths, amidst rising flames, shot up at frequent intervals with loudest detonations, spherical masses of fusing lava, or bright ignited stones......In passing along the eastern side of the crater, we entered several small craters that had been in vigorous action but a short period before, marks of very recent fusion presenting themselves on every side. Their size and height was various, and many which from the top had appeared insignificant as mole hills, we now found to be twelve or twenty feet high. The outsides were composed of bright shining lava, heaped up in piles of most singular form. The lava on the inside was of a light or dark-red color with a glazed surface, and in several places, where the heat had evidently been intense, we saw a deposit of small and beautifully white crystals......In the neighborhood we saw several large rocks of a dark gray color weighing probably from one to four or five tons, which although they did not bear any marks of fire, must have been ejected from the great crater during some violent eruption, as the surrounding rocks in every direction presented a very different appearance. They were hard, and exhibited, when fractured, a glimmering and uneven surface. As we traveled on from this spot, we unexpectedly came upon another deep crater, nearly half as large as the former. The native name of it is Kilauea iki or Little Kilauea [see the surveys of Kilauea in 1865]. It is separated from the large crater by an isthmus nearly one hundred yards wide. Its sides were covered with trees or shrubs, but the bottom was filled with lava, either fluid or scarcely cold, and probably supplied by the great crater, as the trees on its sides showed that it had remained many years in a state of quiescence.[20]

The next year Kilauea is described as follows:[21]

From the time we arrived within two miles of the crater, we had the smoke arising from it directly in our faces, attended with a sulphureous stench. The wind was very strong and brought along with it fine particles of sand so that I found it necessary to draw my hat as close as possible, over my eyes in order to preserve them, carrying my head at the same time pretty low. The travelling was also difficult from the sand which covered the smooth stones on which we had before walked. Into this sand our feet sunk six or eight inches at every step. We however sometimes found the sand sufficiently hard and compact to bear us up......We reached several large crevices from which smoke was issuing at a distance of five miles from the crater. Continuing to advance toward the crater our attention was arrested by a hissing noise like that of the blowing of a furnace, except that it was irregular, the noise being sometimes very low, and then again exceedingly loud. The smoke in which we were now enveloped became so dense that we could see only a small distance before us......We had made the volcano at the southwest end, and we now proceeded round the eastern side hoping to be soon freed from the steam or smoke, which being condensed by the wind, was falling upon us like rain......At the distance of two hundred and fifty or three hundred feet below us was a level platform which appeared to have been formed by the falling in of the wall of the crater. This platform, I believe, extends nearly around the whole of the crater which is supposed to be nearly six miles in circumference. I had little difficulty in descending to this platform. From the side where I descended it extends nearly fifteen rods towards the centre of the crater, where there is another descent of two hundred and fifty or three hundred feet.

1824

---

[20] Ellis, Tour of Hawaii, p. 224.

[21] The writer has been permitted to extract this account from the unpublished journal of Edward Loomis, who was connected with the American Mission, and visited the volcano on June 16, 1824. He approached the crater from Kau on the southwest.

Down this I proceeded, though not without danger, it being in most places perpendicular, and nearly so where I descended. Many of the stones also on which it was necessary to step were loose....I had now reached the ancient bed of the volcano, having, as I supposed, descended six hundred feet. The surface of the lava was smooth though not level, sometimes rising in heaps like cocks of hay, and broken by innumerable fissures crossing each other in various directions.

This lava was of a deep black color, exceedingly porous, and as light as a pumice stone. The steam was constantly issuing from the crevices, and was so hot that I could not hold my hand in it for a moment. On this bed of lava I walked eight or ten rods towards the centre of the crater, when I came to another descent of two or three hundred feet, the volcano having sunk thus far below its ancient bed. The lower bed appeared much like the one on which I stood, but from various parts of it not only smoke, but flames of fire were issuing. The appearance of these small craters where the fire was bursting out, attended with a horrid noise, was indeed awfully grand, but I was disappointed in not finding the lower bed a mass of liquid fire. About a year since when several of our brethren were making the tour of this island, this lower bed of lava was in a liquid state. The surface has now become hard, and I have no doubt would have supported my weight could I have descended to it. This I wished to do, but I looked in vain for a place where I might descend, the sides being in most places shelving over or perpendicular......I proceeded along to the base of the sulphur mountain to collect specimens to carry home. It was in those places from which the smoke was issuing that I found the sulphur most pure, and formed into beautiful crystals.

Mr. Ellis also revisited the crater this year and noticed the greatly decreased activity. The next year, July 28, 1825, Kilauea was visited by the Rev. C. S. Stewart, who described its appearance as follows:

About midway from the top a ledge of lava, in some places only a few feet, in others many rods wide, extends entirely round, at least so far as an examination has been made, forming a kind of gallery to which you can descend in two or three places, and walk as far as the smoke settling at the south end will permit......The gulf below contains probably not less than sixty,—fifty-six have been counted,—smaller conical craters, many of which are in constant action. The tops **1825** and sides of two or three of these are covered with sulphur of mingled shades of yellow and green. With this exception, the ledge and everything below it are of a dismal black. The upper cliffs on the northern and western sides are perfectly perpendicular, and of a red color, everywhere exhibiting the seared marks of former powerful ignition. Those on the eastern side are less precipitous, and consist of entire banks of sulphur of a delicate and beautiful yellow. The south end is wholly obscured by smoke which fills that part of the crater and spreads widely over the surrounding horizon......Two or three of the smaller craters nearest to us were in full action, every moment casting out stones, ashes and lava, with heavy detonations, while the irritated flames accompanying them glared widely over the surrounding obscurity......The great seat of action, however, seemed to be at the southwestern end......Rivers of fire were seen rolling in splendid corruscations among the laboring craters, and on one side a whole lake whose surface constantly flashed and sparkled with the agitation of contending currents......At an inconsiderable distance from us was one of the largest of the conical craters whose laborious action had so impressed us during the night. On reaching its base we judged it to be one hundred and fifty feet high—a huge irregularly shapen, inverted funnel of lava, covered with clefts, orifices and tunnels from which bodies of steam escaped with deafening explosion, while pale flames, ashes, stones and lava were propelled with equal force and noise from its ragged and yawning mouth....Leaving the sulphur banks on the eastern side behind us we directed our course along the northern part to the western cliffs. As we advanced, these became more and more perpendicular, till they presented nothing but the bare and upright face of an immense wall, from eight to ten hundred feet high, on whose surface huge stones and rocks hung—apparently so loosely as to threaten falling, at the agitation of a breath. In many places a white curling vapor issued from the sides and summit of the precipice, and in two or three places streams of clay-colored lava, like small waterfalls, extending almost from the top to the bottom, had cooled evidently at a very recent period.

Lieutenant Malden, of H. B. M. S. Blonde, who accompanied Mr. Stewart, made a plan of the crater which is here reproduced, with the sketch of the crater by Robert Dampier, the artist of the Blonde. Malden calculated the height of the upper cliff from the black ledge at nine hundred feet, making the whole depth of the crater 1500 feet; and the circumference of the crater at its bottom, from five to seven miles, and at its top from eight to ten miles. On the evening of the twenty-ninth, after terrific

FIG. 37. DAMPIER'S VIEW OF KILAUEA IN 1825.

noises and tremblings of the ground, "a dense column of heavy black smoke was seen rising from the crater directly in front of us [Lord Byron's camp was on the isthmus between the main crater and Kilauea iki], the subterranean struggle ceased, and immediately after flames burst from a large cone, near which we had been in the morning, and which then appeared to have been long inactive. Red-hot stones, cinders and ashes, were also propelled to a great height with immense violence; and shortly after the molten lava came boiling up, and flowed down the sides of the cone, and over the surrounding scoriæ, in two beautifully curved streams."[22] At the same time a whole lake opened over an extent two miles in circumference.

In December of the same year Rev. Artemus Bishop found the crater much fuller than when he had visited it with Rev. W. Ellis in 1823. There were many cones from fifty to one hundred feet high on a surface about four hundred feet higher

[22] Byron, Narrative of the Voyage of H. M. S. Blonde to the Sandwich Islands in 1824-1825, p. 190. London, 1827.

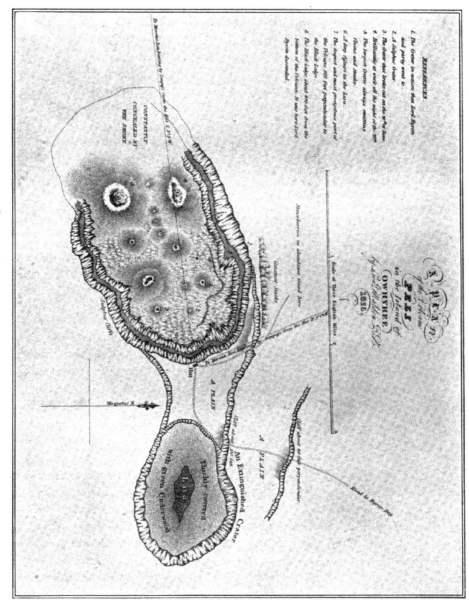

FIG. 38. PLAN OF THE CRATER BY LIEUTENANT MALDEN.

than the bottom of the crater two years before. There were lakes boiling actively, and "every now and then sending forth a gust of vapor and smoke with great noise. The natives remarked that after rising a little higher the lava will discharge itself,

1829 as formerly, toward the sea through some aperture underground."[23] In the early part of October, 1829, the Rev. C. S. Stewart again visited the crater.

He found the lower pit filled up more than two hundred feet; many of the cones had disappeared, and there was much more fire at the northern end. He thus describes two cones which he examined:

> They were in the neighborhood of each other—each about twenty feet in height, not more than sixty in circumference at the base, and tapering almost to a point at the top—being in fact two immense hollow columns formed by successive slight overflowings of lava, cooling as it rolled down, into irregular flutings, ornamented with rude drops and pendants, and long tapering stalactites. Though the ragings beneath must have been intense, from the tremendous roar within, the irresistible force and deafening hiss with which the steam rushed from every opening, and from the flames which flashed up, followed by lava white with an intensity of heat, still the incrustation of scoriæ immediately around seemed firm, and was less hot than in many other places; admitting not only of our coming close to the sides of the cone, but also of clambering some feet up them, till we could run our canes into the orifices at the top, and withdraw with their burning ends, red-hot lava, on which we readily made impressions. Pele did not seem well pleased with this familiarity, however; even the slightest touch with our sticks against the molten lava, produced an increased rush and roar from below, with an angry spitting of the fiery matter high in the air around us."[24]

Four years after, an eruption took place simultaneously with one from the summit of Mauna Loa. Unfortunately we have no account from any eye-witness. In September, 1832, the Rev. J. Goodrich visited Kilauea, and describes the appearance of the emptied crater: "The lavas had previously risen fifty feet above the black

1832 ledge, but were now more than four hundred feet below this level and the action seemed confined to Halemaumau at the south end. In January an earthquake had rent in twain the wall between Kilauea and Kilauea iki, the large crater on the east, producing seams from a few inches to several yards in width, from which the region between the two craters was deluged with lava."[25] The outbreak on the wall was very remarkable, rising as it did in a strip of land four hundred yards wide bounded by precipices on either side some two hundred feet high and apparently as loose as a dry-laid wall. Before this time Kilauea iki had long been free from lava visitations, and its sides were wooded to the bottom. The stream issued from several rents south of the centre of the isthmus and above the lowest part, flowed toward the north a few yards to the lowest part, and then divided and ran east and west into the two craters in a shallow stream; indeed the quantity of lava was so small, that its eruption is hardly more important than the action of slender cones as described by

[23] Missionary Herald, vol. xxiii, p. 53.
[24] A Visit to the South Seas, vol. ii, p. 93.
[25] American Journal of Science (N. S.), vol. xxv, p. 199.

Mr. Stewart. Where the subterranean discharge which emptied the crater and must have been of great volume, is not known. It may have been, probably was, one of the submarine eruptions which have been marked only by a more or less tidal

1834 wave or merely by the number of dead fish along the shore.

David Douglas, the Scotch botanist who lost his life in a cattle trap on Hawaii, and who made the first recorded ascent of Mauna Loa, was at Kilauea in January, 1834,

Perkins. FIG. 39. VIEW OF THE LAVA STREAMS OF 1832 AND LATER.

and measured the depth of the pit at one thousand feet. A lake of boiling lava at the north end was three hundred and nineteen yards in diameter. Halemaumau

1838 was much as described by Ellis.[26]

On the eighth of May, 1838, Captains Chase and Parker visited Kilauea, and their description has been published with a sketch of the crater. The lavas had again nearly reached the black ledge, and all over a surface of four square miles were cones and lakes of fire; twenty-six of the former were counted, eight of which were ejecting

---

[26] Journal of the Royal Geographical Society, vol. iv, 333, 334. Douglas was at Kilauea January 23-25, and his ascent of Mauna Loa was on the 29th. He was killed in July of the same year.

cinders and red-hot lava. Six small lakes were boiling violently, becoming crusted over, cracking, and again boiling. In the Halemaumau was an island which the lava was not seen to overflow; the first notice of a phenomenon observed several times since. The remarkable oscillations in the heat, remarked by all visitors, seem to have taken place on this occasion with more than the usual rapidity. As they were looking at one of the lakes which was boiling violently, they say: "After a few minutes the violent struggle ceased, and the whole surface of the lake was changed to a black mass of

FIG. 40. KILAUEA ACCORDING TO CAPTAINS PARKER AND CHASE. DANA.

scoriæ; but the pause was only to renew its exertions; for, while they were gazing at the change, suddenly the entire crust which had been formed, commenced cracking, and the burning lava soon rolled across the lake, heaving the coating on its surface like cakes of ice upon the ocean surge." As they left the crater, nearly a quarter of the floor gave way, forming a vast pool of liquid lava.[27]

Count Strzelecki was at Kilauea in the late summer of the same year and published what seem to be his undigested observations in the Hawaiian Spectator (vol. i, p. 435)[28], but revised them in his work on New Zealand and Van Diemen's Land in 1845. He made

[27] Silliman's Journal (N. S.), vol. xl, p. 117 (1841). The plate accompanying their description was redrawn from their sketches by a New Haven artist, and it is given in outline in Dana, Characteristics of Volcanoes, p. 60. The floating island "heaved up and down in the liquid mass," and "rocked like a ship on a stormy sea."

[28] Reprinted in Thrum's Annual.

barometric measurements at various points, making what seems to be Waldron's Ledge six hundred feet above the boiling surface of lava, and its height above the sea 4100 feet. He first notices the outer walls of the *ancient* crater, calls the terraces around the present crater vast platforms, and makes the highest point of these ancient walls (now much interrupted) 5054 feet. In all the modern surveys of the crater these "ancient walls" have been neglected, although the early visitors often refer to them, as Ellis saw on one of them on the northeast of Kilauea the ruins of the heiau dedicated to

FIG. 41. WALL ON THE NORTH OF KILAUEA IN 1889.

Pele. The Count described six lakes of boiling lava, four of which were only three or four feet above the general floor, the fifth forty feet, and the last one hundred and fifty; this he calls *Hau mau mau*, which covered nearly a million square feet, while the others he rates at twelve thousand square feet each. His statement that "the lava sank and rose in all the lakes simultaneously" is, considering the difference in level, very improbable, and in cases where there have been several lakes on nearly the same level no such phenomenon has been reported.

1839

Captain John Shepherd was at the crater September 16, 1839. On his way to the great lake he passed several small lakes and cones, the latter twenty to thirty feet high, from whence issued vapors and lava with loud detonations. He speaks of a lake toward the *east* side of the crater a mile long, and half as wide, within a wall a hundred feet above the general floor. This was "in violent ebullition, with an apparent flow from south to north, caused by the escape of elastic fluids, throwing up the spray in many parts thirty to forty feet." He also mentions that this lake (Halemaumau) overflowed at times."[29]

It took Kilauea nine years to fill up after the eruption of 1823; and now for eight years the process had been continued until the lava had reached a level nearly a hundred feet above the level in 1832. The force tending to rupture the mountain may be readily calculated, assuming the pressure of every twelve feet of lava to be fifteen pounds to the square inch; if the crater is emptied to a depth of four hundred feet, and in recent years the depth has been seven hundred feet, we have a pressure of five hundred pounds to the square inch. It must be remembered that the mountain wall is by no means solid and compact, and although successive discharges may strengthen some volcanic mountains, here the effect seems to be quite the contrary, owing to the extreme fluidity of the lava which runs off, leaving tunnels and caverns instead of solid interlacing dykes; consequently the discharges usually follow the same general direction.

There now comes into this history a man whose name has for many years been connected with Kilauea as its faithful observer and reporter; the Rev. Titus Coan, or Father Coan as those of us who knew and loved him preferred to call him. This excellent missionary was stationed at Hilo and the volcano was included in his parish, and he cared for it as he did for all his parishioners. His letters **1840** to the Missionary Herald, Silliman's Journal, Professor Dana, and myself, contain much information of the crater he loved to visit, and will be freely used here. Father Coan was in Oahu when the great eruption of 1840 took place, but on his return to Hawaii he at once began his investigations. In a letter dated September 25, 1840, he gives us the result:

For several years past the great crater of Kilauea has been rapidly filling up by the rising of the superincumbent crust, and by the frequent gushing forth of the molten sea below. In this manner the great basin below the black ledge, which has been computed from three to five hundred feet deep, was long since filled up by the ejection and cooling of successive masses of the fiery fluid. These silent eruptions continued to occur at intervals, until the black ledge was repeatedly overflowed, each cooling and forming a new layer from two feet thick and upwards, until the whole area of the crater was filled up, at least fifty feet above the original black ledge, and thus reducing the whole depth of the crater to less than nine hundred feet. This process of filling up continued till the latter part of May, 1840, when, as many natives testify, the whole area of the crater became one entire sea of ignifluous matter, raging like old ocean when lashed into a fury by a tempest. For several days the fires raged with fearful intensity, exhibiting a scene awfully terrific. The infuriated waves sent up infernal sounds, and dashed with such maddening energy against the sides of the awful cauldron, as to shake the solid earth above, and to detach huge masses of overhanging rocks, which, leaving their ancient beds, plunged into the fiery gulf below. So terrific was the scene that no

---

[29] London Atheneum, Nov. 14, 1840, p. 909.   [428]

one dared to approach near it, and travellers on the main road, which lay along the verge of the crater, feeling the ground tremble beneath their feet, fled and passed by at a distance. I should be inclined to discredit these statements of the natives, had I not since been to Kilauea and examined it minutely with these reports in view. Every appearance, however, of the crater confirms these reports. Every thing within the cauldron is new. Not a particle of lava remains as it was when I last visited it. All has been melted down and recast······I will now give a short history of the eruption itself.

On the 30th of May, the people of Puna observed the appearance of smoke and fire in the interior, a mountainous and desolate region of that district. Thinking that the fire might be the burning of some jungle, they took little notice of it until the next day, Sabbath, when the meetings in the different villages were thrown into confusion by sudden and grand exhibitions of fire, on a

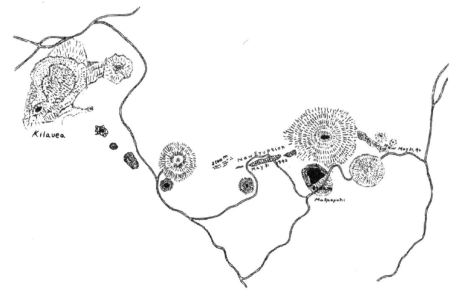

FIG. 42. MAP OF THE REGION OF THE ERUPTION. AFTER WILKES.

scale so large and fearful as to leave them no room to doubt the cause of the phenomenon. The fire augmented during the day and night; but it did not seem to flow off rapidly in any direction. All were in consternation, as it was expected that the molten flood would pour itself down from its height of four thousand feet to the coast, and no one knew to what point it would flow, or what devastation would attend its fiery course. On Monday, June 1st, the stream began to flow off in a northeasterly direction, and on the following Wednesday, June 3rd, at evening, the burning river reached the sea, having averaged half a mile an hour in its progress. The rapidity of the flow was very unequal, being modified by the inequalities of the surface, over which the stream passed. Sometimes it is supposed to have moved five miles an hour, and at other times, owing to obstructions, making no apparent progress, except in filling up deep valleys, and in swelling over or breaking away hills and precipices.

But I will return to the source of the eruption. This is in a forest, and in the bottom of an ancient wooded crater, about four hundred feet deep, and probably eight miles east of Kilauea. The region being uninhabited and covered with a thicket, it was some time before the place was discovered; and up to this time, though several foreigners have attempted it, no one, except myself, has reached the spot.   From Kilauea to this place the lava flows in a subterranean gallery probably at the depth of a thousand feet, but its course can be distinctly traced all the way by the rending of the crust of the earth into innumerable fissures, and by the emission of smoke, steam and gases. The eruption in this old crater is small, and from this place the stream disappears again for the distance of a mile or two when the lava again gushes up and spreads over an area of about fifty acres. Again it passes underground for two or three miles, when it reappears in another old wooded crater, consuming the forest and partly filling up the basin.   Once more it disappears, and flowing in a subterranean channel, cracks and breaks the earth, opening fissures from six inches to ten or twelve feet in width, and sometimes splitting the trunk of a tree so exactly that its legs stand astride at the fissure.   At some places it is impossible to trace the subterranean stream on account of the impenetrable thicket under which it passes.   After flowing underground several miles, perhaps six or eight, it again broke out like an overwhelming flood, and sweeping forest, hamlet, plantation, and everything before it, rolled down with resistless energy to the sea, where leaping a precipice of forty or fifty feet, it poured itself in one vast cataract of fire into the deep below, with loud detonations, fearful hissings, and a thousand unearthly and indescribable sounds······The atmosphere in all directions was filled with ashes, spray, gases, etc.; while the burning lava, as it fell into the water was shivered into millions of minute particles, and, being thrown back into the air fell in showers of sand on all the surrounding country.   The coast was extended into the sea for a quarter of a mile, and a pretty sand beach, and a new cape were formed.   Three hills of scoriæ and sand were also formed in the sea, the lowest about two hundred, and the highest about three hundred feet.

For three weeks this terrific river disgorged itself into the sea with little abatement.   Multitudes of fishes were killed, and the waters of the ocean were heated for twenty miles along the coast. The breadth of the stream where it fell into the sea, is about half a mile, but inland it varies from one to four or five miles in width, conforming itself, like a river, to the face of the country over which it flowed.   The depth of the stream will probably vary from ten to two hundred feet, according to the inequalities of the surface over which it passed.   During the flow night was converted into day on all eastern Hawaii; the light was visible for more than one hundred miles at sea; and at the distance of forty miles fine print could be read at midnight.

The whole course of the stream from Kilauea to the sea is about forty miles.   The ground over which it flowed descends at the rate of one hundred feet to the mile.   The crust is now cooled, and may be traversed with care, though scalding steam, pungent gases, and smoke are still emitted in many places.   In pursuing my way for nearly two days over this mighty smouldering mass, I was more and more impressed at every step with the wonderful scene.   Hills had been melted down like wax; ravines and deep valleys had been filled; and majestic forests had disappeared like a feather in the flames.   On the outer edge of the lava, where the stream was more shallow and the heat less vehement, and where of course the liquid mass cooled soonest, the trees were mowed down like grass before the scythe, and left charred, crisp, smouldering, and only half consumed.   As the lava flowed around the trunks of large trees on the outskirts of the stream, the melted mass stiffened and consolidated before the trunk was consumed, and when this was effected, the top of the tree fell, and lay unconsumed on the crust, while the hole which marked the place of the trunk remains almost as smooth and perfect as the calibre of a cannon.   These holes are innumerable and I found them to measure from ten to forty feet deep, but, as I remarked before, they are in the more shallow part of the lava, the trees being entirely consumed where it was deeper.   During the flow of this eruption the great crater of Kilauea sunk about three hundred feet, and her fires became nearly extinct, one lake only out of many being left in the mighty cauldron.   This open lake is at present intensely active, and the fires are increasing, as is evident from the glare visible from our station, and from the testimony of visitors.   During the early part of the eruption slight and repeated shocks of earthquake were felt, for several successive days, near the scene of action.   These shocks were not noticed

Henshaw.   FIG. 43. LAVA AROUND TREES IN PUNA.

at Hilo. Through the directing hand of a kind Providence no lives were lost, and but little property was consumed during this amazing flood of fiery ruin.

During the progress of the descending stream, it would often fall into some fissure, and forcing itself into apertures, and under massive rocks, and even hillocks and extended plats of ground, and lifting them from their ancient beds, bear them with all their superincumbent mass of soil, trees, etc., on its viscous and livid bosom, like a raft on the water. When the fused mass was sluggish, it had a gory appearance like clotted blood, and when it was active, it resembled fresh and clotted blood mingled and thrown into violent agitation. Sometimes the flowing lava would find a subterranean gallery diverging at right angles from the main channel, and pressing into it would flow off unobserved, till meeting with some obstruction in its dark passage, when, by its expansive force, it would raise the crust of the earth into a dome-like hill of fifteen or twenty feet in height, and then bursting this shell, pour itself out in a fiery torrent around. A man who was standing at a considerable distance from the main stream, and intensely gazing on the absorbing scene before him, found himself suddenly raised to the height of fifteen or twenty feet above the common level around him, and he had but just time to escape from his dangerous position, when the earth opened where he had stood, and a stream of fire gushed out.[30]

The hill where the lava first appeared is called Arare, and is about six miles from Kilauea easterly in the dense forest. The natives say that the lava rose in this crater about three hundred feet, and then sunk again when the fissure opened below, and in 1865 at the time of the author's visit there were evident proofs of this on the crater walls. The course of the stream seems to have led through a high hill (seen in the sketch of Makaopuhi) thus just avoiding this large pit where it might be supposed the resistance would be least, but the hill was probably hollow, being a cone from which the lava had been emptied, and the cavity beneath it perhaps exceeded in size the pit crater.

The elevation of the place where the lava finally reached the surface is given by Wilkes at 1244 feet, and it is twenty-seven miles from Kilauea, twenty-one from the first outbreak, and twelve from the shore at Nanawale. The sand-hills thrown up at this place were found to be one hundred and fifty, and two hundred and fifty feet high eight months after their formation, but since then the sea has removed the whole mass. Even in 1865 they were not a third of the measured height and nodules of olivine were abundant in the sands of the beach at considerable distance.

In November, 1840, when first visited by Professor Dana, the lava was still hot in many places, a few feet below the surface. Small sulphur banks, with deposits of alum and other salts were met with in several places.[11]

The lava of this eruption is chrysolitic to a marked degree; no such lava is found in Kilauea at present; such lava has issued in several streams from Mauna Kea in ancient times, also perhaps from Mauna Loa, if we suppose the large deposits of this lava occasionally found along the coast near Hilo to have proceeded from this

[30] Missionary Herald, vol. xxxvii, p. 283.
[11] Geology of the United States Exploring Expedition, p. 190.

mountain, and it is common in the old flows near Honolulu, and in later flows from Mauna Loa, in Kau. In the crater of Kilauea the olivine is in much smaller particles.

In November of the same year, when visited by Dana, the lava had fallen three hundred and forty feet below the black ledge, or nearly a thousand feet below the highest wall, and only three pools of lava were in action. Halemaumau was fifteen hundred feet long and a thousand feet wide. The black ledge, three hundred and forty

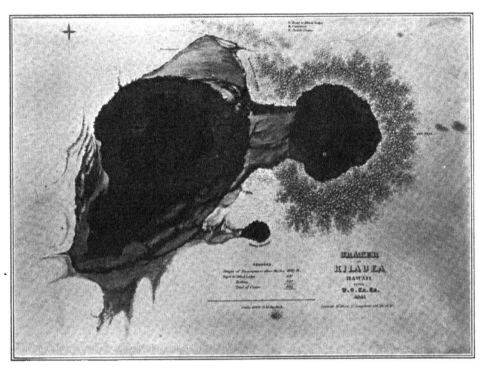

FIG. 44. THE WILKES PLAN OF KILAUEA IN 1841.

feet from the bottom, was from one to three thousand feet wide, and extended completely around the crater. No flames were visible, and there was but little noise.[32]

Unfortunately at the time of Dana's first visit (also at his second in 1887), Kilauea was not in a spectacular condition and he is rather inclined, not unnaturally, in his treatment of the vivid accounts of his predecessors to regard these as rather exaggerated, hence it is pleasing to find in his latest work the following description :[33] "In a night scene from the summit, the large cauldron in place of a bloody glare, now glowed with intense brilliancy, and the surface sparkled all over with shifting points

[32] *Loc. cit.*, p. 171.
[33] Characteristics of Volcanoes, p. 68.

of dazzling light, like a network of lightning, occasioned by the jets in constant play."
My old friend, Dr. Charles Pickering, Dana's companion on the exploration, gave him
the apt comparison to lightning, and Dana admits that Pickering was "a man of very
exact observation and measured words."

1841   In January, 1841, Dr. Pickering describes several considerable variations in
the surface of Halemaumau, a hundred feet or more.   On January 17, two of
the pools discharged large quantities of lava over the bottom of the pit.   The plan of
the crater published by Wilkes, as well as the view by Drayton, one of the artists of the
expedition, show the appearance of Kilauea at this time[14] (Figs. 44, 45).

FIG. 45.   DRAYTON'S VIEW OF KILAUEA IN 1841.

I do not quote much from the narrative of the United States Exploring Expedition, as Captain Wilkes included much in his story that was of merely personal
interest; but there are a few statements about the condition of Kilauea at this time
that should be noticed; and also, as the crater is generally such an amenable subject
that accidents are almost unknown there, and "narrow escapes" seldom occur, it may be
well to tell of one that actually occurred.   I quote from the published report,[15] although
I have heard the substance from Dr. G. P. Judd, who was Wilkes' most useful guide
as well as friend.   He was in the crater to obtain specimens for the expedition: he had
collected gases and was trying to get at the liquid lava:

[14] Narrative of the United States Exploring Expedition, vol. iv, p. 178.
[15] Narrative U. S. Ex. Ex., vol. iv, p. 184, 4to ed.   [434]

Dr. Judd then sought for a place where he might dip up some of the recent and yet fluid lava, but found none sufficiently liquid for the purpose. Failing here he proceeded toward the great fiery lake at the southern extremity of the crater. He found that the ascent toward this was rapid because the successive flowings of the lava had formed crusts which lapped over each other [see the formation in Pls. L and LII]. This rock was so dark in colour as to be almost black, and so hot as to act upon spittle just as iron, heated nearly to redness, would have done......At this time they were very near the great lake but could not see its surface, which was still about twenty feet higher than the spot where they stood......On his return the party passed the small crater which has been spoken of: and which by comparison with the larger one appeared cool. Smoke and a little igneous matter were issuing from a small cone in the centre: but with this exception, a crust of solid lava covered the bottom.

On the sides of this crater Dr. Judd saw some fine specimens of capillary glass, "Pele's hair," which he was anxious to obtain for our collection. He therefore, by the aid of the hand of one of the natives, descended and began to collect specimens. When fairly down he was in danger of falling, in consequence of the narrowness of the footing: but in spite of this difficulty, his anxiety to collect the best specimens enticed him onwards. While thus advancing, he saw and heard a slight movement in the lava about fifty feet from him, which was twice repeated, and curiosity led him to turn to approach the place where the motion occurred. In an instant the crust was broken asunder by a terrific heave, and a jet of molten lava full fifteen feet in diameter rose to a height of about forty-five feet, with a most appalling noise. He instantly turned for the purpose of escaping: but found that he was now under a projecting ledge which opposed his ascent, and that the place where he had descended was some feet distant. The heat was already too great to permit him to turn his face towards it, and was every moment increasing, while the violence of the throes, which shook the rock beneath his feet, augmented. Although he considered his life as lost, he did not omit the means for preserving it, but offering a mental prayer for the Divine aid, he strove, although in vain to scale the projecting rock. While thus engaged he called in English upon his native attendants for aid: and looking upwards, saw the friendly hand of Kalumo....extended towards him. Ere he could grasp it, the fiery jet again rose above their heads, and Kalumo shrank back scorched and terrified, until excited by a second appeal, he again stretched forth his hand, and seizing Dr. Judd's with a giant's grasp, their joint efforts placed him on the ledge......In looking for the natives they were seen some hundreds of yards distant running as fast as their legs could carry them. On his calling to them, however, they returned......Dr. Judd now found that he had no time to lose, for the lava was flowing so rapidly to the north, that their retreat might be cut off, and the whole party be destroyed. They therefore at once took leave of the spot and only effected their escape by running. ....The crater had previously been measured by Dr. Judd and was found to be thirty-eight feet deep by two hundred feet in diameter. The rapidity of its filling (in twelve minutes) will give some idea of the quantity of the fluid mass.

In February, 1842, Mr. Coan writes as follows:

When within four or five rods of the great lake, unaware of our near proximity to it, we saw directly before us a vast area of what we had supposed to be solid lava moving off to the right and left. We were at first a little startled, not knowing but all was about to float away beneath us, especially as the lavas for a mile back were almost insupportably hot, and gases and steam were escaping from numerous openings. On looking again, we perceived that the whole surface of the lake was from six to fifteen feet above the level of the surrounding lava, although at my last visit, it was from sixty to seventy feet below. Within six feet of this embankment we could see nothing of the lake, and in order to examine it we climbed the precipice some fifty feet. The explanation of this strange condition of things, is this: when the liquid contents of the lake had risen to a level with the brim, there was a constant and gradual boiling over of

1842

the viscid mass, but in quantities too small to run off far.   Consequently it solidified on the margin, and thus formed the high rim which confined the lavas.   Twice or at two points while we were there, the liquid flood broke through the rim, and flowed off in a broad, deep channel which continued its flow until we left the volcano.   The view was a new one, and thrilling beyond description.

In July, 1844, Mr. Coan saw the large lake overflow on every side, spreading over the whole southern end of the crater to the base of the black ledge and concealing the outlines of the raised rim.   Two deep fissures extended under the ledge nearly encircling that part of the crater, and one of these was one hundred feet deep.   The

1844 diagram given in Mr. Coan's letter (which has not been published in full) is here reproduced as rendering clearer the geography at the time. Dana considers the canals as mysteries, but the explanation he gives (Characteristics of Volcanoes, p. 77) only substitutes one mystery for another.   We will continue the record and overtake his explanation.

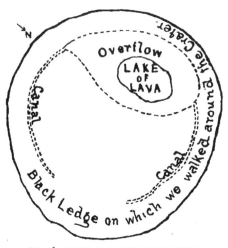

FIG. 46.   DIAGRAM IN THE COAN LETTER.

1846 In June, 1846, Mr. Coan writes[36] that "the repeated overflowings had elevated the central parts of the crater four or five hundred feet since 1840, so that some points are now more elevated than the black ledge."   We may note that the rise in the floor level was due, according to this practised observer, to the overflow of the lake which filled up the lower levels, including the canals.   A month later Rev. Chester S. Lyman was at the crater and found it much as the last observer had reported.   The canal was nearly filled by overflows, and in places nearly obliterated.[37]

A rude sketch which Mr. Lyman left on the islands is here reproduced, and with this chart we may understand the explanation of the rapid rise of the bottom of Kilauea given by Mr. Lyman and adopted by Prof. Dana.[38]   A crescent shaped ridge of rocks is shown on this sketch, and Lyman states that it was a continuous ridge more than a mile long, consisting of angular blocks of compact lava resembling the debris at the foot of a range of trap or basalt.   From this he infers that the ridge once constituted a *talus* or accumulation of debris on the floor of the walls of the lower pit of 1840:

[36] Amer. Journ. Science, 1850, x, 361.
[37] Amer. Journ. Science, 1851, xii, 75.
[38] Prof. Lyman's plan, as given by Dana (Characteristics of Volcanoes, p. 79), is quite different from the plan he left on the spot and which is copied above.   It must have been elaborated at New Haven from notes.

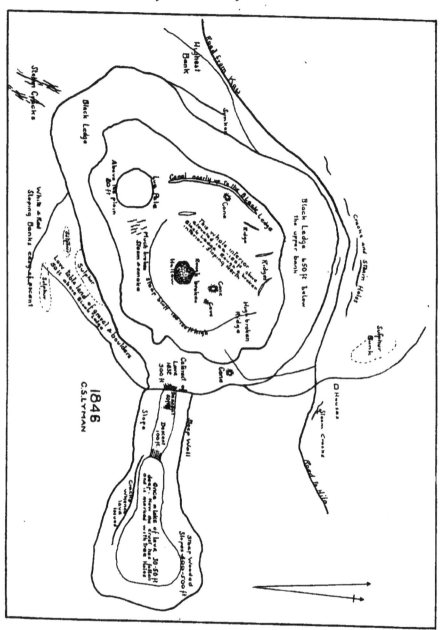

FIG. 47. LYMAN'S PLAN OF KILAUEA IN 1846.

[437]

that the floor with its margin of blocks had been elevated partly by upheaving forces from beneath, and partly by overflows from the Great Lake and other active vents until the talus overtopped the precipice at the foot of which it was accumulated. If these gentlemen had been content with either the elevation or the overflow theory singly, we could understand to some extent the process; we have recently seen the former in the strange obelisk of Mont Pelée, and the latter is the usual way in which the floor of Kilauea is raised. But if either Prof. Dana or Mr. Lyman had seen a lava stream taking a dry stone wall in hand, quietly insinuating its flexible black fingers under and between the stones and raising them _ up and carrying them off, they would have seen the improbability of their wall of stone remaining *in situ* surrounding an overflowing vent of lava. Mr. Coan saw clearly that the rise of the floor of the crater was due mainly at least to the accumulation of overflowing lava; it was acrogenous, and not pushed up from below. The rise of a cylin-

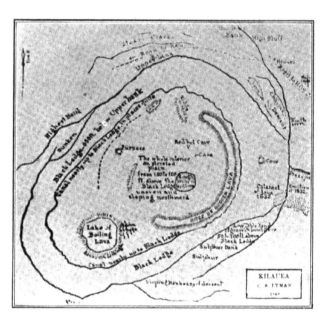

FIG. 48. LYMAN'S CORRECTED PLAN.

der of lava a mile in diameter some two hundred feet would be remarkable, but with an overflowing bowl of lava more than a thousand feet in diameter in its very midst the phenomenon would be incomprehensible. It is also difficult to see what this ascension has to do with forming the canals. When I surveyed the crater eight or nine years after, most of this wall, which did not appear on the original plan as shown above, had disappeared, but in a like position were scattered stones which I could not believe had ever been *elevated* to their then position; they had dropped from the cliffs above—the outer walls—precisely as can be seen today on the trail into the crater huge rocks of the same formation which were hurled down in the earthquake of 1868.

[438]

That there is a daily change of level in the dome-like floor of Kilauea, I cannot doubt. The black surface absorbs the heat of the sun to such a degree as at times to become unbearable to the touch. The casual visitor supposes this terrestrial heat, when it is really solar. The nights here are usually quite cold, and the change from midnight to noon must result in considerable expansion and contraction. In the early morning I have repeatedly heard the tinkling noise caused by the sun's rays on the cold lava as they displace the shadows of the cliffs; and I once measured the change in width of the great crack at the base of the dome on the trail across the crater, at eight inches between early morning and noon on a bright day. If we had a suitable observatory at Kilauea observations could easily be made all over the floor, and on the surface of Halemaumau as well for change of level.

But Mr. Lyman's visits, for he was again at Kilauea in August, were full of information. He saw a thick cone, marked "furnace" on his plan, in full blast on his second visit. Such a furnace as the writer saw in the summer of 1889. Lyman took a few compass bearings in the crater, and with an improvised quadrant obtained the height of walls. The Great Lake (Halemaumau) he made twenty-four hundred by two thousand feet, and the surface ten or fifteen feet below his standpoint on the rim. The lavas had an apparent motion to the southwest.

1847 Halemaumau was, according to Mr. Coan, much in the same condition as the previous year.[19]

1848 The lake was early in the year inactive, and the crust hardened and gradually assumed a convex form. Dana states that soon after this swelling crust two thousand feet in diameter, was raised into a dome two or three hundred feet high, covering the whole lake. Mr. Coan, from whom this information was obtained, adds that in August the dome was raised almost high enough to overtop the lower part of the outer wall of Kilauea and look out upon the surrounding country. From openings in the dome the molten lava could be seen, and occasionally sluggish lava rolled in heavy and irregular streams down the sides. The dome as it now stands has been formed by the compound action of upheaving forces from beneath and of eruptions from the openings forming successive layers upon its external surface. Most of this year no fires were to be seen even at night in Lua Pele.

This is the first appearance of a dome in the history of Kilauea, and it is hard to accept the elevation theory applied to a dome of the brittle nature of crust lava, cracked and fissured in every part, with such a vast diameter, holding together for any length of time even if its foundations were more solid than the brink of Halemaumau affords at its best. To suppose this raised two or three hundred feet without interior

[19] Amer. Journ. Science, 1851, xii, 80.　　　[439]

cross braces or supports is difficult: to suppose it blown up by gases, like a soap bubble, predicates a semifluid or elastic continuous crust which did not exist, for the dome was well punctured at its earliest formation and long before it attained its full height, the top was open like the dome of the Roman Pantheon, and from the lateral apertures flowed lava streams. I do not here dispute the fact that enormous masses have been pushed up to so great an height as five hundred feet from the molten or semi-molten pools in Kilauea,—we shall see many later,—but I must call attention to the difficulty of the problem.

The dome continued to hold together over the quiet pit, like a mausoleum over a dead volcano, and in April, 1849, there came a change; activity was greatly increased; startling detonations were heard from cones around the dome, and from the opening on the top of this lavas were thrown fifty to sixty feet. Elsewhere in the main crater action was so violent as to frighten travelers from the descent to any part of **1849** Kilauea. This excitement did not last long, it suddenly ceased and Hale-maumau was emptied of lava by subterranean discharge, in what direction is unknown, and there followed a period of great quiet. A period of what Mr. Coan aptly calls "steaming stupefaction" continued through the next two years, but early in 1852 boiling lavas could again be seen through the summit aperture of the dome, now one hundred feet in diameter. In July Mr. Coan writes[40] that the orifice had doubled its diameter, which constantly increased by the fall of fragments into the molten pool one hundred and fifty feet below. In the west wall of the dome was a crack from top to bottom, through which lavas were ejected, while vapors escaped from the perforated dome on all sides. In a later letter Mr. Coan writes[41] that at the beginning of 1854 the dome still stood, probably two miles in circumference and three to six hundred feet high. The surface of the main crater floor continued to rise and he estimated it at six hundred feet above the level of 1840.

We are now approaching a period when Pele's activity seems transferred from her everlasting house to her more lofty abode on Mauna Loa, and we can conveniently turn to that grand dome rising ten thousand feet above Kilauea. Henceforth we will record both mountains together, not that I believe they have any more connection than Kea and Hualalai, but for convenience of narrative, as the one in action attracts all the attention; but while Kilauea is generally visited whenever Loa is in action, Kilauea is frequently visited and always now has some one living on the banks, while Loa is seldom ascended, and in the winter season is difficult and even dangerous to ascend. In the winter or rainy months most of the eruptions of Loa have occurred.

[40] Amer. Journ. Science, 1853, xv, 63. Letter dated July 31, 1852.
[41] Ibid, 1854, xviii, 96. Letter dated Jan. 30, 1854. [440]

We must retrace our steps to the first recorded eruption of Mauna Loa in 1832. It is strange that no traditions of the natives point definitely to any previous one. They might have seen the fires from the summit crater Mokuaweoweo, or even the fire fountains from the cracks on the flanks, but even the hunters did not care to venture

1832 into the elevated waste where cold and winds and rain divided the realm with gods and wandering spirits of lower degree and even less morals. All that concerned the aborigines was the descent of a destroying lava stream into their fertile fields or over the sand beaches and into the bays, so important to a fishing population. The impelling spirit was always Pele, and from which of her many abodes she came mattered little to these children of Nature.

On June 20, 1832, Mauna Loa began to eject lava from the summit on several sides, and continued three or four weeks, with such brilliancy as to be visible at Lahaina, more than a hundred miles distant.[42] As no one ascended the mountain it is not known whether this eruption was from Mokuaweoweo or from some of the many vents dotted over the broad flat summit. Through the summer earthquakes were frequent on Hawaii, although not severe, and finally Kilauea burst into activity as described in the account of that volcano (p. 46).

After an interval of eleven years Mokuaweoweo again broke out. In 1837 Douglas made the first ascent of Loa by a foreigner (if not by any human being), and unfortunately wrote a letter to Dr. Hooker of Kew, England, in which he gives a wild and impossible account of the condition of the crater. In his journal, and in a later letter

1843 to Captain Sabine he gave a sane account of the crater which was quiescent.[43] He remarks that there was little in the upper part of the mountain to interest a naturalist. Mr. Douglas was all the time a botanist. The Wilkes expedition made the ascent in January, 1841, and found no activity beyond a few steam exhalations. Lieutenant Eld, by taking angles from the bottom of the crater, made the western wall 784 feet high, and the eastern 470 feet. Dr. G. P. Judd accompanied Eld in the descent into the crater. The accounts of the eruption of 1843 are as follows, the first from Dr. Andrews in a letter dated February 6, 1843:

Smoke was first seen near the summit of the mountain, on Monday, January 9th. During the succeeding night a brilliant light was emitted from the same spot. The great distance of the mountain from Hilo—about forty miles—prevented our seeing anything more than the intense glare

[42] Amer. Journ. Science, xxv, 199.

[43] Dana says in a note on page 59 of his Characteristics of Volcanoes, in speaking of the letter to Dr. Hooker, which caused an unjust doubt to fall on all his reports, "His words indicate a mixing up and magnifying of what he had seen at the Kilauea and Mauna Loa craters, which can be explained only on the ground of temporary hallucination. He may have dined that day with his friend the British consul. Mr. Douglas was an excellent Scotchman, and all the rest of his writings are beyond questioning." The journal appeared in the Companion of the Botanical Magazine, ii, 79-182, in 1836. In the Journal of the Royal Geographical Society, 1834, iv, 333, is an important letter to Captain Sabine, and in the Magazine of Zoology and Botany, 1837, i, 582, are extracts from his journal including the letter to Dr. Hooker.

sent forth by the boiling mass, which apparently was pouring forth and rolling down the side... During the day vast volumes of smoke were constantly pouring forth, concealing everything beneath. At times the smoke rose in a nearly perpendicular column, not less, as I judged, than one or two thousand feet high. Before the close of the week the light disappeared from the upper part of the mountain, and broke out anew near its base in the valley between it and Mauna Kea.[44]

The Rev. Titus Coan writes under date of February 20, 1843.[45] After describing the brilliancy of the light he says: "For about four weeks this scene continued without much abatement. At the present time, after six weeks, the action of the fire is greatly diminished, though it is still somewhat vehement at one or two points along the line of eruption. The flow of the lava has probably extended twenty miles." Soon after this he was able to visit the scene of eruption, and ascend the mountain, and writes in a letter dated April 5: "The eruption has flowed from the summit of Mauna Loa to the base of Mauna Kea, where it separates into two broad streams, one flowing toward Waimea, and the other towards Hilo. Another great stream has flowed along the base of Mauna Loa towards Mauna Hualalai in Kona. These streams are still flowing, and they have reached a distance of from twenty-

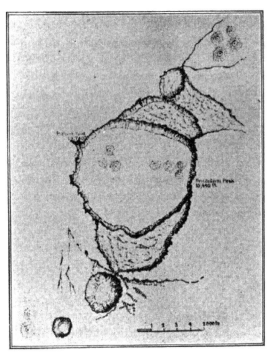

FIG. 49. WILKES' SURVEY OF MOKUAWEOWEO, 1841.

five to thirty miles from the crater on the top of the mountain. The quantity of lava is immense, it being many miles wide. There are two great active craters in close contiguity near the summit. Lava does not flow from these craters now; it is conveyed down the side of the mountain in a subterranean duct from fifty to a hundred feet below the surface, at the rate of from fifteen to twenty miles an hour."[46] Soon after this visit the flow ceased. Mr. Coan threw stones into the stream as it appeared through the openings in the crust, and they did not sink but were instantly carried along out of sight. Mounds, ridges and cones were thrown up along the lava stream, and from

[44] Missionary Herald, xxxix, p. 381.   [45] Ibid, 463.   [46] Missionary Herald, xl, 44.

the latter, steam, gases and hot stones were ejected. The angle of descent for the whole distance is 6°, but in many places the stream was continuous at an inclination of 25°. Kilauea was visited by Mr. Abner Wilcox during this eruption, but it showed no signs of sympathy with the summit crater.

1849 In May, 1849, there was seen for two or three weeks a brilliant and lofty column of light over the mountain. Mr. Coan, who furnishes this note, says nothing of any outflow of lava or earthquakes.[47] In 1851 a slight **1851** eruption occurred on the summit of Mauna Loa, described by Mr. Coan as follows:[48] "On the 8th of August last a new eruption was seen on the western slope of Mauna Loa, a few miles from its summit. All we could see at Hilo was a white pillar of smoke by day and a brilliant fiery pillar by night....At Kau the view was less obstructed....The eruption continued but three or four days." This eruption broke out about a thousand feet below the summit, or two hundred feet below the bottom of the terminal crater. Some observers declare that the smoke proceeded partly from Mokuaweoweo, but no one ascended the mountain. No jets were thrown up and the fissure soon closed. From the portion of this stream that I visited in 1864, I should estimate its dimensions at ten miles in length, but less than a mile in average breadth, or in volume one hundred and sixty million cubic yards of lava. The greater part of this lava is pahoehoe, although some aa occurs, and the whole flow bears marks of rapid cooling. It followed very nearly the track of an eruption which broke down the western rim of Mokuaweoweo and flowed through Kealakeakua.

1852 February 17, 1852, only six months after the slight eruption just mentioned, Mauna Loa again broke out and our faithful chronicler writes as follows:[49]

Old Kilauea has been quite tame since I last wrote you......At half-past three on the morning of the 17th ult. a small beacon light was discovered on the summit of Mauna Loa. At first it appeared like a solitary star resting on the apex of the mountain. In a few minutes its light increased and shone like a rising moon. Seamen keeping watch on deck in our port exclaimed, "What is that? The moon is rising in the West!" In fifteen minutes the problem was solved. A flood of fire burst out of the mountain, and soon began to flow in a brilliant current down its northern slope. It was from the same point, and it flowed in the same line, as the great eruption which I visited in March, 1843. In a short time immense columns of burning lava shot up heavenward to the height of three or four hundred feet, flooding the summit of the mountain with light, and gilding the firmament with its radiance. Streams of light came pouring down the mountain, flashing through our windows, and lighting up our apartments so that we could see to read large print. When we first awoke, so dazzling was the glare on our windows that we supposed that some building near us must be on fire; but as the light shone directly upon our couch and into our faces we soon perceived the cause. In two hours the molten stream had rolled, as we judged, about fifteen miles down the side of the mountain. This eruption was one of terrible activity and surpassing splendor, but it was short. In about twenty-four hours all traces of it seemed to be extinguished.

---

[47] American Journal of Science, 1851, xii, 82. Letter dated January, 1851.

[48] Ibid, xi, 395. A letter to Rev. C. S. Lyman.

[49] Ibid, xii, 219.

At daybreak on the 20th of February, we were again startled by a rapid eruption bursting out laterally on the side of the mountain facing Hilo, and about midway from the base to the summit of the mountain. This lateral crater was equally active with the one on the summit, and in a short time we perceived the molten river flowing from its orifice direct towards Hilo. The action became more and more fierce from hour to hour. Floods of lava poured out of the mountain's side, and the glowing river soon reached the woods at the base of the mountain, a distance of twenty miles.

Clouds of smoke ascended and hung like a vast canopy over the mountain, or rolled off on the wings of the wind. These clouds assumed various hues,—murky, blue, white, purple or scarlet—as they were more or less illuminated from the fiery abyss below. Sometimes they resembled an *inverted* burning mountain with its apex pointing to the awful orifice over which it hung. Sometimes the glowing pillar would shoot up vertically for several degrees, and then describing a graceful curve, sweep off horizontally, like the tail of a comet, further than the eye could reach. The sable atmosphere of Hilo assumed a lurid appearance, and the sun's rays fell upon us with a yellow, sickly light. Clouds of smoke careered over the ocean, carrying with them ashes, cinders, charred leaves, etc., which fell in showers upon the decks of ships approaching our coast. The light was seen more than a hundred miles at sea, and at times the purple tinge was so widely diffused as to appear like the whole firmament on fire. Ashes and capillary vitrifactions called Pele's hair fell thick in our streets and upon the roofs of our houses. And this state of things still continues, for even now while I write, the atmosphere is in the same yellow and dingy condition; every object looks pale, and sickly showers of vitreous filaments are falling around us, and our children are gathering them.

As soon as the second eruption broke out I determined to visit it. Dr. Wetmore agreeing to accompany me, we procured four natives to carry our baggage, one of them, Kekai acting as guide. On Monday the 23rd of February, we all set off and slept in the outskirts of the great forest which separates Hilo from the mountains. Our track was not the one I took in 1843, namely the bed of a river; we attempted to penetrate the thicket at another point, our general course bearing southwest. In ancient days an Indian trail had been beaten through in this direction, but it was now entangled with jungle so that all traces of it were nearly obliterated. However, we plunged into the forest with a long knife, hatchet and clubs, and cut and beat our way at the rate of one and a fifth miles an hour. At night we slept in the bush and listened to the distant roar of the volcano. On Wednesday the 25th we gained a little eminence in the woods, from which we could see the lava-stream which was now opposite us on our left, distant six miles. This fiery flood was now half way through the forest, and more than three-fourths of the way from the crater to the shore, sweeping all before it. Apprehending that it might reach the sea in a day or two, and that the ladies at the station might be alarmed, Dr. Wetmore determined to return. Taking one of the natives and leaving three with me, he retraced his steps while I pushed on through jungle and bog and dell, beating every yard of my way out of this horrible thicket. On the 26th we emerged from the forest but plunged at once into a dense fog more dark than the thicket itself. Pushing up the mountain we encamped for the night on a rough bushy ridge. A little before sunset the fog rolled off, and Mauna Kea and Mauna Loa both stood out in grand relief; the former robed in a fleecy mantle almost to its base, and the latter belching out floods of fire from its burning bowels. All night long we could see the glowing fires, and listen to the awful roar of the fearful crater.

We had now been out four nights, and were within twenty miles of the crater, with the long brilliant river of fusion on our left shining in a line of light down the side of the mountain [see the illustration of the flow of 1887] till it entered the woods. We left our mountain aerie on the 27th, determined if possible to reach the seat of action on that day. Taking the pillar of fire and cloud as our mark, and still having the great river of lava on our left, we pushed on over a rough and almost impassable surface—the attraction increasing as the square of the distance decreased. Our intense interest mocked all obstacles. At noon we came upon the confines of a tract of naked scoriæ so intolerably sharp and jagged that our baggage-men could not pass it. Here I ordered a halt;

stationed the two carriers, gave an extra pair of strong shoes to my guide, gave him my wrapper and blanket, put a few crackers and boiled eggs into my pockets, took my compass and staff, and said to Mr. Salt Sea (Kekai), ''Now go ahead, and let us warm ourselves tonight by that fire yonder.'' Thus equipped we pressed up the mountain, over fields of indescribable roughness; now mounting a ridge of sharp and vitreous scoriæ (aa), where the fiery pillar stood full in view, and then plung-ing into some awful ravine or pit, from which we slowly emerged by crawling upon all fours. But I soon found that my guide needed a leader. He was too slow. I therefore pressed ahead, leaving him to get on as best he could. After half-past three P. M. I reached the awful crater and stood alone in the light of its fires. It was a moment of unutterable interest. I seemed to be standing in the presence and before the throne of the eternal God; and while all other voices were hushed, His alone spake. I was ten thousand feet above the sea, in a vast solitude untrodden by the foot of man or beast; amidst a silence unbroken by any living voice, and surrounded by scenes of terrific deso-lation. Here I stood almost blinded by the insufferable brightness; almost deafened by the startling clangor; almost petrified with the awful scene. The heat was so intense that the crater could not be approached within forty or fifty yards on the windward side, and probably, not within two miles on the leeward. The eruption as before stated, commenced on the very summit of the mountain, but it would seem that the lateral pressure of the embowelled lava was so great as to force itself out at a weaker point in the side of the mountain; at the same time cracking and rending the mountain all the way down from the summit to the place of ejection······The eruption first issued from a depression in the mountain, but a rim of scoriæ two hundred feet in elevation had already been formed around the orifice in the form of a hollow, truncated cone. This cone was about half a mile in circumference at its base, and the orifice at the top may be three hundred feet in diameter······ The eruptions were not intermittent but continuous. Volumes of the fusion were constantly ascend-ing and descending like a *jet d'eau*. The force which expelled these igneous columns from the orifice, shivered them into millions of fragments of unequal size, some of which would be rising, some fall-ing, some shooting off laterally, others describing graceful curves; some moving in tangents, and some falling back in vertical lines into the mouth of the crater. During the night the scene sur-passed all powers of description. Vast volumes of lava, at a white heat shot up continuously···A large fissure opening through the lower rim of the crater gave vent to the molten flood which constantly poured out of the orifice and rolled down the mountain in a deep, broad river at the rate, probably, of ten miles an hour.

The stream stopped about ten miles from Hilo beach; the eruption lasted twenty days. Early in March Messrs. H. Kinney and Fuller made the ascent and they confirm Mr. Coan's description of the terrific noise, but are inclined to enlarge his estimates in some particulars. Mr. Kinney made the height of the jets four to eight hundred feet: he noticed great whirlwinds about the jet, stalking like sentinels. Mr. Fuller states[50] that the diameter of the crater from which the jets played was about a thousand feet; height of crater, a hundred to a hundred and fifty feet; height of the jet, two to seven hundred feet, and rarely below three hundred feet; diameter of the jet, one to three hundred feet, and rarely perhaps reaching four hundred feet. In July Mr. Coan again ascended to the crater and found no fire. He found an unusual supply of limu or basaltic pumice. He says in writing of this, "We found it ten miles

[50] American Journal of Science, 1852, xiv, 258. Letter dated Waiohinu, March 28,

from the crater, and it grew more and more abundant till we reached the cone, where it covered the whole region to a depth of five or ten feet.[51]

All this time Kilauea was quiet and remained so all through 1854, but the next year the old activity returned. Underneath the dome the lava was throwing up jets to the height of perhaps two hundred feet; vents had opened around the edge of the floor of the main crater, and Mr. Coan, in May and June, could count sixty lakes of leaping lavas. There was one great pool in the northeast region near where **1855** the path meets the bottom, and other boiling cauldrons not far distant, so that access to the crater was cut off.[52] On July 6th Dr. Titus Munson Coan was at the crater, and found this northeast pool crusted over except at the edge where the lavas were splashing. Halemaumau was estimated to measure four hundred by two hundred and fifty feet in its diameters, while the lava was seventy-five feet below the rim. The walls of this pit were tufted with Pele's hair, and two islands were in the northwest part of the lake. In October the crater was still active, but less so than early in the summer. The dome over Halemaumau had fallen in. It is thought that the lavas had passed out as at the last so-called eruption in 1849. But there was more important work going on in the Hawaiian lava ducts.

In a letter dated September 27, 1855, Mr. Coan writes: "On the evening of the eleventh of August, a small point glowing like Sirius, was seen at the height of twelve thousand feet on the northwestern slope of Mauna Loa. This radiant point rapidly expanded, throwing off corruscations of light, until it looked like a full-orbed sun."[53]

Sixty-five days later, the fissure which permitted the escape of lava was still open and in awful activity. The stream was flowing directly towards Hilo and there were no valleys or ridges of sufficient size to turn its course. The inhabitants of this beautiful village were exceedingly anxious, and made frequent excursions to the scene of the lava-flow. On the second of October, Mr. Coan with a party of friends passed through the thick forest, following the course of the Wailuku river, and on the fifth reached the lava-stream early in the morning, at a narrow point where it was about three miles wide. "In some places it spread out into wide lakes and seas, apparently from five to eight miles broad, enclosing, as is usually the case, little islands not flooded by the fusion." Mr. Coan continues in this letter, which is dated October 15, 1855:[54]

Early on Saturday, the 6th, we were ascending our rugged pathway, amidst steam and smoke and heat which almost blinded and scathed us. At ten we came to open orifices down which we looked into the fiery river which rushed furiously beneath our feet. Up to this we had come to no open lake or stream of active fusion. We had seen in the night many lights, like street lamps, glowing along the slope of the mountain at considerable distances from each other, while the stream made

[51] American Journal of Science, 1853, xv. 63.   [53] Ibid, xxi. 144.
[52] Ibid, 1856, xxi, 100, 139.   [54] Ibid, 139.

its way in a subterranean channel, traced only by these vents. From 10 A.M. and onward, these fiery vents were frequent, some of them measuring ten, twenty, fifty, or one hundred feet in diameter. In one place only we saw the river uncovered for thirty rods and rushing down a declivity of from ten to twenty-five degrees. The scene was awful, the momentum incredible, the fusion perfect (a white heat), and the velocity forty miles an hour. The banks on each side of this stream were red-hot, jagged and overhanging, adorned with burning stalactites and festooned with immense quantities of filamentose or capillary glass, called Pele's hair. From this point to the summit crater all was inexpressibly interesting.

Valve after valve opened as we went up, out of which issued fire and smoke and brimstone, and down which we looked as into the caverns of Pluto. The gases were so pungent that we had to use the greatest caution, approaching a stream or an orifice on the windward side, and watching every change or gyration of the breeze. Sometimes whirlwinds would sweep along loaded with deadly gases, and threatening the unwary traveler. After a hot and weary struggle over smoking masses of jagged scoriæ and slag, thrown in wild confusion into hills, cones and ridges, and spread out over vast fields, we came at one P.M. to the terminal or summit crater (not Mokuaweoweo).

This we found to be a low elongated cone, or rather a series of cones, standing over a great fissure in the mountain. Mounting to the crest of the highest cone, we expected to look down into a great sea of raging lavas, but instead of this the throat of the crater, at the depth of one hundred feet was clogged with scoriæ, cinders, and ashes through which the smoke and gases rushed up furiously from seams and holes. One orifice within this cone was about twenty feet in diameter, and was continually sending up a dense column of blue and white smoke which rolled off in gases and spread over all that part of the mountain, darkening the sun and obscuring every object a few rods distant. So toppling was the crest of this cone, so great the heat, and so deadly the gases, that we could find no position where we could look down the throat of the orifice; and could we have done so, it is not probable that we should have seen the deep fountain below us, as the lavas were forced up its horrid chimney from the burning bowels of the earth.

The summit cone which we ascended was about one hundred feet high, say five hundred feet long, and three hundred broad at its base. Several other cones below us were of the same form and general character, presenting the appearance of smoking tumuli along the upper slope of the mountain. . . . The molten stream first appears some ten miles below the fountain crater, and as we viewed it rushing out from beneath the black rocks, and, in the twinkling of an eye, diving again into its fiery den, it produced indescribable feelings of awe and dread. The summit crater I estimate at twelve thousand feet elevation; the principal stream (there are many lesser and lateral ones) including all its windings, sixty miles long; average breadth, three miles; depth from three to three hundred feet, according to the surface over which it flowed. The present eruption is between those of 1843 and 1852, and from our high tower we could see them both and trace their windings.

Early on Monday we decamped and set our faces for Kilauea, distant some thirty-five miles, hoping by a forced march to reach it at night. At eight A.M. we passed the seat of the grand eruption of 1852, and travelled for miles on its cinders. A little steam only issues from that cone whose awful throat in 1852, sent up a column of glowing fusion to the height of a thousand feet. We explored Kilauea and on Thursday reached Hilo.

Hilo is now in a state of solemn and thoughtful suspense. The great summit fountain is still playing with fearful energy and the devouring stream rushes madly down towards us. It is now about ten miles distant,—nearly through the woods, following the right bank of the Wailuku, and heading directly for our bay.

October 22. It is now seventy-two days since the eruption commenced, and the fountain is in full force. The matter disgorged is of the same general character as in former eruptions. We saw nothing new. Among the salts, sulphur and sulphate of lime are the most abundant. They are scattered freely at several points along the line of flow.

[447]

Mr. Coan, it will be seen, struck the flow at a point above the terminus and followed it to its source. On his return he determined to cut through the forest and meet the stream. Following a branch of the Wailuku in a drenching rain which made the river almost impassable, he thus describes the scene:[55]

So soon as we entered this stream we found it discolored with pyroligneous acid from burning wood, whose odor and lustre became more and more positive the further we advanced up the stream. The discoloration also became more apparent as we proceeded, until the water was almost black. This showed that the lava-flow had crossed the head waters of the stream and its small tributaries, consuming the forest and jungle, and sending down what could not be evaporated of the juices to mingle with the stream.

A little before sundown our guide led us at right angles from the stream we had been threading for six hours, and in a few minutes the fires of the volcano glared upon us through the woods. We were within six rods of the awful flood which was moving sullenly along on its mission towards Hilo. Thrusting our poles into the lava, we stirred it, and dipped it up like pitch, taking out the boiling mass, and cooling all the specimens we desired. We were on the right or southern verge of the stream, and we also found that we were about two miles above its terminus, where it was glowing with intense radiance and pushing its molten flood into the dense forest which still disputed its passage to the sea. We judged the stream to be two or three miles wide at this point, and over all this expanse, and as far as the eye could see above, and down to the end of the river, the whole surface was dotted with countless fires, both mineral and vegetable. Immense trees which had stood for hours, or for a day, in this molten sea, were falling before and below us, while the trunks of those previously prostrated were burning in great numbers upon the surface of the lava.

You are aware that the great fire-vent on the mountain discharges its floods of incandescent minerals into a subterranean pipe which extends at a depth of from fifty to two hundred feet, down the side of the mountain. Under this arched passage the boiling lava hurries down with awful speed until it reaches the plains below. Here the fusion spreads out under a black surface of hardened lava some six or eight miles wide, depositing immense masses which stiffen and harden on the way. Channels, however, winding under this stratified stratum, conduct portions of the lava down to the terminus of the stream, some sixty-five miles from its high fountain. Here it pushes out from under its mural arch, exhibiting a fiery glow, across the whole breadth of the stream. Where the ground is not steep, and where the obstructions from trees, jungle, depressions, etc., are numerous, the progress is very slow, say one mile a week.

On the evening of our arrival we encamped within ten feet of the flowing lava, and, as before stated, on the southern margin of the stream, some two miles above its extreme lower points. Here under a large tree, and on a bank elevated some three feet above the igneous flood which moved before us, we kept vigils until morning. During the whole night the scene was indescribably brilliant and terribly sublime. The greater portion of the vast area before us was of ebon blackness, and consisted of the hardened or smouldering flood which had been thrown out and deposited here in a depth of from ten feet to one hundred.

Not only was the lava, as aforesaid, gushing out at the end of this layer, but also at its sides. These lateral gushings came out before and behind us, and two-thirds surrounded our camp during the night, so that in the morning, when we decamped, the fusion was just five feet by measurement, in front of us, six feet in our rear, and three feet, or the diameter of the trunk of our camp-tree, on our left. The drenching rain and our chilled condition induced us to keep as near the fire as we could bear it. Evening and morning we boiled our tea-kettle and fried our ham upon the melted lavas, and when we left, our sheltering tree was on fire.

[55] American Journal, xxi, 237. The letter is dated Nov. 16, 1855.

Mr. Coan made several attempts to cross the lava-flow, "but the hardened surface of the stream was swelling and heaving at innumerable points by the accumulating masses and the upraising pressure of the lava below; and valves were continually opening out of which the molten flood gushed and flowed in little streams on every side of us. Not a square rod could be found on all this wide expanse, where the glowing fusion could not be seen under our feet through holes and cracks in the superincumbent stratum on which we were walking. The open pots and pools and streams we avoided by a zigzag course; but as we advanced, these became more numerous and intensely active, and the heat becoming unendurable, we again beat a retreat after having proceeded some thirty rods upon the stream. It may seem strange to many, that one should venture on such a fiery stream at all, but you will understand that the greater part of the surface of the stream was hardened to the depth of from six inches to two or three feet; that the incandescent stream flowed nearly under this crust like water under ice, but showing up through ten thousand fissures and breaking up in countless pools. On the hardened parts we could walk, though the heat was almost scorching, and the smoke and gases suffocating. We could even tread on a fresh stream of lava only one hour after it had poured out from a boiling cauldron, so soon does the lava harden in contact with the air."

Although the stream of lava continued to move for more than a year after in parts of its course, its front became cold and fixed on the banks of the river, and a merciful Providence listened to the prayers of the people of Hilo.

Prof. Dana considered it most probable that a fissure had extended completely down the mountain side, and that the lava issued from many vents along this line.[56]

March 7, 1856, Mr. Coan writes:

The great fire-fountain is still in eruption, and the terminus of the stream is only five miles from the shore. The lava moves slowly along on the surface of the ground, and at points where the quantity of lava is small, we dip it up with an iron spoon held in the hand. During the last three weeks the stream has made no progress toward Hilo, and we begin to hope that the supply at the summit-fountain has diminished. There is, however, still much smoke at the terminal crater. You

1856 will understand that the molten flood is all poured out of the fissures on the summit and for a few miles down the slope of the mountain. At first this disgorgement flowed down and spread wide on the surface of the mountain, as blood flows down a punctured limb. This phenomenon continued until the stream had swept down some thirty miles, which it did in about two days. It now came upon a place were the angle of slope was small, say one degree. Here its progress became slow, it spread more widely, and refrigeration was more rapid. The surface of course hardened first. But this refrigerating process went deeper and deeper like the congelation of water, and extended higher up the mountain, until at length all the lava was covered, except at occasional vents—as heretofore described—for the escape of steam and gases.

The process of breaking up vertically and spreading out afresh upon the hardened crust, was occasioned by obstructions at the end of the stream, damming up the liquid, and thus obliging the accumulating lavas to force new passages and outlets for disgorgement. In this way the stream was

---

[56]American Journal, xxi, 241.

widened by lateral outgushings, divided into several channels, swayed to the right and left, and raised to great heights by pushing up from below and heaping mass after mass upon what *had been* its upper stratum. Often when the stream had been flowing briskly and brilliantly at the end, it would suddenly harden and cool, and for several days remain inactive. At length, however, immense areas of the solidified lava, four, five or six miles *above* the end of the stream, are seen in motion—cones are uncapped—domes crack—hills and ridges of scoriæ move and clink—immense slabs of lava are raised vertically or tilted in every direction, while a low sullen crash is heard from below. While you gaze in mute amazement, and feel the solid mass of rock, often thirty, fifty, or seventy feet thick, moving under your feet, the struggling lava oozes out through ten thousand orifices and fissures over a field of some four or five square miles. More than once have I been on such a field, and heard, and seen, and felt more than is here or can be described. And yet the action of the lava is so slow, in the conditions described, that there is no fear, and little danger to one well acquainted with such phenomena.

During the night of the 29th of January, the molten stream poured continuously over a precipice of fifty feet, into a deep, dry basin half filled with flood-wood. The angle down which this fire cataract flowed, was about seventy-five degrees: the lava was divided into two, three, and sometimes four channels from one to four yards wide, and two or three feet deep. The flow was continuous down the face of this precipice from two P.M. until ten the next morning when we left. During the night the immense basin under the fall was filled, the precipice converted into an inclined plane of about four degrees, and the burning stream was urging its way along the rocky channel below. But the scene on the night of the 12th of February was, in some respects, more gorgeous still, as it combined the element of water with that of fire. A stream of lava from twenty to forty yards wide had followed the rocky and precipitous bed of a river, until it was two miles in advance of the main lava-flow, which was nearly two miles broad. Beating our way through the thicket we came upon the terminus of this narrow stream of lava, near sunset. It was intensely active, and about to pour over a precipice of thirty-nine feet (by measurement), into a basin of deep water, large enough to float a ship. Before dark the lava began to fall into the water, first in great broken masses, like clots of blood; but in a short time in continuous, incandescent streams, which increased from hour to hour in volume, in brilliancy, and in rate of motion. [See Plate XLI, which represents exactly similar action at a later period.] The water boiled and raged with fearful vehemence, raising its domes and cones of ebullition ten feet high, and reflecting the red masses of fusion like a sea of fire mingled with blood.

We encamped on the bank of the river, about fifty feet below the fiery cataract, and exactly opposite the basin of water into which the lava was flowing, twenty feet only from its rim. The face of this precipice was an angle of about eighty degrees, and the lava flowed down it briskly and continuously in streams from one to four feet deep, during the night. Before morning this whole body of water, some twenty feet deep, was converted into steam, and the precipice became a gently inclined plane.

To make the fact that the fissure did not extend to the base of the mountain more clear, Mr. Coan again writes under date of October 22, 1856; he had then visited the flow seven times:

A fracture or fractures occurred near the summit of the mountain, which extended in an irregular line from the terminal point, say five miles down the northeast slope of the mountain. From this serrated and yawning fissure, for two to thirty yards wide, the molten flood rushed out and spread laterally for four or five miles, filling the ravines, flowing over the plains, and covering all those high regions, from ten to one or two hundred feet deep. Along this extended fissure, elongated cones were formed at the points of the greatest activity. These cones appear as if split through their larger diameter, the inner sides being perpendicular or overhanging, jagged and hung with stalactites, draped with filamentous vitrifications, and encrusted with sulphur, sulphate of lime and other salts. The outside of these cones are inclined planes, on an angle of forty to sixty degrees, and composed of pumice, cinder, volcanic sand, etc. You will not, however, understand that these semi-cones were once entire, and that they have been *rent*. They are simply masses or ridges of cinder and dross deposited on each side of the fractures where the action is greatest. *It is all a new deposit.* [See a similar cone painted by D. Howard Hitchcock in the eruption of 1899.] After you leave the region of open fissures, near the summit of the mountain, all below *appears to be a flow on the surface*.

1st. We can *see* no chasms or fractures except those always found in the surface flows. There is no visible evidence that the old substrata had been fractured except on the higher regions of the mountain.[37]

2d. Where there is a throat extending down to the fiery abyss below, there will, we think, always be a column of smoke and gaseous vapor ascending to mark the spot, so long as action continues. This is true of Kilauea, and it is also true of *all* the eruptions I have noticed. Now if you were at Hilo, you would see a continuous volume of smoke ascending from the terminal point, and another from the terminus of the stream—separated in a direct line forty miles, and by route of the flow seventy miles—while between these extreme points you see no smoke and have no evidence of fire beneath[38] except the radiation of heat as you pass up. The smoke at the fountain is mineral, that at the end of the stream is from vegetation, and only here the fusion now makes its appearance, having come, as I believe, all the way from the mountain under cover, without showing itself at a single point. I do not mean that it has tunnelled the mountain, or melted a lateral duct through its mural sides. The process is this: lavas flowing on the surface and exposed to the atmosphere, unless moving with great velocity, as down steep hills, soon refrigerate on the surface. This hardened surface thickens, until it extends downward from one to two hundred feet, as the case may be. Under this superstratum the lava remains liquid; consequently at the termini and sometimes along the margins of the hardened streams you see the fusion gushing out in lines and points, and in irregular masses. When lavas refrigerate through the whole stratum, and thus rest on an ancient or previous formation, they form dams which divert the stream of lava from above, unless this obstruction is broken up, tilted, or overflowed by fresh lava. Down the steep sides of the mountain such obstructions occur more rarely; consequently the lava ceases to reach the surface either at the fountain or down the sides of the mountain, but is confined to channels, mostly covered with fresh, solidified lavas, where it finds a free and rapid passage to the plains below. Here the movement is slow, the obstructions more numerous, and the force to overcome them less patent. This accounts for the spreading laterally, the upliftings, and the ten thousand irregularities which diversify the ever-changing surface of lava streams. I have seen a dome, some three hundred feet in diameter at base, raised one hundred feet high and split from the summit in numerous radii, through which the red and viscid fusion was seen; and I have mounted to the top of such a dome in this state, thrust my pole into the liquid fire and measured the thickness of its shell, which was from two to five feet. Wherever vegetable matter is being consumed there is smoke; when this is exhausted there is none. Consequently I argue that there are no fissures extending to the central fires of the earth, except for a few miles near the summit of the mountain.

3d. Again, and what is more reliable, I have surveyed the ground upon which lava-streams have been approaching, for distances of five to twenty miles, and have seen the burning flood move on, covering today the ground on which I traveled yesterday, and consuming the hut where I slept; and the process is so familiar that it is difficult to see how I can be mistaken. I *think* that this stream

[37] A careful examination of the line of eruption resulted in the conviction that the fissure was originally very small, not exceeding three or four feet, and did not extend below the point where the lava first reached the surface.

[38] This has been the case for some eight months. At first the whole ridge of the mountain was lighted with fusion on the surface; afterwards no fire was seen except at the end of the stream near Hilo [Note by Mr. Coan].

of lava is *now flowing* more than sixty miles longitudinally under its own refrigerated cover; but I may be mistaken. No fire is *seen* anywhere except at the end of the stream. Here it still pushes out and spreads and heaps with little abatement, while the great mountain furnace sends up large and continuous volumes of smoke.[59]

To this exceedingly full and minute account, I need only add that I visited in 1865 the terminus of the stream, where it ceased to flow, and found the whole appearance of the stream in strict accordance with Mr. Coan's account. The surface was horribly rough and piled with slabs of hardened crust in vast ridges extending for miles. I slept on the fresh lava and examined the structure minutely, and found nothing to distinguish this stream from other eruptions, except its broken condition, arising from the wet soil over which it passed, which raised the surface into huge blisters. Where the lava fell into the water it was shivered into coarse sand like the deposit (known as "black sand") near Punchbowl in Honolulu, and as the water was evaporated the pahoehoe covered the ground almost entirely and even penetrated its mass. The angles down which the continuous stream of lava fell were as large as Mr. Coan mentions, and the lava does not seem much more cellular here than on level ground.

At the lowest edge of the lava-flow, I found, on the more ancient rock, rounded masses of red earth (ferruginous oxides) of the consistency of putty, and as large as a man's head. They were in considerable number, and seemed to have been pushed along by the lava; their softness was owing to the rain, as when dried they became as hard as dried potter's clay. The surface of the stream lava was covered with a minute lichen on which great numbers of succineas were feeding.

After flowing fifteen months this important eruption ceased. Professor Dana still thought the lava supply came from fissures along its track, but I cannot see any reason for this opinion. Mr. Coan and those who have followed in his steps are convinced of the contrary, and the *opinion* of an observer with such unequaled experience is worthy of great consideration. Those who have never seen a lava-flow, cannot well understand its action. I believe that Mr. Coan's briefest account conveys a better idea of what such a flow is than the most elaborate theorizing of those who have never seen one, or who see one for the first time.

In October, 1856, Mr. Coan reports Kilauea as declining in activity since the summit eruption began, there was but little sluggish lava in Halemaumau, but much escaping vapor.[60] In June, 1857, Kilauea was still quiet.[61] The lava in Halemaumau was a hundred feet below the brink and only five hundred feet across. In August, 1858, this pool "boiled and sputtered lazily at the centre of a deep basin which occupied the locality of the old dome. The action alternated between general refrigeration and a

---

[59] American Journal, xxiii, 435.   [60] Ibid, 438.   [61] Ibid, xxv, 136.

breaking up of the whole surface with intense ebullition."[61] In 1862 the lava pool had increased to six hundred feet in diameter. Within the central depression there was, a quarter of a mile from the pool, a driblet cone of remarkable form with turrets which Mr. Coan called the Cathedral, and which, two years after, I found a very convenient object in my survey of the crater, as it was visible from the entire outer rim. In October, 1863, Mr. Coan reported an awakening in Halemaumau and indeed all around the crater.[63] We must now look at Mauna Loa. A letter from Prof. R. C. Haskell, of Oahu College, gives the following account of the important eruption of 1859:[64]

FIG. 50. THE CATHEDRAL FROM WEST AND NORTHWEST.

Our party consisted of Prof. E. G. Beckwith, Prof. W. D. Alexander and myself, with some students of the college. The eruption broke out on the 23d of January. No earthquake was felt in any part of the island at the time, but dead fish were noticed on the 21st and a few days afterwards, to the east of Molokai, and between Molokai and Oahu. The fish gave no evidence of disease, but seemed to have been parboiled. At Honolulu, two hundred miles from the eruption, the atmosphere was exceedingly thick and hazy. So much was this the case that it caused considerable excitement, before the news of the eruption arrived.

Rev. Lorenzo Lyons, of Waimea, states that on Sunday afternoon, January 23, smoke was seen gathering on Mauna Loa. In the evening lava spouted up violently near the top of the mountain on the north side, and apparently flowed both towards Hilo and towards the west side of the island. This continued but a few minutes, when at a point considerably farther below the top, and farther west, another jet spouted up. Accounts from Hilo say, that on the night of the 23d, it was so light there that fine print could be read without difficulty. After the 23d the light was much less. At Lahaina, more than one hundred miles distant, the whole heavens in the direction of the eruption were lighted up.

Our party started from Honolulu, February 1st, and reached Kealakeakua on the 3d. Here we learned that the stream from the eruption had reached the sea on the 31st of January, at Wainanalii, about forty [sixty] miles from the place of eruption. This makes the average progress of the stream above five [seven] miles per day. After procuring guides, natives, pack-oxen and mules, we started for the source of the flow on the 5th. About noon we had a view of the source, distant from us, probably, twenty-five miles in an air-line. The crater was about one hundred and fifty feet high, and two hundred feet in diameter (as we afterwards estimated). From within this crater liquid lava was spouting up to the height of three or four hundred feet above the top. In shape and movement it resembled a mighty fountain or jet of water, though more inconstant. At one moment it was uncommonly high and quite narrow at the top, at the next not so high but very broad. At night, and from a good position near, the view of the jet, according to Mr. Faudrey (the only man who reached the crater while the jet was spouting), was grand beyond all description.

[61] Amer. Journ., xxvii, 411. Letter of Feb. 3, 1859.   [64] Ibid, xxxvii, 415. Letter of Oct. 6, 1863.
[63] Ibid, xxxv, 296. Letter of Nov. 13, 1862.   [453]

THE SCRIPPS INSTITUTION
OF OCEANOGRAPHY
OF THE
UNIVERSITY OF CALIFORNIA
LA JOLLA, CALIF.

Owing to an accident which befell one of our party, and the failure of water where it was supposed to be abundant, we were delayed two days and induced to divide our party into two divisions. One part returned to visit the flow at a point some twenty miles below, by another and easier route. The party who went on, consisting of twelve white persons and thirty kanakas, reached the crater Wednesday evening February 9th, and encamped about two miles from it. Here all fears about water were at an end, for we found snow in abundance within half a mile of our camping ground. In the evening the view was magnificent. The jet had ceased to play; but two craters, about eighty rods apart, were sending up gas and steam, with appearances of flame. This apparent flame, however, we afterwards ascertained, was only fine particles heated to redness. The noise attending this action was like that of an ascending rocket, very much increased of course, but quite irregular. About half a mile below the lower of the two craters, the stream first made its appearance. For five or six miles its course was well defined, and there were no side streams. From this point the main stream divided more or less, and on the plain between the three mountains Hualalai, Kea and Loa,

the branches extended over a breadth of three or four miles. Some of these streams were very broad and sluggish and partially cooled, some were narrow and running, as it seemed, at the rate of two or three miles per hour, burning the jungle and trees before them, and vying with each other in their work of destruction.

For the first few miles the stream appeared to be a succession of cataracts and rapids. As it approached the plain between the two mountains, it gradually changed into a network

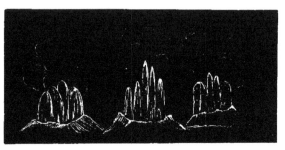

FIG. 51. VIEWS OF LAVA FOUNTAIN SEEN FEBRUARY 6 AND 7, 1859.

of streams, or a lake of fire, embracing numerous islands and sending out streams on all sides. The color of the stream on its first appearance was a light red approaching to white: on the plain a deep blood-red. From the plain towards Wainanalii the stream was narrow, varying from half a mile to a mile in width, and showing only a dull reddish light......The next morning we were able to make some explorations about the craters. On the windward side we could ascend them and look in, though the heat was so great that we could look for a moment only, before turning our faces away. The sulphurous gases also were so strong that we were obliged to close our mouths and noses as we approached to look in. The craters were both very irregular in shape not only on the outside but on the inside. No liquid lava was seen in either at the time. In each there were two or three separate holes where gases and steam were issuing. The sides of these holes, and indeed the entire bottom of the craters, were at a white heat. The lava-stream appeared to be running underneath these craters, and the holes within seemed to be merely vents for the escape of gases. The craters were formed of fragments of light scoriæ and lava combined. The lower of the two (the one from which the jet was thrown up for fifteen days) was now open on the lower side. This was not the case while the jet was thrown up, according to Mr. Faudrey......The upper crater was closed on all sides.

Above these two craters we visited a third not then in action, but still hot. This was smaller and open on the lower side, and broken down somewhat on the upper side. This was formed not so much of scoriæ as of old lava. Above this we could see others of the same kind......The next morning we visited the point where the stream first made its appearance. Here we found the lava rushing out of its subterranean passage, and dashing over cataracts and along rapids at such a rate that the eye could scarcely follow it. The lava was at a white heat, and apparently as liquid as water. Only a few feet from where the stream issued, small masses of lava were thrown up from ten to fifty feet into the air which cooled in falling······About three hours afterward we returned to the same place, and found that the action had greatly increased. Gases were escaping at two other points [Fig. 52, B and C] a few rods below the point first seen. Pieces of lava were thrown as high as one hundred and fifty feet, and at the lowest of the three points [Fig. 52, A] there was a fountain twenty-five feet high. The bits of lava thrown up cooled as they fell, and had already formed craters ten feet high around two of the points where gases were escaping······

Prof. Haskell followed the stream down some distance, and was struck with the great rapidity of its motion. The slope was considerable, and cascades and cataracts followed each other. The width of the stream here was from twenty to one hundred feet. His description of the formation of aa (which he does not distinguish from clinkers) is as follows:

The clinkers are always [generally] formed by deep streams, and generally by wide ones, which flow sluggishly, become dammed up in front by the cooling of the lava, and in some instances cooled over the top, forming, as it were a pond or lake. As the stream augments beneath, the barriers in front and the crust on the surface are broken up, and the pieces are rolled forward and coated over with melted lava which cools and adheres to them more or less. Then from the force of the melted lava behind and underneath, the stream rolls over and over itself. In this way a bank of clinkers ten to forty feet high, resembling the embankment of a railroad, is formed. Often at the end of the stream no liquid lava can be seen, and the only evidence of motion is the rolling of the jagged rocks of all sizes, down the front of the embankment.[65]

FIG. 52. LAVA FOUNTAIN OF FEBRUARY 10, 1859.

In another letter Prof. Haskell writes under date of June 22, 1859:

I have just returned from a second visit to the scene of the lava-flood on Mauna Loa. There is one fact which I observed that I desire to communicate to you. The real source of the flow is about four miles above the two craters which in February seemed to be the source. From this point down to the two craters, a crack in the mountain can be traced nearly all the way. At first it is no more than two inches in width, but gradually increases to two feet. At the present time heat can be perceived in the crack within a few feet of the higest point. But little lava has issued from this crack above the two craters. During the first quarter of a mile lava has oozed out in different places a few rods apart, to the amount of three or four cubic feet. Below this point there is a stream, now cold of course, a few rods in width. In this flow, therefore, there is no doubt that there is a continuous crack in the side of the mountain for four miles. How much farther this crack extends down the mountain cannot be ascertained, now at least, for the craters are still sending forth immense volumes of sulphurous vapors, and the stream of lava is still flowing below them. This stream, however, is much smaller than it was in February, and is entirely subterranean for the first twenty-five or thirty miles, except that there are a few holes where the running lava can be seen. In some instances this stream is as much as forty feet below the surface.

During this trip I went to the top of Mauna Loa. There is no perceptible action in the crater of Mokuaweoweo. The source of the present flow is probably 11,000 feet above the level of the sea.[66]

[65] American Journal, xxviii, 66. [66] Ibid, 284.

I will here insert some of the valuable observations of the careful observer of Hawaiian volcanic action, Mr. Wm. Lowthian Green, given in his Vestiges of a Molten Globe. Of the entry of the stream of lava into the sea at Wainanalii, he says:

It ran over a low shelf about ten feet high, and extended perhaps 500 or 600 feet wide, and fell into the sea where it was about twenty or thirty feet deep. It came from under the crust in great red-hot flattened spheroidal masses, having something the appearance of masses of moderately thick porridge as it is poured from a saucepan. The spheroidal masses, however, being perhaps ten feet to fifteen feet wide, and four to six feet deep. There was no steam, vapor or gas whatever to be seen coming from this lava till it went under water. Indeed the first contact with the red-hot spheroids did not seem to produce a particle of steam, and it was only when each had gone under water and become partially cooled off, that a puff of steam rose above the surface. The molten lava from this 1859 opening 10,000 feet up on Mauna Loa, for several months quietly *ran over* without any visible steam, noise, earthquakes or commotion of any kind.—(Part II, p. 163.)

Again the explosions so common during the flow of lava from the Hawaiian mountains, he correctly explains as follows:

In 1859, on the evening of the day just referred to, I started with two guides—goat hunters—to visit the orifice of eruption of the lava we had been observing spreading itself over the plateau between the mountains Loa, Kea and Hualalai. We camped about nine o'clock on the flat between these mountains close to a portion of the lava stream which was spreading itself plentifully over the ground, and all night long we heard loud explosions like the reports of heavy cannon. At the time I did not know the cause of them, but on my return I happened to be close to an explosion under a stream of lava, and which was evidently caused by the white-hot molten lava flowing over a hollow in one of the innumerable old lava streams. It is to be observed that in this part of the mountain there is no water. All the apertures of some underground cavern having been sealed up by the molten lava, it is only a question of time how soon an explosion of confined, highly heated air will occur. The molten lava may sometimes run into these caverns and so assist both the heat and compression (l.c., p. 270).

We have not yet exhausted all that Mr. Green can tell us of this flow, which will help our understanding of all others on this island. He continues (p. 274):

When we pitched our tent on our way to the 1859 crater, in the neighborhood of the loud explosions already referred to, it being then quite dark, we had a fine view of the pillar of fire at the crater on the side of the mountain fifteen miles above us, and which all day had shown as a pillar of cloud or smoke. This at night became illuminated by the glare of the white-hot lake of lava in the crater. We were on our way to it early next morning, and although we did not rest more than an hour during the day, it was dark again when we arrived alongside the great pillar of fire which rose ten thousand feet at least above our heads. We had for some time been crunching our way over the glass-foam which had evidently proceeded from the great lava fountain which had now ceased spouting; and close to the crater a steep escarpment appeared, up which we climbed, and when nearly abreast of the centre of the crater, and a little below the level of the edge, we pitched our tent and laid our blankets in a hole in a lava-bespattered crag which was partially filled with the same glass-foam. This lava-fountain seemed—as I found in the case of the 1868 outbreak afterwards—to have broken out at the intersection of two fissures, one leading to the top of the mountain and the other more or less at right angles to it. After our evening meal, I climbed over the rough lava a short distance to get a good view of the scene. It was unique. From the whole interior of the crater rose the great illuminated column of smoke, apparently about five hundred feet wide. The sight was grand and fascinating. Perhaps the circumstance which impressed me most was the dead silence which reigned. The noisy explosions of the night before had been left far behind. There was no wind, and the now illuminated smoke rose as it had done the day before in a well-defined perpendicular column, but spreading out on all sides at a great height in the atmosphere. I gazed at it long and steadily. I had toiled all day to get to this spot and to learn something, perchance, about volcanic action, but here at the crater, the only idea which I seemed capable of realizing, was my own utter insignificance amongst this waste of fire, smoke and lava, and as I turned from the view a moment to look back at the little white tent, tinged with a lurid red, perched amongst a chaos of black slags, I felt as an astronomer might, who, looking through his telescope at the surface of the moon should suddenly discover a habitation; the difference being that here I seemed to be in the moon, or at least in a spot which was equally unearthly and unsuited for human existence. The exertion of the last two days made my bed of pumice welcome, and after retiring I slept till daylight, not a single sound having disturbed us. On looking out in the morning, the great, steadily rising pillar of cloud beside us was reassuring. The colour of the smoke, by daylight, seemed to be about the same as that of a steamer burning Welsh or semibituminous coal after she first fires up. It rose gently, curling in great wreaths and folds, just as it might from the funnel of a huge steamer. I made an attempt to climb the edge of the crater and look in, but after scrambling for some time out of one sulphury crack into another, a thick fog crept up the mountain side and enveloped me, so that I could see nothing in any direction, and was glad, when on retreating, I found myself within hail of my guides, although I could neither see them nor the tent. In the course of an hour or two the fog cleared up, and we started down the mountain, our provisions and water being only sufficient for half a day longer. In descending I kept as near as possible to the lava stream which was running from the lower part of the crater, in the usual covered passage formed by its own cooled crust. At the lower side of the crater, just where the slope became moderate, we observed some vitrified breakers. The molten glass-foam had run over the lip of the crater in great waves and now stood on the gentle slope below, like petrified combers on the sea shore. The likeness was the more remarkable because the break of the waves was up the slope, and the falling crests were in the opposite direction, mechanically speaking, to those of the ocean waves......In some places the wave seemed to have bent, fallen and doubled upon itself, and the vesicular glass had solidified in great folds of a delicate green shade, looking like the folds of satin as they are sometimes displayed in a shop window.[67] The material of the waves seemed to be identical in composition and colour, with the usual Hawaiian pumice or glass-foam [limu], and the semi-transparent glaze covered the whole outer surface.

We got belated, and were compelled to go supperless to rest on the ropy pahoehoe, which, with nothing but a blanket to interpose, was not so comfortable to lie upon as the pumice at the crater. It was, however better than aa, and rising early next morning, we arrived at the camping ground just in time to hail the native, who was leaving with our horses, and who had been instructed to wait for us: the rest of the party having left for Kailua the day before. We could hardly have blamed him for leaving us to get to the coast as best we could. He had concluded that we were *make* (dead). Few Hawaiians could have been found to remain a night alone amidst the fires and thunders of their offended goddess Pele.

The immense columns of smoke which so constantly rise from the orifices of eruption on Hawaii, may often be largely composed of the vapor of water. When the lava breaks away, great red-hot chasms must often be left, and percolating surface water may well find its way into them and escape at the only opening, that is where the lava escapes. At the time of my visit to the 1859 crater, the top of the mountain was covered with snow, which would be one source of percolating water.... One important ingredient in most Hawaiian volcanic smoke so-called, is the excessively light,

---

[67] This identical formation appeared also in the eruption of 1880-81 according to a painting by Mr. Furneaux now before me. It is shown, although not so clearly as I could wish, in the right foreground.

glassy threads, films and vesicles, which the heated air first forms, and then raises to a great height in the atmosphere......The next time I visited this river of molten stone was some months afterwards at the sea-shore at Wainanalii, where it had never ceased running into the sea. It finally ceased in July.

In 1864, Mr. Horace Mann and the author approached Kilauea from the southwest on the Kau trail. For ten miles we had seen the cloud of smoke over the crater, and for more than half that distance we had traversed beds of pahoehoe, and large tracts of sand deep and difficult for our horses. No aa and but little scoriæ were visible

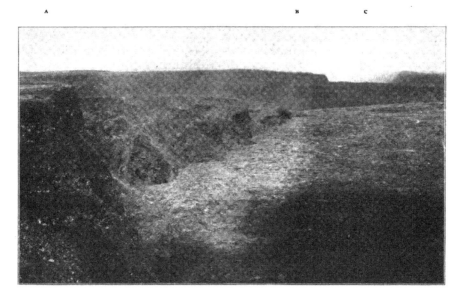

FIG. 53. NORTH END OF KILAUEA FROM WEST BANK. A, SITE OF HOTEL. B, BOTTOM OF DESCENT.
C, KILAUEA IKI WITH A SHOWER OF RAIN.

from the path. The eruption of 1789, is said to have thrown out the sand, but the winds have entirely changed its original location. It is dark, fine and uniform, and it now lies covering the pahoehoe in places to the depth of several yards. Soon after one o'clock we came upon the brink of the crater near Uwekahuna, the highest part of

1864   the bounding wall, and from here in the afternoon is a favorable view of Kilauea, perhaps the best. From below us steam and sulphurous vapors rose in a sluggish column, but we saw no fire and heard no noises. The great sunken plain before us, covering four or five square miles, looked bright in the clear sunlight, and even the walls on which we stood were of a light gray color. The whole circuit of the walls on the west and north sides is much cracked and interrupted. We rode along over several cracks, one of which, a little more than a yard wide, had opened about a year since, accompanied by an explosion heard distinctly at a distance of twenty miles. Some of the cracks were parallel with the edge of the abyss, others were at right angles to these, and in one place the small cracks were so numerous as to resemble a geometric spider's web.

Passing over the high cliffs on the northwest, the road leads down by a steep descent of fifty feet to a plain a mile long, and three-quarters of a mile wide, gravelly, and covered sparsely with a growth of dwarf ohia and ohelos, and dotted with small

FIG. 54. THE NORTHERN SULPHUR BANK IN 1889.

oval or circular fumaroles, from which steam was issuing silently and abundantly. The steam had no odor, and ferns and other plants grew luxuriantly over the openings. Around these steam holes the muddy and tenacious red soil retained pools of excellent water condensed from the steam. There was no trace of sulphur or acid in it that could be detected by the taste or by the more delicate test papers. The rock through which these steam holes passed was completely decomposed from a hard gray clinkstone to a red loamy earth, soft and worn smooth by the ascending vapors. It was quite evident that these fumaroles were not originally formed by the vapor, but were simply cracks through which the steam escaped, and the circular shape resulted from the falling in of the surface gravel and soil. The steam was quite hot, and we saw the remains of several cattle who had gone too near in search of water.

On the northern edge of this plain are extensive sulphur beds, that is to say, they cover a large space although containing but little sulphur, under a perpendicular ledge of clinkstone nearly a hundred feet high.   They are simply great piles of decomposed lava through which steam and sulphurous vapors constantly escape through a thousand apertures, depositing beneath the cool crust the most beautiful, almost acicular crystals of sulphur.[68]   The soil formed by the decomposition of the rock by sulphurous vapors is quite unlike that resulting from the action of steam alone; it is

FIG. 55. FUMAROLE IN SIDE WALL WITH SULPHUR CRYSTALS, 1889.

light gray or yellow, and does not form a plastic mud as readily as the latter, which is red and smooth to the touch.   In some places the sulphates of oxides of copper, iron, sulphates of soda, lime and alumina were forming within minute fissures, and the silica thus set free was gradually consolidating the earth into a firm crust whenever the supply of steam ceased, and we could often raise large slabs of this curious conglomerate.   Metamorphism was progressing rapidly under the combined influence of heat and moisture.   Twigs and leaves were fast passing into the condition of fossils in this hardening earth.   All the sulphur found here is deposited from the vapor, seems to be tolerably pure and is of a light yellow color indicating the absence of

[68] Although the two illustrations of the sulphur bank were taken by the author twenty-five years after this visit, there is little change in the first and none in the second so far as the deposit of crystals is concerned.   In 1864 the sulphur proved too strong for the wet plate process then used.

selenium. At first it seemed that this plain had sunk, but farther examination convinced me that this was once the floor of the ancient crater,—a black ledge.

As soon as our men came up with the blankets, we engaged guides and went down into the crater. The descent was steep and winding, and we passed over several terraces which were the result of a sinking or falling in as their strata were inclined and much broken, and came under the grand wall of compact lava figured in the Narrative of the United States Exploring Expedition.[69] A descent of some four hun-

FIG. 56. KILAUEA IN 1864. PERRY.

dred feet brought us to the bottom, and we stepped from a gravelly, shelving bank on to a black lava which had broken out last year under the north bank, and overflowed this end of the crater. Where it touched the gravel bank it had glued to its under surface the small fragments of stone, but had not altered their appearance, and all along the edge it was cracked, and laid up on the bank as if, on cooling, the lava had fallen about a foot. The surface was covered with a thin, scaly, vitreous crust, which crumbled beneath the tread, sounding like snow on a cold morning, and thus a very distinct path was made to the Halemaumau, the enduring house of Pele. The lava beneath this crust, however, was so hard as to strike out abundant sparks as the steel

[69] Named "Waldron's Ledge" for the purser of the expedition. Vol. iv, p. 171.

nails in my shoes scraped upon it. When hard it was often iridescent, like some anthracite coal, and so closely resembling this mineral that the difference would hardly be detected on a cursory examination. The fresh lava closely resembled that from Mauna Loa in the flow of 1859. Three-quarters of a mile over this uneven lava, and we came to a wall of fragments of every size of compact light-colored lava, very solid

and heavy and containing many small grains of olivine quite different in appearance as well as size from that in the lava of 1840; and this wall, which is roughly concentric with the outer wall of Kilauea, is said by the natives to rise and fall and sometimes disappear. The stones so closely matched the outer walls, that I had no doubt that they had fallen from these walls, loosened by some of the many slight earthquakes

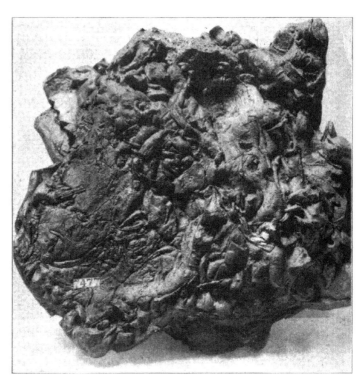

FIG. 57. PORTION OF THE FLOOR COVERED WITH SPATTER.

and floated out to its present position. An unpractised eye could see no marks of fire on the rough granite-like masses. All over the floor caves, cracks and ridges make the surface very uneven, and after walking two miles we came to several large cracks of great depth, but not more than a yard wide, and then a wall enclosing an amphitheatre down which we climbed on the loose slabs of lava.

The whole bottom of the crater is above what Prof. Dana describes as the Black Ledge, and although no fire is visible over the northern and eastern portions, steam constantly rises from many cracks, and the caves are often uncomfortably warm.

When we were near Halemaumau, we came to a cone formed of spattered lava and cemented scoriæ, some twenty-five feet high, with a bright light at its apex. This was the first fire we had seen, but we passed by, eager to reach the great lake. This we reached after ascending a gradual incline. It was eight hundred feet in diameter, and the lava was fifty feet below the cliff on which we stood, covered with a dark crust which

FIG. 58. BOTTOM OF THE FRAGMENT (FIG. 57), SHOWING THREE LARGE DROPS.

was broken around the edges, and there the blood-red lava was visible, surging against its walls with a dull, sullen sound. The smoke was blown away by the wind so that we were able to stand on the very verge of the pit; but the heat was so great that we were compelled to hold our hands before our faces.

The wall on which we stood, and where we intended to sleep, was thickly covered on the side towards the pit, with waving, woolly Pele's hair, which we saw forming continually. The drops of lava thrown up drew after them the glass thread, or sometimes two drops spin out a thread a yard long between them, and the hair thus formed either clings to the rough sides or is blown over the edge, where it catches on any projecting point. The drops are always black, or a very dark green on the surface, but light green within, porous and quite brittle, and the thread is transparent, and when first formed, of a yellow or greenish color. Occasionally a crack would open across the lake, and violent ebullition commence at various points along its surface. There were two small islands in the lake which the lava seemed seeking to destroy. The current would often set in toward the banks, and it appeared as if the whole lake was about to be drawn in as cake after cake broke off from the surface and disappeared. But it would soon cease, and then run toward another point of the wall, and I could not see that it was oftener on one side than another. As a crack opened, the red lava rose above the crack, running on the surface, and as the crack grew wider, cooling rapidly, and being drawn out much like molasses candy. While white-hot, the lava was liquid as water, but it rapidly assumed the viscid condition, and then the solid. I threw a stick of dry wood on the surface the instant it became fixed after a violent bubbling, and it was ten minutes before any smoke was made, and it was only when a crack opened under it that it was consumed. The motion was always from the centre, except when the lava was thrown back in spray from the caverns which extended under much of the wall.

We laid down in our blankets on the eastern edge where the wall was highest, and the wind drove away the smoke, and soon fell asleep. About nine o'clock I got up and moved to the very edge of the pit to view the molten mass to better advantage, and warm myself, as the wind from Mauna Loa towering ten thousand feet above us was quite cold. The moon was up and almost full, but her orb was pale beside the fires of Pele. Finding the place quite comfortable, I lay down and went to sleep. At twelve I awoke with a start, and found myself in the midst of a shower of fiery drops, some of which were burning my blankets. I shook myself and jumped back, looking at my watch to note the time, for I thought a great eruption at hand, and then stood gazing at the strange scene for some time before I thought of calling my companions. The whole surface had risen several feet and was boiling violently and dashing against the sides, throwing the red-hot spray high over the banks and causing the providential rain of fire which awoke me to see this grand display. There was no noise except the dash and the sullen roar. When I could think of anything else, I called the others, who were asleep several rods from the edge, but only succeeded in awakening the guides, and just then a drop came plump on to a greasy paper in which we had brought our supper, and it blazed up so suddenly that one of the kanakas thought that a new jet was opening at our feet, and ran off to some distance. Failing to arouse my companions by calling, I threw a handful of small stones at them but without effect, and I had to climb down and shake them roughly. When they had got to the edge the action had greatly diminished, and in a few minutes more the dark crust again covered the central portion, and we all went to sleep.

I was glad to see such distinct flames, as it had been denied that they exist in Kilauea. They burst from the surface, and were in tongues or wide sheets a foot long and of a bluish-green color, quite distinct from the lava even when white-hot; they

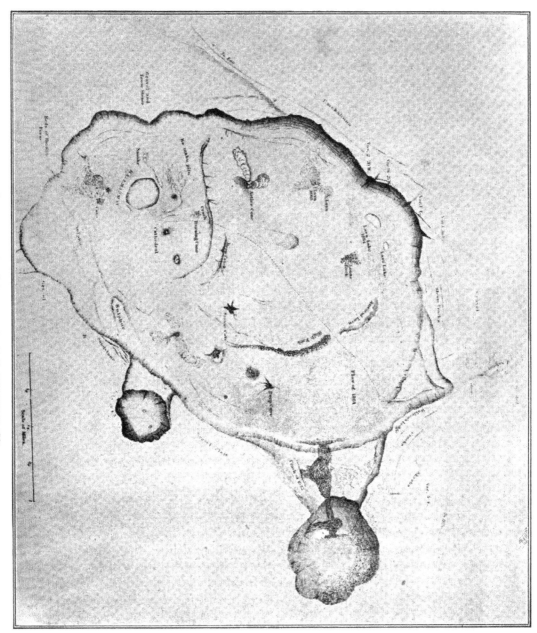

FIG. 59. SURVEY OF KILAUEA BY WM. T. BRIGHAM IN 1865.

played over the whole surface at intervals, and I thought they were more frequent after one of the periodical risings of the surface in the pit.

In the morning we found it very misty, and the mist soon turned to rain, but we went to the cone we had seen the evening before, and climbing its sides looked into its red-hot mouth. It was nearly full of melted lava, but although we tossed in scoriæ we could not excite it. Another cone with several pinnacles called the "cathedral" we did not visit, as no fire was visible, although smoke poured from it copiously. The rain caused steam to rise from the cracks over the whole surface of the crater, and we got quite wet, and our views were wholly cut off. At half-past seven we were in the saddle on the way to Hilo, which was only twenty-nine miles distant, but the road was so rocky in some places and so muddy in others that we were obliged to walk our horses all the way, and it was twelve hours before we dismounted at the house of the excellent missionary who has done more than all others to record the volcanic phenomena which have taken place on Hawaii during his long and useful pastorate.

August 2, 1865, I again visited Kilauea to make arrangements for a survey. The appearance was much the same as last year, although the bottom had evidently risen, and several new cracks had opened, while others had closed. The banks of Halemaumau had changed considerably; the platform on which I had slept before was gone, and the diameter was now at least a thousand feet. The islands had disappeared, and the lava was not more than thirty feet below the top of the bank. We went down in the crater in the evening, and fell asleep with the usual resolve to wake up now and then to enjoy the fireworks; but we were so weary with the tiresome ride from Hilo, that we slept till after midnight, when a puff of sulphurous vapor from a crack under our heads, waked us up choking, and we beat a hasty retreat. In a few minutes, however, the gas ceased to blow, and after enjoying the changing fire of the pool for half an hour, we slept until five in the morning, when our guide advised us to return, as we were to breakfast on the upper bank some three miles distant. We went round by a new pool which had opened during the winter on the northern side near the bank. It was small, hardly two hundred feet long and fifty wide, but the melted lava was not more than a foot below the bank, so that we could work it with our sticks. It was blood-colored and very viscid, and exhibited the same motions as the larger pool,—the currents to the sides, and the cracking and bubbling, but on a much smaller scale. Fire was visible at night at various points between this and Halemaumau.

The next night I slept on the upper bank, in the grass house, while several of our party spent the night in the crater. They could not approach the place where we had slept the night before, owing to the change of wind, and during the night the whole shelf fell in with a loud noise. This formed a small island which was soon broken and melted by the boiling lava.

August 22, I returned to Kilauea from Hilo, having since my last visit explored the district of Puna and the pit craters on the course of the flow of 1840. I brought with me surveying instruments and photograph apparatus (wet-plate most unsuitable

FIG. 60. KILAUEA IKI.

to the vicinity of sulphur fumes), and after spending a day in selecting stations and drilling my kanakas in chaining, commenced the survey from the grass house on the northern bank. Going eastward the ground was covered with bushes and full of steam cracks which made chaining very difficult. Waldron's Ledge looks like a continuation of the wall behind the northern sulphur bank, and on meeting the crater edge it turns eastward toward the large lateral crater Kilauea iki, enclosing this with a circular wall four thousand feet in diameter, and deeper than the main crater at present. Descending the steep precipice we came upon the western edge of the gravelly isthmus which separates the two craters. In the midst of this issued the lava stream of 1832 which ran down into both. Its appearance is still fresh, and where it descended into Kilauea over a precipice of 60° and more than two hundred feet high, it has formed a fine lava-fall perfectly continuous, although for a short distance it is nearly perpendicular. It is hollow and of small volume.[70]

FIG. 61. FRAGMENT OF THE 1862 LAVA-FALL.

The ascent from this isthmus is not so steep on the southern side, and above, the soil is gravelly and barren, supporting but few plants. The wall of Kilauea is much cracked and broken on this side and is also much lower. The second lateral crater, Keanakakoi on the southeast is much smaller than Kilauea iki. Its walls are quite perpendicular on the side towards Kilauea, and the depth is greater than that of the main crater. The bottom is gravelly, level, except where a small mound rises near the northern side. Near the edge of Kilauea was a ledge of sandstone much split into vertical parallel plates and evidently formed by the cementation of the volcanic sand common on the banks of this side. There were many curious circular depressions in the hard gravelly soil, about three feet in diameter, and from six to eight inches deep, which I did not at first understand. I soon found that they were over cracks in the subjacent rock, and the sand, which is quite loose a foot below the surface,

had settled into these small fissures, causing the depression in the sandstone above, which is almost as flexible as Itacolumite. There were evidences of severe showers over this plain, as the torrent channels were numerous and deep, and always emptied into the crater. The traces of the ancient adz-making, which gave Keanakakoi (the

---

[70] Only the ruins of this fall are to be seen at present (1909). Specimen hunters and earthquakes have perhaps contributed equally to this result, but forty-four years ago it was the most remarkable lava-fall to be seen on the island. The wall behind it is much cracked and broken, but the remaining fragments have still the fresh appearance noted in the text.

workshop of the adzes) its name, were abundant, but the fragments of the adzes usually abundant in such quarries were not noticed.[71]

At the edge of Keanakakoi, as it was late in the afternoon, my natives built a stone house to shelter the instruments, and we decided to cross Kilauea as the nearest way home. We climbed down a steep gravel bank apparently formed by the action of sulphurous vapors on the rock of the walls, crossed a small sulphur bank from which steam was issuing, and continued our way over the portion of Kilauea which

FIG. 62. KEANAKAKOI IN 1889.

was overflowed the year before. It was very disagreeable walking, as the crust was quite thin and brittle, and we constantly broke through, only a few inches perhaps, but there was a constant feeling of insecurity, for we could not know but that the breaking crust covered a deeper crack in the harder lava beneath. Half way across we found a cone three or four feet high covered with spatters of lava of various colors. Crossing the crater again the next morning in the rain it was difficult to find our way owing to the steam, but we at length reached the bank. It was two o'clock before the mist cleared away enough to permit the use of the theodolite. The large sulphur bank near this end of Kilauea was of a bright green color owing to a large proportion of

---

[71] Every trace of stone-working has been hidden by a subsequent flow of lava which has for more than twenty-five years covered the bottom of this crater. [469]

sulphate of protoxide of iron which seemed to be constantly forming.[72] Much of the sulphur is in large amorphous masses as if melted.

The ground on this side of the crater is smooth, free from stones, and so terraced and sloped that it is difficult to define the boundaries of the great pit. As no rock is visible it is impossible to determine the direction of the disturbing forces, but the present condition of the bank seems to indicate a falling in of the walls in several places, probably over one or more of the subterranean streams of lava that have deluged Puna. The side of the mountain is weaker here than elsewhere, and most of the subterranean eruptions have forced their way through it, forming several lines of cracks and craters extending to the sea. One of Wilkes' signal posts was found rotted off at the base, but otherwise sound.

On the southwest side the smoke from Halemaumau was very suffocating, and I was obliged to pass through it with a wetted handkerchief to my face; so little aqueous vapor was in the smoke that the cloth dried with great rapidity. The ground was covered with Pele's hair, which collected on the leeward side of the ridges and stones, and also extensive beds of the Hawaiian pumice or limu. This limu is identical with that seen on Mauna Loa, and is the froth of the burning lake. As the steel chain was drawn through it the links were completely polished. The deposit was so loose and friable that in one place I sank up to my waist in it. Stones and fragments of scoria were lying about apparently loose, but we found it almost impossible to break them off, so firmly were they cemented to the gravel rock below. The action of the sulphurous vapor seems to speedily dissolve the Pele's hair, and this with the silica in the rock itself makes a solid cement. There is an easy descent into the crater at the southwest end, and beyond this the nearly perpendicular rock wall rises rapidly to the highest point at Uwekahuna.

I reached the highest point on the Kau trail about dark, and sent home the instruments, while I followed slowly along the bank, watching the fires which were gleaming brightly seven hundred feet below. The small new pool close beneath the bank was exceedingly beautiful, as it emitted but little smoke, and constantly cracked and broke up its crust, forming an everchanging network of fire. A line of fire was burning all the way from this to Halemaumau, but the level of the new pool is more than fifty feet below the old.

Saturday it was rainy and impossible to obtain sights with the instruments, so I went into Kilauea to explore the caves. Halemaumau was not in a very lively condition, and passing beyond that, I went into a cave of considerable extent, where the

---

[72] A few years after this (1867), a flow from Halemaumau reached this long bank and set it afire; the combustion was slow but complete, and the gravelly residue is covered on the sides with coarse ferns.

curious silicious tubes had formed on the rock roof, and obtained many of these fragile specimens, some of which were coated with beautiful white crystals. This cave was more than fifty feet below the level of the lava in the main pool, and the walls did not seem very secure. A small lava stream had recently poured into the mouth of the cave, but there were no vapors, nor any uncomfortable heat. Taking advantage of a change of wind, I passed around Halemaumau, and ascended a cone with two peaks formed by lava spatters, but completely closed on the top, as nearly all the others in the crater were, and found steam hissing from many apertures. On breaking off the crust fine crystals of various salts were found thickly coating the inner surface, and in one place we found much potassa nitrate. I went from cave to cave, from cone to cone, collecting many kinds of lava and some salts, and finished by a bath in a steam cave, where the steam issued from the floor at an agreeable temperature, and condensed on the roof falling in rain. The water was quite sweet, and no smell of sulphur was noticeable in the cave. On the roof the little tube stalactites were constantly forming by the solution of the silica in the rock above, and I broke off the twisted, brittle tubes sometimes a foot long. On the floor the drops had made stalagmites of various forms (see Plates XLVIII and XLIX).[73] This steam bath was most delightful after the smoking I had just experienced in a cave where the end was red-hot, and into which my natives did not dare to follow me.

Sunday was the first bright day I had had, and the pulu[74] pickers from the region came to my hut after the morning service, and told me the names of the various parts of the crater, and legends of various eruptions.[75] Monday was rainy, but I completed my measurements, and in the evening made a series of observations to determine the declination of the magnetic needle. The electric currents in the lava and the large amount of iron in the rock, made strange work with the compass: I have seen the needle turn suddenly through an arc of forty degrees. The remainder of the week was too stormy to take photographs, and I was reluctantly obliged to send back my instruments and return to Hilo.

---

[73] These stalactitic formations have been fully described and figured in the section on the lava forms. No one can well understand the formation unless able to watch the process as I have repeatedly done at this visit, checking my results at subsequent visits to these and other caves, and I am not surprised that Dana, who never saw them *in situ*, should question the accuracy of my observation. After many years I do not care to alter my original description, which I believe true, and have quoted in full in the section referred to.

[74] Pulu is the silky covering of the opening fronds of several species of tree ferns, and was formerly exported in large quantities to California for bedding, etc. The material proved undesirable in a dry climate, the export ceased, and the present generation knows nothing of this interesting business.

[75] It was here that I got the name Poli o Keawe (bosom of Keawe, or place of torment of Keawe), which I gave to the larger lateral crater on my map of this survey instead of the name given by Ellis, which I now resume. The name of Poli o Keawe was certainly applied to some place in the immediate vicinity of Kilauea, but I have not been able to identify it. It may be added that the natives have generally lost the accuracy of local knowledge possessed by their fathers, and when they do not know the name of any place will not own to their ignorance, but often give any name that occurs to them. [471]

Pit Craters in Puna a Part of the Kilauea System.—A region that has been the chosen path so often for the escape of the Kilauean lava, would naturally excite the strong interest of a geologist, but until within a few years the whole district was an almost impenetrable wilderness. The Rev. Titus Coan was the first who discovered the craters on the line of the eruption of 1840. Dr. Charles Pickering extended his explorations to a greater distance and mapped some of the larger craters, work after adopted as official on the chart of this region published with the Wilkes report.[76] In the early sixties the business of picking and packing pulu had become so important that trails cut by the many natives thus employed, opened the crater country far more than ever before, and at this time I was fortunate enough to go through the fern forests with Father Coan, and although I have been several times through the strange path of Pele, cutting it here and there, I was more impressed with this first visit and will transcribe from my note book what I saw.

Here and there on the way from the coast at Panau we passed lava streams. Ohia trees were growing on these, thin and tall, suggestive of alpine regions; indeed I have seen similar forests on the Swiss mountains, and there was a peculiar grace, which, while pleasing the eye yet conveyed the idea of a struggle for existence amid the storms which sweep the rocky slopes of Mauna Loa. At the height of eighteen hundred feet we entered the fern forest. The fruit of the poha (*Physalis*) and ohelo (*Vaccinium*) was abundant, and sandal-wood was occasionally met with at an elevation of two thousand feet. As we came to the fern region, we turned into a path cut through the jungle, and, as the soil was a soft black mould, it had been paved with the stems of the tree-ferns about six inches in diameter. This "corduroy" road was constructed with great labor by the natives, and we calculated that forty thousand pieces of fern were used to build it. The ferns are cut in lengths of six feet, and many of them sprout and make a green edging to the roadway. Nearly two miles along this tropical and attractive road, and we came to a tract of pahoehoe where was the pulu station to which the roads had been cut. This was the residence of a remarkable Hawaiian who had leased the whole district for the pulu business,—Kaina, the district judge. His house was directly on the line of craters, and only a few rods from steam cracks where his men cooked their food. It was well built, and surrounded with a substantial stone wall. The interior was furnished with bedsteads, rocking-chairs, and other conveniences; and our supper table was supplied with fresh wheaten bread, milk, butter, eggs and delicious ohelo berries.

West of the house was a large open field where the silky, golden fibre of the pulu is dried before packing, and beyond in the woods, I found curious tubes of lava

[76] See outline of this chart on page 51. The names given by Wilkes are not those at present used and have been omitted.

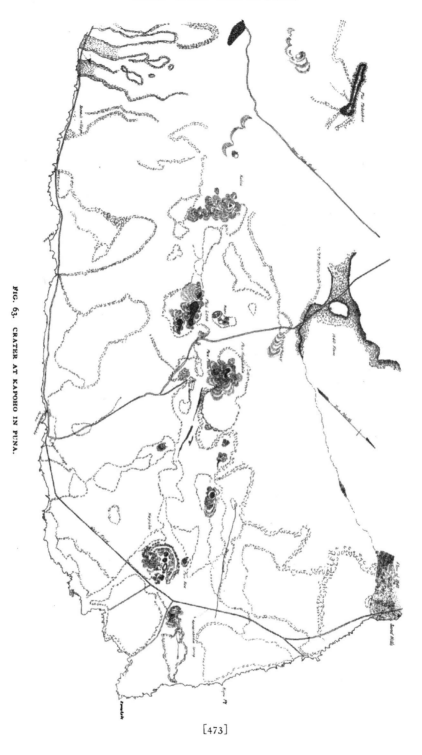

FIG. 63. CRATER AT KAPOHO IN PUNA.

on an ancient flow, one of which was seven feet high, eighteen inches external diameter, and with a bore of eight inches. It was brittle, and on breaking it off, I found the hole was six feet deep, making its whole length thirteen feet. Others of the same height were near by, and their sides were always thicker towards the source of the flow, Externally they are rough like aa, but the top was smooth and sometimes projected like an umbrella. Where several were in close proximity a slab of lava was supported

FIG. 64. CRATER MAKAOPUHI IN PUNA.

like a roof on columns (see Fig. 43). The lining of the tube was smooth and much more compact and vitreous than the exterior. The trees which served as cores, if not burned have entirely decayed, and were mostly tree ferns, although I think that I detected some ohias. I followed the stream down some distance to learn the cause of its subsidence, which must have been rapid, and found that a fissure had opened and swallowed most of the lava. Judging from the great size of the trees growing over its surface, the flow must be quite ancient. The surface of the casts gave fresh indication of the process by which aa is formed and seems to prove that the more refractory particles of the lava cool at an appreciable time before the general molten mass ceases to be liquid, much as the less soluble salts in a saline solution crystallize first on cooling;

here the first cooling part is not fully crystalline, and if the mother liquor is withdrawn the rough already solidified part remains as aa.

Tuesday I went with my boy Ioane to explore the woods. As I followed a path made by the pulu pickers through the dense forest, I came upon a large hole on the edge of the path which proved to be the entrance to a cave of great depth. The path had been turned aside to avoid it, and in the dark it would be very dangerous. Such holes are common in this part of Puna, and natives occasionally disappear mysteriously. Brushing through the bushes I came to a precipice forming the edge of a crater nearly three-quarters of a mile in diameter and seven hundred feet deep. The sides were quite perpendicular, and in most places impassable. The bottom was level and gravelly, with a thin growth of ohia, and at the western end, directly under the wall, was a much deeper pit, indeed the deepest I had seen on Hawaii. Beyond this was a cone of some size, near which the eruption of 1840 reached the surface, first passing under the cone (see Fig. 64). Half a mile beyond this is another pit crater, smaller, and covered on the bottom with black lava. Following the line down in a southeasterly direction, I came to the steam cracks, which extend for several hundred feet, and since tradition existed have furnished the natives of the neighborhood with the means of cooking. The pahoehoe has been decomposed into a soft red muddy soil, covered with a hard crust, which may be raised in slabs. Under these are most beautiful crystals of sulphur in clusters, but too fragile to be removed.

Beyond these cracks was a much larger crater, elliptical, with a major axis a mile long and a depth of nearly five hundred feet. The perpendicular walls presented basaltic columns in various places, and at the west end were rent asunder affording an easy descent to the bottom, which was gravelly, level, and free from cracks or holes. The walls of all the craters that I visited were compact gray clinkstone in deep strata like the walls of Kilauea, and no recent lava was visible. Several dykes were seen at right angles to a line from Kilauea to Kapoho.[77] The line of these cones and craters may be seen on the map, but the principal group at Kapoho, near the coast, deserves more notice. These cones and craters seem to extend in several nearly parallel lines toward the mountain. One very interesting group much broken down, and apparently among the oldest, contains in its midst the beautiful Green Lake (Fig. 66). This occupies a deep crater but the water is of constant level, with no outlet and no apparent

[77] These craters are now (1909) easily accessible by a good trail from the Volcano House. Many of these pit craters have the walls more or less covered with ferns, and one had the name Halema'uma'u (House of fern). From this perhaps arose the pedantic mistake of calling the Halemaumau (House that endures) of Kilauea by this other very inappropriate name. Pele had her Halemaumau, always there, however the form might change, and on her accustomed path to the sea she had her temporary lodging, a mere fern-covered house (Halema'uma'u). Father Coan, whose critical knowledge of the Hawaiian language was certainly as great as that of any one now living, recognized only Halemaumau in Kilauea, but more than one Halema'uma'u in Puna.

supply except from the rainfall on the sloping sides of the crater; it is about twenty feet deep, and although viewed from above the water looks very green, it is quite sweet and colorless in a glass. The natives assured me that its waters become yellow and then black during an eruption of Kilauea, a statement I much doubt. An adjoining crater contains many coconut trees: the walls between the craters of this group are thin as some of those in Hualalai, and like those pit craters are walled with stony lava and not tufa.

Half a mile from this group is a cone about two hundred and fifty feet high, and crowned with an ancient heiau or temple, and a clump of coconut trees. This cone is largely composed of lava, and is doubtless of great age as the soil is several

FIG. 65. VIEW OF THE PUNA CRATERS FROM THE NORTH.

feet deep upon it in some places. At its base is a large cleft in the rock some three hundred feet long and sixty wide, in which is a remarkably clear pool of warm water, twenty or thirty feet deep and of a temperature at the time of my first visit of 90°. Thirty-four years after I found it five degrees above the air temperature. At a later visit to test more accurately I found the pool occupied by a gang of Japanese field hands. The water is not mineral to the taste, but the dark-colored bodies of natives swimming in it seem almost wax-colored, and a white man in the pool resembles marble. The sound of water trickling down within the cliff is distinctly audible after a rain. Three-quarters of a mile from this is a deep narrow cavern into which one may climb guided by the natives with their bambu torches. There is a steep descent of nearly fifty feet to a pool of very warm water which is said to extend more than half a mile under ground.[78] All along the shore for twenty miles, warm springs are common near

[78] In 1864 the writer saw several natives swim nearly that distance holding their torches clear of the steaming water, and the indistinct view thus obtained of the cavern, led to the conclusion that it was a deep crack, over which a subsequent lava-flow had formed a roof.   [476]

low-water level. No mineral waters are found here, nor is there anywhere on the Hawaiian Islands even a carbonated or sulphur spring. The ground is mostly covered with aa through the whole district of Puna, and all the rain that is not held by this sponge-like form of lava sinks to the sea level and issues from clefts on the shore. As there is hardly any soil, it might be supposed that Puna would be a barren region, but the reverse is the case. Groves of coconut trees extend for miles, growing more thriftily than elsewhere on these islands, and the natives have no difficulty in raising

FIG. 66. THE GREEN LAKE.

pines, bananas and other fruits. The aa is often so rough that unshod horses cannot stand on it outside the beaten road, without a carpet of pandanus leaves or seaweed.

The slopes of Kilauea are quite regular in this district, and many eruptions have flowed down this way; at least twenty may be counted in thirty miles. Tradition declares that formerly Puna was a fertile region surpassing in the productiveness of its soil any district of Hawaii, and that during the absence of the chief, Pele, the goddess of the volcano, left her abode in Kilauea to pay him a visit. From the appearance of the streams of lava it is not impossible that many of them were synchronous, and that the larger portion of Puna was overwhelmed by the same eruption of Kilauea. None of the lavas of Mauna Loa have flowed this way. The pandanus flourishes greatly in this region, and innumerable caves found in the streams of ancient lava afforded the weavers cool and damp shelters well adapted to mat-making. Other caves whose roofs have not fallen have, from early times been a favorite depositary for the remains of the dead.

[477]

This digression from the chronological record of the Kilauean eruptions seemed necessary to explain the geography of the emptyings of its great cauldron, and will save time later when our notes are more condensed. I have been through Puna many times, and have tried to trace from native tradition this or that eruption in the lava flows that, generally speaking, look all of an age, but I am not certain that any prior to that of 1840 can be correctly identified. I put no faith in the identification of that of 1823 on one of the government surveys, for Ellis closely questioned the natives and

FIG. 67. BLUE POOL.

could not hear of any outbreak from the natives of Puna who met him both in Puna and Hilo. That or any other may be the flow of 1823 if that flow came to the surface on the Hilo side, which it probably did not, so far as the evidence goes.[79]

1868 Since 1865 the great crater of Kilauea had been slowly filling up by the overflow of the northern lakes of 1864, and of various cones between these and Halemaumau until the whole central portion was considerably elevated.[80] Mauna Loa had also been more or less active since visited by Mr. Horace Mann and myself in 1865. Then the great summit crater Mokuaweoweo was quite still, and apparently cold and extinct, exhibiting hardly any signs of recent action; only on one

[79] The evidence strongly favors the identification of the short flow on the other side of Kilauea as that of 1823, and I have so considered it on the map of Hawaii herewith.

[80] The following account was published in 1869 in the Memoirs of the Boston Society of Natural History, vol. i, 564. I have here united the eruptions of the two volcanoes, as the same cause seems to have effected both, and the subsidiary phenomena—earthquakes, landslide, and tidal wave, belong to either or both.

of the lower walls a little steam floated up from the cracks below. No one has ascended this mountain since our visit three years ago, but from the shores the glare of its crater has been distinctly seen more than once in the interval. As it was winter, and the snows and storms rendered the ascent dangerous, no one attempted it, and as no lava stream flowed down, little attention was paid to these distant and temporary volcanic displays.

During the past ninety years ten great eruptions have taken place on Hawaii, averaging one for every nine years, the last occurring in 1859, when a large stream of lava flowed from Mauna Loa some sixty miles into the sea. The lava had accumulated in the reservoirs which supply this mountain and was ready to break forth. To this brief statement of the condition of the Hawaiian volcanoes previous to the present outbreak, may be added the fact that the season had been exceedingly rainy, and the mountain streams were much higher than usual.

March 27, 1868, about half-past five in the morning, persons on the whale ships at anchor in the harbor of Kawaihae saw a dense cloud of smoke rise on the top of Mauna Loa, in one massive pillar, to the height of several miles, lighted up brilliantly by the glare from the crater Mokuaweoweo. In a few hours the smoke dispersed, and at night no light was visible.[a]

About ten o'clock A.M. on the 28th (Saturday), a series of earthquakes began, which has continued at intervals nearly eight months. The shocks commenced early in the morning; the first was followed at an interval of an hour by a second, and then by others at shorter intervals and with increasing violence, until at one o'clock P.M. a very severe shock was felt all through the southwest part of the island. From this time until the 10th of April the earth was in an almost constant tremor. In the district of Kona as many as fifty or sixty distinct shocks were counted in one day; in Kau over three hundred in the same time; while near Kilauea and about Kapapala it was difficult to count them. It is said that during the early part of April two thousand distinct shocks occurred in Kau, or an average of one hundred and forty or more each day. The culminating shock occurred on Thursday, April 2d, at twenty minutes before four in the afternoon. Every stone wall, almost every house, in Kau was overturned, and the whole was done in an instant. A gentleman riding found his horse lying flat under him before he could think of the cause, and persons were thrown to the ground in an equally unexpected manner. Mr. F. S. Lyman was at Keaiwa, near the point where the motion was greatest, between that and the centre of vibration,

---

[a] Rev. J. D. Paris writes from Kona, Hawaii, "In less than half an hour these columns of smoke had shot up along the slope of the great mountain southward to the distance of ten or fifteen miles. We thought it was from a stream of lava.....but the clouds soon shut in the whole mountain, and nothing more was seen during the day..... During the whole night no light nor smoke were to be seen. All was clear and still as death."

which was not very distant, as the angle of emergence was almost 90°, or nearly coincident with the seismic vertical, and he reported as follows:

> First the earth swayed to and fro north and south, then east and west, round and round, then up and down and in every imaginable direction, for several minutes; everything crushing around us; the trees thrashing about as if torn by a mighty rushing wind. It was impossible to stand, we had to sit on the ground, bracing with hands and feet to keep from rolling over. In the midst of it we saw burst out from the pali [precipice] about a mile and a half to the north of us, what we supposed to be an immense river of molten lava (which afterwards proved to be red earth), which rushed down its headlong course and across the plain below, apparently bursting up from the ground, throwing rocks high in the air, and swallowing up everything in its way, trees, houses, cattle, horses, goats and men, all in an instant, as it were. It went three miles in not more than three minutes time, and then ceased. Some one pointed to the shore, and we ran to where we could see it. After the hard shaking had ceased, and all along the sea-shore, from directly below us to Punaluu, about three or four miles, the sea was boiling and foaming furiously, all red, for about an eighth of a mile from the shore, and the shore was covered by the sea. We went right over to Nahala's hill with the children and our natives, to where we could see both ways; expecting every moment to be swallowed up by the lava from beneath; for it sounded as if it was surging and rushing under our feet all the time, and there were frequent shakes. In places the ground was all cracked up, and every rock or pali that could fall had fallen. At Hilea we saw a small stream of black smoking lava, and outside of Punaluu a long black point of lava slowly pushed out to sea and soon disappeared.

Ten miles to the southwest of Keaiwa, at Waiohinu, the great stone church was levelled to the ground (Fig. 68), and nearly all the other buildings were destroyed. The earth opened all through the district, and often left dangerous fissures, although it usually closed. The meizoseismic curve (or that of maximum overthrow) seems to have been elliptical, with a major axis of about ten miles in a southwest and northeast direction, while the isoseismic curves were rather crescent-shaped, having their convexity towards Mauna Loa. In Kona the shocks were severe, but less so than in Kau; At Kohala they did very little damage, not even injuring the tall chimney of the Kohala sugar mill; while at Hilo, on the other side of the mountains, the violence of the vibrations was about the same as in Kona. The mountains seem to have deadened the shock, and simply transmitted it through their solid cones to the axes of the other islands of the group, where the shock of April 2nd was felt as a vibration from the central mountain to the sea. This was the case even in Kauai, nearly three hundred miles distant from the supposed seismic vertical. No damage was done except in these southern districts of Hawaii, where the undulations seemed to bend around the base of the mountain, forcing the isoseismic curves far from the meizoseismic curve in Kau.

At Hilo, although the shock was not so severe as at Waiohinu, more damage was done, for the houses were larger and more numerous. A correspondent writes: "I was coming from the tannery to my store, when I heard a loud, rumbling noise like a number of iron carriages drawn over a rough road by wild horses. Soon the shock came. The horses in the pasture took fright, and ran and snorted, the dogs howled, and the pigeons flew about as if somebody had been shooting at them. The shock lasted a good while, how long I cannot say, but long enough to make me feel sea-sick, and it was with difficulty that I could stand. All the stone walls about the town were flat. Fissures opened, and the brooks ran mud; in one place a fissure opened about a foot, and when it closed the two sides were several inches from coincidence."

The land-slide referred to by Mr. Lyman, is well described by the Rev. T. Coan, whose letter will be given presently. The most destructive feature of the whole catastrophe, however, was the sea-wave which swept the shores of Hawaii from Kahuku to Kapoho and was felt at the most distant shores of the group. At Hilo the sea receded a hundred and fifty or two hundred feet, and when it returned rose about ten feet above

FIG. 68. CHURCH AT WAIOHINU WRECKED BY EARTHQUAKE.

high-water mark. Along the shore between Kapoho and Kalae, villages were swept away, and even heavy stone houses disappeared before the destroying waves.

The earth continued to vibrate, but the shocks were not very severe, until on Tuesday night, April 7th, lava broke out in Kahuku, and flowed some ten miles then into the sea. The exact locality of the flow was afterwards determined by Mr. Coan. The schooner Oddfellow was cruising along the coast of Hilo, Puna and Kau, about the time of the sea-wave and the eruption, and from the report of a passenger the following notes are extracted. As she touched at many points, the information is of considerable interest.

Saturday, March 28.—Lakes in Kilauea active. Portion of the southwest cliff thrown down. *Sunday, 29.*—Shakes frequent but slight; one of them very peculiar in its motion commencing from northwest to southeast, shook a moment, and then shifted to northeast and southwest. North lake quite active. Shocks appear to have been stronger on the beach at Keauhou than they were at the volcano. *Thursday, April 2.*—Severe shock at Hilo. Keauhou and other villages in the neighborhood swept away. *Friday, 3.*—Shocks very violent in Kilauea. Fire in Kilauea-iki, the south lake terribly active, and enlarging rapidly. *Saturday, 4.*—Saw fire on the hills at Kapoho; could not tell whether it was a lava-flow or not. *Sunday, 5.*—Made Kealakomo, Puna, at daylight. The houses nearest the beach gone; same at Kahue. All swept clean at Apua. Reached Keauhou, Kau, at seven A.M. and anchored. Found the anchorage and boat-landing all right. Every building, eleven in all, washed away; not a stick or stone of them left standing. Portions of the wreck washed inland over the flat about eight hundred feet; heavy ohia sticks and a large spar were carried that distance. In some places the ground appeared to have sunk, and the sea was flowing a fathom deep where houses formerly stood. Men who were at work near the beach at the time of the shock (April 2), say that the walls of stone buildings were thrown outward by the shock, which was so severe that they were themselves thrown off their feet; then the sea came pouring over the rocks which lined the shore, and they escaped being overtaken by the hardest kind of running. No one was hurt. A messenger from Kilauea reports that hardly a sign of fire was to be seen in the crater. Got under way and ran down to Punaluu. *Monday, 6.*—Too rough to attempt a landing. The stone church and all the other buildings near the sea gone. At Ninole but three houses were left. Smoke or steam is issuing from the hills back of Hilea. Came to anchor at Kaalualu at noon. The houses, wharf, etc., all gone here, and the rocks inland strewed with the wreck for a distance of six or eight hundred feet. Dense clouds covered the summit of Mauna Loa, but no sign of fire, and no reflection from Kilauea. *Tuesday, 7.*—The deck covered this morning with very fine ashes. Procured animals, and rode along the beach to the south point. The sea had been inland in some places, a hundred and fifty yards, and the whole coast was lined with house timbers, lumber, broken canoes, dead animals that had drifted ashore. At Halii found the body of a native woman lying among the rocks, the right leg bitten off at the knee, and the body otherwise horribly mutilated by the sharks. The shock of the earthquake was evidently slight in this direction, for many of the stone pens were not much damaged, and at Kalae, the extreme southerly point, there was no sign of any disturbance. Weighed anchor at three P.M., and ran past Kalae. At six P.M., when the point was about ten miles astern, bearing E. by S., a volume of flame shot up from the mountain Loa, in what appeared to be the neighborhood of Kahuku. The heavens were lighted up at once, and the reflection extended rapidly in the direction of Waiohinu and Kaalualu. After the first outburst we saw the fire but once or twice, and then it appeared to be the grass burning on the edge of the cliff which extends inland from the south point. There was no flow of the lava over the cliff, nor toward Kona, and the stream probably ran down on the Kahuku flat or between there and Waiohinu to the neighborhood of the Kaalualu landing. It reached the sea somewhere in that direction at nine and a half P.M., when an immense body of steam at once arose, through which flashes resembling lightning were constantly darting as long as we were in sight. The top of the mountain was concealed by the dense clouds of smoke.

From a schooner at anchor off Lanai the light of this lava-stream was seen about midnight, over the mountain, while flashes like chain-lightning shot up into the clouds. From Lahaina the same light was seen, and the next day a column of smoke in the same direction. From Kona the light was first seen about eleven P.M. The Rev. S. E. Bishop, president of Lahainaluna Seminary on Maui, contributes the following observations:

During the night of April 7th a bright but varying crimson light over the volcano was visible from the Seminary at the distance of one hundred and twenty statute miles as measured on Wilkes' chart. This light was a reflection from a mass of cumulus cloud through which vivid lightning was constantly darting. After daylight and through the morning of the 8th, this stupendous column of cloud was visible pouring rapidly up to the ether, with ever varying shape. It was usually well defined on the westward side, where it, at times, presented a perpendicular wall of miles in height. On the east it was ill-defined. Above, it often spread out, especially toward the east, as if borne off by the southeast wind of the upper air. The base, so far as visible, appeared to be commingled with murky brown strata. The apparent altitude of this cumulus above the horizon, when at its highest was 3°30' which reduced for a base of 120 miles with 500 feet altitude of the point of observation, gives a height of 7.8 miles. This morning, the 9th, our atmosphere is charged with smoky haze, and a very distinct odor of sulphurous acid.

At Kapapala, on the 7th, the ground was still in violent agitation, with a long undulatory motion. At night a very large flow of lava was seen running down the mountain to the sea. The next day smoke was seen issuing from cracks in this neighborhood. Mr. H. M. Whitney visited the scene of the eruption on the 10th, and from him we learn the following particulars:

As we approached the flow the rumbling noise became more and more distinct. The ground was covered with what appeared to be cinders, but on examining them we found they were fragments of [basaltic] pumice-stone which had been carried by the wind a distance of over ten miles. Mixed with these cinders was *Pele's hair*, which we found floating in the air, and when it was thick we had to hold our handkerchiefs to our nostrils to prevent inhaling it; our clothes were frequently covered with it. We hurried on and reached the flow shortly after noon, when from a ridge to the west of it the whole scene opened before us. Between us and the crater was a valley five hundred yards wide and ten miles long, which had recently been overflowed throughout its entire breadth and length from the mountain to the sea where it widened to two or three miles. The lava was of the smooth or pahoehoe variety, from ten to twenty feet deep, and partially cooled over, though flames, smoke and gas escaped from numerous crevices. On Tuesday afternoon, April 7th, at five o'clock, a new crater, several miles lower down than that referred to, and about two miles back of Captain Brown's residence, burst out. The lava stream commenced flowing down the beautiful grass-covered plateau, towards and around the farm-house, and the inmates had barely time to escape with the clothes they had on; the path by which they escaped was covered with lava ten minutes after they passed over it.

On ascending the ridge we found the eruption in full blast. Four enormous fountains, on a line a mile long, north and south, were continually spouting up from the opening. These jets were blood-red, and yet as fluid as water, ever varying in size, bulk and height. Sometimes two would join together, and again the whole four would be united, making one continuous fountain a mile in length. From the lower end of the crater, a stream of very liquid, boiling lava flowed out and down the plateau, a distance of two or three miles, then following the road ran down the precipice at an angle of about 30°, then along the foot of the pali or precipice, five miles to the sea, the stream being about eight or ten miles in length, and in some places half a mile wide. One peculiarity of the spouting was that the lava was ejected with a *rotary motion*, and as it ascended both lava and stones rotated always in one direction towards the south. This was the only stream which reached the sea, and flowed into it at Kailikii. It lasted only five days, the eruption ceasing entirely on the night of the 11th, or morning of the 12th. During its continuance, the atmosphere was filled with smoke so dense that the sun appeared like a ball of fire, and the whole island was shrouded in darkness. The smoke came from the rent or crater, and was highly charged with sulphur.

As the lava entered the sea, clouds of steam and smoke rose up, and flames of bluish fire were emitted, rising from the water to a height of from ten to twenty feet. During the night we were at the volcano, the air was highly charged with sulphurous gas and electricity, and frequent flashes of lightning were seen directly over the lava stream, accompanied with short claps of thunder. These flashes were also observed less frequently further up the mountain. About four thousand acres of good pasture land were destroyed, besides which the lava ran over an immense district of worthless land. On the night of the 6th of April, prior to the eruption, there was a shower of ashes and pumice-stone, which came from this crater, and covered the country to a distance of ten or fifteen miles each way. Generally the ashes were not more than one or two inches in depth, but in some places were found to be fifteen. The pumice-stone was very light, and appears to have been carried by the wind a great distance. Pieces two and three inches in diameter floated ashore at Kealakeakua, forty-five miles distant.

[483]

During the early part of April an observer in Kona kept a careful record of the principal shocks felt there, but in other places no observations were made. The only certain thing, among various and somewhat extravagant reports, is that the vibrations were very frequent and not very severe. In some places they were almost silent, but usually accompanied by subterranean detonations and rumblings, with a noise as of boiling, surging waves in the bowels of the earth. No observations were made on the gases said to have been emitted from some of the fissures.

When the eruption of lava was made known at Honolulu, many residents at once set out for Hawaii, and among them a gentleman of distinguished attainments in botany, Dr. William Hillebrand, who has given us so accurate and full an account of what he saw in passing through the disturbed region that it seems worthy of a more permanent record than would be its lot in the local newspaper in which it first appeared. He writes as follows:

I started from Hilo with a few friends for Kilauea April 17th; descended the crater on the 18th; examined the extensive fissures near the Puna road on the 20th; the so-called mud-flow on the 21st; and the lava streams in Kahuku on the 23rd. On the 24th we crossed the lava stream on the road to Kona, and reached Kealakeakua Bay on April 26th.

Of Hilo I have little to say, as your correspondents have communicated to you the most remarkable events from that place. I saw several fissures in the earth near Wahiawa River, of from eight inches to one foot in width, which were caused by the earthquake of April 2nd, and run in the direction of Mauna Loa. The earthquake waves all moved from southwest to northeast, and over-turned movable objects standing at right angles with that line. A heavy book-case in the Rev. T. Coan's library, holding that relation to the wave, was overturned, while another heavy case, filled with shells and minerals, which stood parallel to the wave, remained standing.

Kilauea.—The ground around the crater, particularly on the eastern and western sides, is rent by a number of fissures, one near the Puna road more than twelve feet wide, and very deep; others of lesser size run parallel to and cross the Kau road, so as to render travel on it very danger-ous. The lookout house is detached from the mainland by a very deep crevasse, and stands now on an isolated overhanging rock, which at the next severe concussion must tumble into the pit below. Many smaller fissures are hidden by grass and bushes, forming so many traps for the unwary. The Volcano House, however, has not suffered nor is the ground surrounding it broken in the least. From the walls of Kilauea large masses of rock have been detached and thrown down. On the west and northwest sides, where the fire had been most active before the great earthquake of April 2nd, the falling masses probably have been at once melted by the lava and carried off in its stream, for the walls there remain as perpendicular as they were before; but that this part of the wall has lost portions of its mass, is shown too evidently by the deep crevices along the western edge just spoken of, and the partial detachment in many places of large prisms of rock. But it is on the east and northeast wall particularly, that the character of the crater has undergone a change. Along the descent on the second ledge large masses of rock, many, more than one hundred tons in weight, obstruct the path and form abutments to the stone pillars—small buttress hills similar to those ob-served in front of the high basaltic wall of Koolau, Oahu. So also in the deep crater itself the east-ern wall has lost much of its perpendicular dip, and has become shelving in part.

The crater itself was entirely devoid of liquid lava; no incandescence anywhere; pitchy dark-ness hovered over the abyss the first night. I say the first night, because during the second night of our stay between twelve M. and one A.M., detonations were heard again, and light reappeared for a short time in the south lake Halemaumau. White vapors of steam issued from the floor in a hundred places, but of those stifling sulphurous and acid gases, formerly so overpowering in the neighborhood of the lakes and ovens, only the faintest trace was perceived here and there.

The heat was nowhere so great that we could not keep our footing for a minute or more, although in many places it would forbid the touch of the bare hand. The great south lake Halemaumau is transformed into a vast pit, more than five hundred feet deep, the solid eastern wall projecting far over the hollow below, while the remaining sides are falling off with a sharp inclination, and consist of a confused mass of rough aa. More than two-thirds of the old floor of Kilauea has caved in, and sunk from one hundred to three hundred feet below the level of the remaining floor.

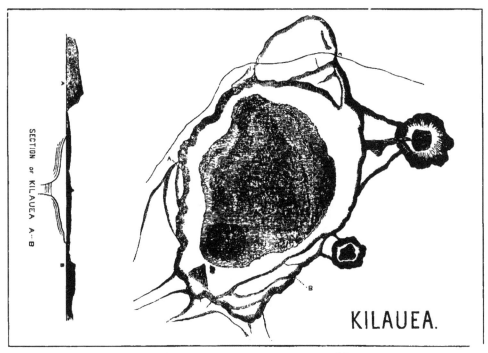

FIG. 69. KILAUEA AFTER THE ERUPTION OF 1868.

The depression embraces the whole western half, and infringes in a semicircular line on a considerable portion of the other half. This is greatest in the northern, and rather gradual and gentle in its southern portion. Entering on the depressed floor from the southern lake, it was some time before we became fully aware of its existence, and it was only on our return from the northwest corner, where it is deepest, that there presented itself through the mist in which we were enveloped, a high wall of three hundred feet, grotesque and fanciful in outline. At first we were quite bewildered, fancying that we beheld the great outer wall of the crater. On nearer approach we soon satisfied ourselves that this singular wall represented the line of demarcation of a great depression in the floor of the crater—a fact that surprised us the more, as a bird's eye view from above had altogether failed to apprise us of its existence. As we had been informed that the principal activity of the crater before the great earthquake had been in the northwest corner, we proceeded in that direction on leaving the south lake. Having arrived at about the middle of the depression a considerable rise in the ground presented itself on our left—to the west. Having ascended this, we found ourselves at the brink of a fearful chasm, which fell off on our side with a beetling wall to the depth of several hundred feet and extended about half a mile from north to south. Very hot air rose from it. Around it, towards its northern extremity, the lava is thrown up into an indescribable confusion; pile upon pile of aa gorge and ridge by turns.

The caving in of the floor seemed to be still in progression, for twice during our exploration of the crater, our nerves were disturbed by a prolonged heavy rumbling and rattling noise, as from a distant platoon-fire of musketry, coming from the northwest corner.

Kilauea iki, which in 1865 was covered with shrubs on its side and partly on the bottom, was now overflowed with black, shining lava. It has been free from fire since 1832.

Thus far as to what we have seen. Now allow me to relate what I learned from Kaina [the District Judge, and a most intelligent Hawaiian], who has resided near the volcano without inter- ruption for the last five months, and whose strong nerves sustained him during the fearful catastrophe introduced by the earthquake of April 2nd. He and the Chinaman who keeps the house, were the only persons who remained at Kilauea. He says that for two months preceding the first shock, namely, from January 20th to March 27th, the crater had been unusually active; eight lakes being in constant ebullition and frequently overflowing. During all this time (the date of its first appear- ance could not be ascertained exactly), there was in the northwest corner a blow-hole, from which at regular intervals of a minute or less, with a roaring noise, large masses of vapor were thrown off, as from a steam engine. This ceased about the 17th of March. At the same time the activity of the lakes became greatly increased, and Kaina anticipated mischief. March 27, the first shock was perceived. Two days later Mr. Abraham Fornander found the bottom of the crater overflowed with fresh lava, and incandescent.

Thursday, April 2nd, at a few minutes past four P.M., the big earthquake occurred, which caused the ground around Kilauea to rock like a ship at sea. At that moment there commenced fearful detonations in the crater; large quantities of lava were thrown up to a great height; portions of the wall tumbled in. This extraordinary commotion, accompanied with unearthly noise and sway- ing of the ground, continued from that day till Sunday night, April 5th, but *from the first the fire began to recede.* On Thursday night it was already confined to the regular lakes; on Saturday night it only remained in the great south lake, and on Sunday night there was none at all; Pele had left Kilauea. The noises now became weaker, and were separated by longer intervals. By Tuesday quiet reigned in Kilauea. On that afternoon the lava burst out at a distance of forty miles, south- west, in Kahuku.

April 2nd, from six to ten P.M., Kaina observed fire in the direction of Puna, which, at the time, caused him to believe that the lava had found a vent again in that direction, as it did in 1840; but he subsequently satisfied himself that it was only a reflection from lava in Kilauea iki. It was not seen afterward.

Iu Kapapala we are told that fire had been seen several nights in a southeast direction, and that natives had reported flowing lava there. We rode over in the morning of April 20th. At a dis- tance of five miles from Mr. Reed's dwelling, where the Puna road turns off from the Kilauea road, heavy clouds of white vapor were seen to issue from the bush, which sparsely covered the pahoehoe, makai[83] of the road. Half an hour's ride brought us up to the place, but we were obliged to leave our horses some distance before reaching the spot, on account of fissures. After having crossed a number of them, heading for the heaviest cloud of vapor, we at last came to a deep crevasse in the pahoehoe, at least twenty-four feet in width, no bottom visible. It narrowed and widened out in places, but nowhere was less than eight feet wide. Its length we estimated at four hundred feet.

[83] Makai is the Hawaiian for "towards the sea". [486]

Parallel with this great crevasse, constituting a belt about six hundred feet in width, were a number of smaller ones on each side, diminishing in size with distance from it, from six feet to a few inches. From the larger openings in the former, heavy white columns of hot steam issued, which had a decidedly alkaline smell. Smaller jets of vapor to the number of thirty, rose from the smaller fissures. We could not discover fire in any place, but it is very probable that during dark nights the reflection of the underlying lava should be thrown up, for as the steam did not seem to contain combustible material, it is unlikely that the light seen should have been produced by it. The mean direction of all the fissures was N.E. 9° N., S.W. 9° S., or nearly the direction of a line connecting Kilauea with Waiohinu and Kahuku. The distance of these fissures from Kilauea is thirteen miles.

As in this district the earthquake of April 2nd culminated to its greatest intensity, so as even to rend in twain the frame-work of a mountain-side, and hurl down on the plain a portion of its flank, it is necessary to give a short description of the country in order to insure a proper understanding of the disturbance. The locality in question is that comprised between the ranch stations of Messrs. Reed and Richardson, on the east, and Mr. F. S. Lyman on the west, a distance of five miles. The government road connecting these two places runs through a fine grassy plain, which has a very gentle fall towards the sea, its elevation being about 2000 feet. Into this plain project from the slope of Mauna Loa three parallel hills or spurs, each about one mile in length, and from 800 to 1800 feet in height. They include two broad valleys between them. The upper portions of these valleys rise with a steep incline towards a ridge which runs at right angles with the spurs, and is covered with a dense pulu forest, which extends far up the gentle slope of the dome of Mauna Loa. In the second one of these valleys—that next to Mr. Lyman's—the so-called mud-flow took place, but very extensive land-slides, confined simply to the loose earth and conglomerate, also occurred in the other valley.

The ground around Reed and Richardson's station is torn up into numerous small cracks and fissures, running in every direction. Some are large enough to engulf horse and rider, a fact which actually occurred a few days after the earthquake. A large cistern, built in solid masonry and covered with an arched stone roof, was rent to pieces, and the roof entirely broken away. Not a single stone fence is standing; their places are indicated by flat belts of stone on the ground. The dwelling house—a good wooden framed one—exhibits a wrench across its roof, so that the gutters empty themselves in the sitting room; the cook-house is thrown off its foundation; other out-buildings are completely overturned; and of the grass houses, some are smashed down, others greatly inclined. But all these signs of destruction are thrown in the shade by the grandeur of the force which shook off the side of the pali, burying in a minute thirty-one human beings, many hundred head of cattle, and entire flocks of goats, and ending four miles from its beginning in a mighty river of mud. Before reaching this mud-flow from Reed's house, we passed two considerable streams of muddy water, of a reddish-yellow color, emitting a strong odor of clay, such as may be perceived in potteries. Both streams have their origin in the land-slide of the first valley. When we passed them again, two days later, they had nearly disappeared; they evidently owed their origin to the drainage of the fallen mass. The mud-flow is met with three miles from Reed's. It projects itself from the spurs of the hills two miles down in the plain; begins at once with a thickness of six feet, which, towards the middle, where it forms a small hill, rises to thirty feet; averages about three-fourths of a mile in width, and contracts towards its end. From this end a long queue of boulders bears witness to the violent action of a torrent which shot out of the mud after it was deposited, and which has since perpetuated itself in a stream of some size, quite muddy, and emitting the above mentioned pottery odor when we saw it first, on April 20th, but perfectly clear and inodorous when we passed it three days later. A little higher up a koa grove gives still stronger evidence of the strength of the propelling force. The trees first seized are snapped off and prostrate, yet the mud in that place is only a few feet deep. The mass itself is nothing but the loose red soil of the mountain side, with a good sprinkling of round boulders, with here and there stumps of trees, ferns, *hapuu* and *amaumau*, and entire lehua trunks. Near the lower end a vigorous, healthy taro-plant stood erect in the mud as if it had been planted there. From the sides of the mass protruded portions of the bodies of many cattle and goats, overwhelmed in their flight; a gain of one second of time might have saved them. The surface of the mud in this lower course was rather smooth, as if it had been forced down by the agency of water, and it was still so soft that the feet sank deep into it.

After we had flanked it for some distance along the side of the hill, the mud became solid enough to bear our weight, and we walked upon it to the head of the pali. The surface gradually became more rough; the boulders increased, and detached portions of earth and stone were scattered beyond its borders, which also flattened out gradually. The ascent soon became steep, and here, on a short spur, just in the middle of the mud, stands a native house on an island of grass and kalo, flanked by two trees. A poor woman who happened to be in it at the time of the outbreak, escaped the awful fate which doomed the remaining members of her family, and was removed from her perilous situation a few days after, when the crust had become solid enough to bear a man's weight.

As we went on the mass became more rough and hard, tree trunks and boulders increased, even angular rocks appeared, until at last the mud ceased entirely and gave place to a sea of huge rocks, all angular and exhibiting fresh fractures, large trunks of trees crushed between and under them, and streamlets of fresh, clear water meandering between them. This continued for the last three hundred feet of rise, and ended in a perpendicular wall of solid rock, some twenty feet high, after having climbed which, we reposed under the refreshing shade of tall fern trees, for we had entered at once the great pulu forest. Seated on the trunk of a prostrate tree, we could survey the whole scene of devastation we had just traversed. Immediately at our feet the rocky framework of the pali was torn up, and its contents turned topsy-turvy in dire confusion. The rocky wall we had just climbed, continued until it reached the sides of the two flanking hills. A perpendicular cut in the sides of the latter laid open some forty feet of red earth and conglomerate. On looking behind us we saw that the rock we were resting on was separated from the mountain by a deep crevasse, parallel to the wall, and only partly visible, as it extended under the dense trees. To our left a clear sparkling mountain stream leaped in a bounding cascade over the crag, and after losing its course amid the maze of rocks, gathered itself again, flowing over the solid bed-rock in a deep gorge cut in the mud. This stream had existed here before, but ere it reached half down the pali, became lost in the soil. It can easily be imagined what an amount of subsoil water must have been deposited here. Bearing this in mind, and the great depth of soil and conglomerate on this slope, as indicated by the cuts in the hill-sides, there seems to be no great difficulty in explaining how such enormous masses of earth, at first propelled horizontally through the air, hurled down the valley by the tremendous force which tore off the side of the mountain, should then have been seized by the propelling force of the now liberated subsoil water and carried in a mighty stream far beyond the place where at first they were deposited.

All this destruction was the work of the great earthquake of April 2nd. During the five days preceding it, over one thousand shocks had been counted. On that afternoon Mr. Harbottle, at Reed's, with his men, was driving cattle across the hill towards Hilo, when suddenly the earth shook violently and a great detonation was heard behind them. Horses and cattle turned round involuntarily. The whole atmosphere before them was red and black. In a very short time this subsided—some say in one minute, others in five minutes; but a black cloud continued to hover over the scene for some time. From that Thursday to Sunday the earth constantly rocked and swayed; the hills seemed to alternately approach and recede. Most people became seasick. Strange roaring and surging noises were heard under the ground. When the ear was applied to the earth it would often receive a distinct impression as if a subterranean wave struck against the earth's crust. The prevailing direction of the earthquake waves was said to have been from northeast to southwest.

Here follows a portion of Dr. Hillebrand's account that covers ground already trodden by Mr. Whitney. After he arrived at Kahuku his account gives us the appearance of the lava after the flow had ceased. He continues:

As the principal interest was the discovery of the main source of the stream, we at once went to that part of it, where, according to common report, the lava had issued. A very light, dark brown, glistening pumice stone lay scattered about long before the lava was seen. Near the flow it increased so much that the animals' feet sank deep into it at every step. We soon reached the ridge of a hill from which we surveyed the place where, according to our guide's account, the fountains of lava had been seen. The upper portion of the lava stream fills a broad valley or depression, between two parallel low hills of not more than three hundred feet in height, both running almost due north and south. From the western one of these hills Mr. Whitney had witnessed the eruption. From the eastern hill we in vain looked for a crater or cone. We did not make out any indication of an eruption until we had crossed nearly three-fourths of the stream, which here is not far from a mile wide. Then our attention was attracted by an accumulation of scoriæ. Nearing this we were struck by a current of hot air, and, a little farther on, found ourselves on the brink of a deep gap in the lava about twenty feet wide, but narrowing and continuing northward. We walked round the southern end of the gap, and followed it up on the western or lee side. Before long we came to another enlargement of the fissure, like the former, emitting hot air charged with acid gases which drove us back. Still continuing our march on the west side of the fissure as close as the hot gases would allow, we came in sight of a pretty miniature cone, built up most regularly of loose scoriæ to the height of twelve feet, and located right over the fissure. It encloses a chimney crater of about twelve feet diameter, with perpendicular sides, the depth of which could not be ascertained. Hot gases issued in abundance. On account of the exhalation of the latter we were obliged to cross the chasm, on the bridge formed by the side of the cone, to the windward side, along which we followed up steadily.

This crack or fissure tends south six degrees west to north six degrees east and is in the slope of the hill that forms the west boundary of the lava-stream. Its lava cover therefore is quite thin in many places, so that you can see how it sinks in the original rock of the hill. Its depth cannot be ascertained anywhere. More than four-fifths of the lava is on the eastern side, as it followed the declivity of the hill-slope to fill the trough of the valley, where it assumed a general downward course. It is from the entire length of this fissure that the lava has welled up simultaneously. The waves of lava for some distance from it are all parallel to its course, while in the middle of the stream they stand at a right angle to it. The edges are somewhat raised above the remainder of the stream, and scoriæ covers it in most parts, forming quite heavy layers where the stream has blowholes. Isolated flakes of brittle lava, resembling cow-dung, probably blown out at the end of the eruption, with fitful spouting of steam and gas, are seen all along its course. Nearing the upper end of the valley, where I expected to find the end of the fissure, I was surprised at the sudden appearance of a veritable cataract of lava coming down the precipitous side of the eastern hill, a height of at least three hundred feet. Having ascended it with considerable toil, I found myself again alongside the big crevasse, which in passing across the valley had deflected from its former course to a nearly N.E. direction, heading direct for the summit of Mauna Loa.

From here onward, the incline increasing considerably, the lava commenced to be very rugged and broken. As here it had passed over and destroyed a dense forest, a number of grotesque shapes met the eye. Wherever the lava had met a tree of some size, it had surrounded it with a perfect mould which either still held the smouldering remains of the trunk, or exhibited hollow cylinders bearing on the inside the markings of the bark of the tree. The leaf stalk scars of fern-trees were almost perfect. A few of the moulds contained still entire trunks with the unconsumed branches. In the bifurcations of these, heavy masses of lava had accumulated, hanging down in wavy points like so many stalactites. Wherever there was a fern stump standing upright, it bore a cap of lava; everything indicated that the liquid mass had been thrown upwards by the violent rush of steam and gas. As I said before, this part of the flow was lined by a dense forest. It soon became apparent that the sides of the forest closed in upon each other, and from an eminence alongside the fissure I could see that the lava-stream contracted at some distance beyond to the apex of an isoceles triangle. The crevasse which ran straight up to the apex, was continuous, wider than below, and emitted in great profusion sulphurous and other acid gases. Its borders, which were of the color of red brick, commenced to be covered with the efflorescence of salts and sulphur, and in places they assumed altogether the appearance of sulphur banks. The heat of the lava increased so as to be unbearable in some places. Ashes and scoriæ covered every hollow in the floor, and the edge of the woods for some distance.

Having arrived at the apex of the triangle, I found that the crevasse, over which the trees almost closed from both sides, still extended a few hundred yards higher up in the woods, as indicated by a continuous line of white and yellow smoke. The choking nature of the latter forbade my marching along the edge of the fissure, while the impenetrable thicket, with the ground thickly covered by ashes, proved another effectual bar to my further progress. In fact, while hurrying out of an overpowering cloud of the smoke, I got one leg caught in a lateral fissure hidden under the ashes, where it received such a lively impression of heat that I made quick time to retire from that neighborhood. Just then I heard a deep, hollow, rumbling, prolonged sound, while the air and earth remained perfectly still. Subsequently I learned that it had been caused by the rolling down of large masses of pumice stone from the hill to the lower lava stream, but at the time being fearful of another catastrophe, I hurried back as fast as circumstances would permit, and felt a great relief in rejoining my friends who had remained behind, at the lower part of the stream. From the height above the cataract I saw two other lines of smoke running through the woods, taking their origin from the valley below, indicating two other fissures. Thus it appears that at the head of the valley the main fissure divided itself into three parts: the first and largest, running northeast; the middle one almost due north, and the third about north-northwest. The two latter did not seem to have thrown off much lava, if any, for there appeared no gap in the woods along their courses.[5]

From a letter addressed to me under date of August 27, 1868, by the Rev. T. Coan, I extract the following important facts and accurate descriptions:

I left Hilo on the fourth of August, on a missionary tour through Puna and Kau, and was absent eighteen days. During this tour I made careful observations with measurements and notes, on the remarkable volcanic phenomena of the past five months. The action of tellurial forces on our little island shell has been marvellous. The subsidence along the coast of Puna, from the east cape at Kapoho to Apua on the western line, is four to seven feet, varying in different localities. The great sand beach at Kaimu has been forced back into the young and beautiful coco-palm grove, and also into the groves of pandanus, so that trees now stand eight feet deep in sand, and many stand in the water. The plain of Kalapana has sunk about six feet, and water four to five feet deep now covers some twenty acres of what was once dry land. The old stone church is buried nearly to the eaves in sand, and the tide rises and falls within it.

This plain of Kalapana was doubtless at some former time buried much deeper beneath the sea. A coral reef of several yards thickness stretches half across the valley, and formed a barrier against further encroachments of the sea. It was three or four feet above high water mark, and formed a convenient site for the village. The church that Mr. Coan mentions was on this coral mound towards the shore. As the wall of rock which bounds the plain on the southerly side shows clearly that some former subsidence resulted in a rupture of the crust forming the floor of the plain from this wall, it would have been well to note any change at this point. Mr. Coan observed none, and the loose rocks knocked down by the protracted earthquakes would perhaps obliterate any traces of so slight a dislocation as a fall of six feet would cause.[84]

At Kealakomo the salt-works are destroyed and the fountain on the shore sunk. Apua, the last village in Puna, was swept clear [by the tidal wave of April 2nd] and sunk. Its pretty sand beach and miniature bay rendering it a resort for fishermen, are no more; the sea stands some six feet deep where the houses once stood. The same is true of Keauhou, the first village in Kau, and an important pulu station; coconut trees stand seven feet in the water, and all the buildings were swept away by the tidal wave. Passing on to Punaluu, this wave rose twenty feet and swept all before it. The great sand barrier which protected the beautiful pond and the cold, limpid spring, was first swept into the sea and then brought back and deposited in the pond, filling it up and changing the shore line. I got the height of this wave by measurement on a palm tree, and also upon the surrounding ridge of scoriform lava, making the rise above common high water about twenty feet.

From Punaluu onward to Honuapo, all houses were swept away except two standing on high lava ridges. The road was strown with boulders and fragments of rocks, and in some places it has sunk, so that it is with great difficulty, and not without a guide, that the traveler threads his zigzag way along this coast for five miles. Not a house remains in the considerable village of Honuapo: the sea occupies the site of former dwellings. The wave here corresponded with that at Punaluu, as shown by measurements on coconut trees. There were points where the influx of the sea was greater than at other places, and this seems to have been caused by the approach of the wave from the southwest, or at an angle of 45° to the shore, and by striking headlands and projecting points causing the waters to heap up within the points of tangency, while the current swept on at a lower mark where the coast presented no lateral obstructions.[85]

In crossing over the great lava fields from Puna to Kau, I passed about nine miles to the south and leeward of Kilauea, the great volcano flanking us on the right. The country through which we passed was terribly rent by the earthquake of April 2nd, and in some places we were obliged to deflect widely from the old track to avoid fissures. For several miles the cracks were so numerous and so wide, that a stranger would be utterly unable to find his way through this mural network of fractures. Our guide zigzagged us everywhere, our animals often demurring, trembling, and refusing to go. The whole atmosphere was filled with sulphurous smoke, through which the sun shone with sanguine rays. After passing most of these fissures, I requested my guide to turn to the left and follow the line of fissure seaward, hoping to find the locality of a disputed eruption which it was affirmed by some and denied by others had taken place in that wide and wild field of ancient lavas. After an hour of hard search amidst hills and ridges of aa and fields of pahoehoe, we found a veritable eruption······The fused lavas had been thrown out of the fissures at five different points, on a line of less than a mile in length. The largest batch was one thousand feet long and six hundred feet wide, with an average depth of ten feet, and with a steaming and tumulated surface. This series of small eruptions is about eleven miles southwest of Kilauea, and it shows distinctly the subterranean path taken by the igneous flood which left that seething cauldron on the night after the rending earthquake of April 2nd. That shock doubtless opened a pathway for the struggling fires, and they went off in a southwestern course under the highlands of Kau, uniting with the subterranean

[84] In crossing this plain twenty-five years later I found my surmise correct and the former wall had been covered by the confused fragments.

[85] To the casual traveler no signs of this shore catastrophe remain. Wharves and villages replace those destroyed, and even a sugar-mill and its surrounding hamlet occupies one of the points where the ravages were greatest.

fires of Mauna Loa, and finding a fuller vent at Kahuku on the seventh of April. This is the theory, and it is rendered probable by the great and constant trembling of the earth along that whole line, by subterranean noises heard by the people of Kapapala, Keaiwa, Waiohinu, and other places, and by the issuing of steam at several points from fissures along that line.

When it was found that Kilauea had discharged its contents, the first supposition was that the course of the eruption of 1840, or towards the southeast, had been followed, and this was strengthened by the report of fire seen at the bottom of some of the numerous pit craters on that line; but while it is possible that lava may have been injected in earthquake fissures opened in this direction even so far as the pit craters (see map, p. 51), the probable path was that indicated by Mr. Coan, which is apparently the same as that of the eruption 1823. When the Rev. William Ellis went over the ground the next year he found deep fissures extending in a southwest direction, some of them ten or twelve feet across, and emitting sulphurous vapors at a high temperature.[86] In one place where the chasm was about three feet wide, a large quantity of lava had been recently vomited. I do not agree with Mr. Coan that the lava from Kilauea and that from Mauna Loa effected a juncture before reaching the surface. It seems more probable that the former passed into the sea near Punaluu, as did that of 1823, not appearing above ground except at Kapapala. The fact that the openings on the side of Mauna Loa above Kahuku were much higher than those mentioned at Kapapala, seems to indicate conclusively that the lava of Kilauea did not flow out in the stream that deluged the height above Ka Lae. The lava of both these volcanic vents is so similar that nothing can be inferred from that of its individual source.

Landslide.—Between Kapapala and Keaiwa in Kau, I examined what has incorrectly been called the Mud Flow. I went entirely around it, and crossed it at its head and center, measuring its length and breadth which I found were severally three miles long and half a mile wide. The breadth at the head is about a mile, and the ground on the side-hill, where the cleavage took place, is now a bold precipice sixty feet high. Below this line of fracture the superstrata of the earth, consisting of soil, rocks, lavas, boulders, trees, roots, ferns and all tropical jungle, and water, slid and rolled down an incline of some 20°, until the immense masses came to the brow of a precipice near a thousand feet high, and here all plunged down an incline of 40° to 70° to the cultivated and inhabited plains below. The momentum acquired by this terrific slide was so great that the mass was forced over the plain, and even up an angle of 1° 30', at the rate of more than a mile a minute. In its course it swept along enormous trees, and rocks from the size of a pebble to those weighing many tons. Immense blocks of lava, some fresh as of yesterday, and others in all stages of decomposition, were uncovered by the slide. The depth of the deposit on the grass plains may average six feet: in depressions at the foot of the precipice it may be thirty or even forty feet.[87]

Eruption in Kahuku.—From the land-slide I went on to the igneous eruption in western Kau. Rents, tiltings, and other disturbances of the strata were seen along the shore, while the wooded and grassy hills on the right were scalped, scarred, cracked and striated, some of the once

---

[86] Ellis's Polynesian Researches, London, 1859, vol. iv, p. 220. See also quotation on p. 39 of the present work.
[87] I have a map of the landslide constructed for me by the late Latimer Coan, son of Rev. T. Coan, but it seemed unnecessary to reproduce it here, the descriptions are so definite.

green hills looked as if a gigantic cultivator had been driven down their sides, tearing off the sward and exposing the soil in wide parallel grooves, and leaving broad belts of vegetation resembling rows of sugar cane. In passing from Waiohinu to Kahuku, we started a little after sunrise and rode westward. About three miles from Waiohinu we crossed a lateral arm of the eruption, about one-sixteenth of a mile wide, and some two miles long, from where it left the parent stream. It was a high ridge of aa, say twenty-five feet deep, and running in a southeasterly direction. Crossing this and riding half a mile over verdant and beautiful fields, we come to another lateral outgush of similar character, and dimensions. Then came a third, which flowed some four miles and threatened to fill the harbor of Kaalualu. This was longer and broader than the other two, but of the same general character. After another half mile we crossed a fourth rugged stream of aa, and then moving southwest we rode rapidly over a fine surface of soil down a slope of about 3° to the ends of the two large parallel streams that entered the sea at Kailikii. Over all this wide field of pasturage, cinder and pumice had been scattered, and the grass had been consumed as by a prairie fire.

This portion of the eruption went into the sea about one mile northwest of Ka Lae, the south cape of the island. On the left flank of the stream is a high and very steep ridge (four hundred to five hundred feet high), extending from the cape up the southern slope of Mauna Loa. The outburst of April 7th commenced about ten miles from the sea by the opening of a horrid fissure in the forest on the upper side of this precipice. For about three miles the burning river flowed down partly above and partly below this precipice. The area above was rich and beautiful land for cultivation and pasturage; that below was simply pahoehoe. The four lateral streams before mentioned all ran off upon the beautiful highlands, covering several thousand acres, but without reaching the sea. Some three miles from the head the main stream went altogether over the precipice, and pursued its rapid course over the pahoehoe some seven miles to the sea which it reached in two hours. There it formed, as is usual when lava streams enter the sea, two cones of lava sand, or lava shivered into millions of particles by coming in contact with water while in an intensely heated state. There is no island there and there is nothing but what is common under similar circumstances. This stream is about half a mile wide, and it entered the sea some three-fourths of a mile from the high pali before spoken of. After running a day or two, in this channel, partial obstructions occurred, by cooling masses, when the shell of the stream was tapped some five miles from the sea, and a torrent of white-hot lava pushed out on the east side, running off to the great precipice and following its base in a breadth of half a mile down to the sea, and thus forming an island five miles long and a quarter of a mile wide, surrounded on three sides by fire. Three houses stand unscathed on this islet, and about thirty head of cattle were inclosed by the igneous flood.

The route taken by this lava flow was substantially that of a stream of unknown date, but whose smooth surface of hard pahoehoe looks fresh and undecomposed. Where this ancient stream originated is not known, for no one has ever taken the trouble to trace up the various flows that radiate like the spokes of a wheel from the cone of Mauna Loa.[88] The pali referred to was probably formed by the subsidence of the ground over which the successive streams of lava have flowed, and it forms the boundary of a fine pasture land, which appears to have been exempt from these lava inundations for many ages; the outcropping ledges of lava are weathered and lichen-covered until they resemble the gneiss and granite rocks of New England, at least from a distance.

---

[88] It will be seen from the map of this island that the government survey has done much in tracing the flows of known date, but much remains to be done, although it is probably impossible to fully trace other than the superficial flows.

The flow of 1840 which reached the sea at Nanawale, formed conical hills which lasted many years although composed of the loose gravelly rapilli resulting from the sudden shivering of the lava, and the same form of cinder piles is seen at the junction of lava and sea-water in this flow of 1868. It is not universally the case, however, that lava is broken up in this way when passing into the sea. Sometimes the heat has been so intense as to induce the spheroidal state preventing the actual contact of the water, and the melted rock has run on under the water, forming submarine ledges of pahoehoe.

From the shore we rode up on the elevated plateau with the two parallel streams of cooled lava on our left, some five hundred feet below, with nothing to obstruct a full bird's eye view of the scene. At length we came to the great trunk at Kahuku, from which all the lateral branches had been sent off. At our right on one of these branches were the ruins of the large stone church of Kahuku. The great earthquake had shaken down the walls, and the roof was lowered and standing over the ruins, around which the sea of molten lava had flowed, leaving them upon a small island unconsumed and uncovered. One-eighth of a mile above this, and on the same stream, we saw three small thatched houses, where four natives had been surrounded by the burning sea and confined for ten days in this fiery prison. The whole inclosed island contained about an acre, and before the people were aware of it, no avenue of escape was left. The hot clinkers came rolling along in a great stream within twenty-five feet of one of the houses, and cooled in a ridge as high as the top of the house. We climbed over this rough mass and visited the people who still live in this awful but now romantic inclosure. They seemed cheerful and were right glad to see us. On inquiring how they felt and how they spent their time during those days of fiery trial, they replied that in expectation of certain death they were calm and resigned, looking up to God and spending most of their time in prayer.

Passing up the main stream, we came to the place where Captain Brown's houses once stood; just in the rear of this was an awful vent from which fiery jets were thrown hundreds of feet high, with fearful hissings and belchings. Beyond this we saw numbers of green islets, of two to five acres in extent, formed by the surging sea of fire as it seethed and boiled and swept around these reserved places. On some of these islands cattle were feeding, and twenty head were taken from one islet of less than two acres, after the lavas were partly cooled. They were terribly heated and frantic, and some of them died. Still pursuing our course upward, we veered to the right, and once more took the soil on the uplands which bordered the stream. Here the great trunk of the stream was in its full breadth and I hired two men to measure across, while we rode through a charred forest and deep cinders more than one hundred feet above the shining lava fields which lay on our left. At length we descended again to the stream of fresh and warm pahoehoe, and rode nearly a mile upon its crackling surface. We soon came to a region of fissures and blow-holes, and where the evidences of Plutonic fury were unmistakable. From these infernal orifices amazing jets had been thrown hundreds of feet heavenwards, forming ridges, hills and jagged cones of every contour, and leaving the products of raging seas and rivers of fire, such as must have been appalling to near witnesses of these fiery dynamics. Here we left our horses, and with great effort struggled over the sharp and confused masses which were heaped wildly around. Climbing a rough hillside some two hundred feet high, and on an angle of forty-five degrees, we came upon the great head fissure from which the first lavas were disgorged. We followed this to the terminal point in the woods, over ridges and heaps of cinder, pumice and scoria. From this high terrace we could overlook the stream below for about three miles. The great vent or fissure extended longitudinally and in an irregular line for two and a half miles or more, and at many points along this line the steam and smoke were still rising with no little heat. No fire was, however, seen; it all disappeared in less than four days after the commencement of the eruption. The fissure opened from two to twenty feet wide, and there are places where it is interrupted or so narrow that it can be crossed.   [494]

Near the head of this fissure a small quantity of sulphur is found, as also alum, gypsum, Glauber's and other salts; none of these are abundant, and the products of this eruption are identical with those of all former eruptions on this island. Returning to the point whence I had sent the men to line across the stream, I regretted to find that they had measured until they came to the great fissure, and seeing no way of crossing it, had returned. They had measured half a mile, and thought they were half way across, but from sight I judged they were only one-third across, giving a mile and a half as the estimated width at this point, which was about the widest place of the undivided or trunk stream. I would say that the average width of the flow by uniting all the branches would be one and a half miles, the length ten miles, and the average depth fifteen feet. Where it entered deep basins and gorges it is fifty to a hundred feet deep, but where it spread over grass fields and unbroken surfaces, we find it from two to fifteen feet deep. The course of the main stream, the one that entered the sea, is due south. The flow upon the surface was short and energetic, some say three and some five days,—we give it as four days. The scene was brilliant and awe-inspiring; obstructions along the line of flow often opened vents through which fiery jets were thrown up to the height of five hundred to seven hundred feet, with amazing brilliancy and a force which made the earth tremble. All the southern coast of Hawaii was illuminated with the dazzling glare; but the amount of matter discharged is small compared with the eruption of 1855.

Kilauea.—In going to Kau my route was along the shore road through Puna; my return was via Kilauea. At this place I spent a day and a night, and examined the changes. Previous to the great earthquake, the fiery abysses of Kilauea had been in a raging condition as if seeking vent. The molten sea had broken up vertically in the bottom of Little Kilauea, and had left a burning stratum upon the old deposits of 1832. The terrible rendings of April 2nd tore up the earth, opened great fissures everywhere around Kilauea, sent down thundering avalanches of rocks from the high surrounding walls, and probably opened a subterranean passage for the igneous flood to the southwest. That night Pele decamped in this underground passage, and the central area of the great crater subsided about three hundred feet, leaving or rather forming a new Black Ledge of unequal width, all around the crater. In some parts the central depression left the ledge a perpendicular or beetling wall with a serrated line, but in most parts the centre sagged away gently forming a large concave basin with an angle of 20° to 70°. The surface of this concave was once the crowning or convex central portion of the crater, where ferns and ohelos have been growing for nearly twenty years. This superincumbent plateau has been depressed so quietly that the surface is very little disturbed, and the ferns and bushes are still growing in the basin three hundred feet below their position on the first of April. Some parts, however, of this great area have been covered with fresh lava, and some ferns have been killed by heat and gases.

From the black ledge I passed down and across this depression (about a mile), and then up the ascent on the other side for half a mile to the rim of Halemaumau. This is all changed; it has gone down some five hundred feet below the highest point on the black ledge, and about two hundred feet below the depression in the basin before mentioned. The walls have fallen on all sides, and the pit resembles a vast funnel, half a mile in diameter at the top and about fifteen hundred feet across the bottom. There are two places where visitors can descend into this great pit, with some difficulty and risk. Much of the time this pit is filled with smoke and sulphurous gases, with little visible fire: occasionally explosions, detonations, and fiery demonstrations occur in this awful pit.

On the fourteenth, fifteenth and sixteenth of this month (August), the sea was agitated around our entire group, rising and falling from two to four feet above and below the ordinary marks, once in ten, fifteen and twenty-five minutes; the accounts of rise and time vary as noted in different places by different observers, and I give the range.

The sea-waves of which Mr. Coan speaks were doubtless caused by the terrible earthquake which on the thirteenth of August shook the whole western coast of South

America, and drove an oceanic wave to the shores of New Zealand and these islands. But although this was decidedly a foreign volcanic or seismic demonstration, the vibrations of the land of Hawaii have not ceased, and it is not at all improbable that the reservoirs of lava are emptying themselves beneath the sea; certainly the lava is in motion. The destruction of life and property on Hawaii was comparatively small, owing to the nature of the district affected. The losses in Kau were as follows:

Houses destroyed by land-slide.......	10	Deaths, 31
Houses destroyed by sea-wave	108	Deaths, 46
Houses destroyed by earthquake	46	Deaths, 0
Houses destroyed by lava-stream	37	Deaths, 0
Totals	201	77

One life was lost in Puna by the sea-wave, and one in Hilo by a falling cliff. A shock of no greater violence in the city of Boston would probably have killed fifty thousand people, and laid most of the city in ruins.

The data for determining the direction and force of the vibrations are quite different from those used by Mallet in his remarkable investigation of the Calabrian earthquake of 1857. The houses are mostly of wood and grass, and stone walls are built of angular blocks of lava, often without any cement; a brick wall or wall of hewn stone, is not to be found in Kau. On the other hand the rocks which form the upper crust are of uniform composition, the direction of the strata is well known, and there are no strata of sedimentary rock to mislead by reflection of earth waves. On the whole, Hawaii offers many advantages for the study of seismic as well as volcanic phenomena. (Published March, 1869.)

Forty years have passed and I have little to add to the careful record of these observers, nearly all of whom have passed from earth. Neither have I much to correct in my own observations on the record. Many times I have passed through the country so terribly shaken, and every time I have cause to wonder, not at the rapidity of the destructive force of the earthquakes and lava streams, but at the rapid healing in the skin of Mother Earth in this climate. The great cones, the wide chasms are there, but how changed! Quiet and peaceful, they add so much to the grandeur if not to the beauty of the scene. The avalanche of earth, stone and water that was so much more fatal to life than the volcanic outbreak, has now disappeared beneath vegetation, and while I could trace it easily in 1880, when I passed that way a few months ago I could not point it out to my companions.

The seismic studies are not much advanced here, although the island of Oahu boasts a seismometer. No scientific body has built an observatory on the brink of Kilauea, and no competent observer has established himself in our midst.[89]

[89] Since the above was written two of the Professors of the Massachusetts Institute of Technology, Messrs. Jaggar and Daly have visited Kilauea with a view to determine the desirability of establishing an observatory there under the control of that institution.

In July of the next year Mr. Coan was able to descend into the pit of Hale-maumau and measure across the cooled surface which was then four hundred feet below the rim. Its diameter was "five-sixths of a mile," and the Halemaumau must have been quiet, but by no means "dead," for in that condition volumes of smoke are

1869 generally emitted from the pit (see Fig. 26), and now he could see lava in ebullition far below the surface, perhaps a hundred feet below, through some of the many cracks in the hardened crust.[90] In 1871 Halemaumau was full

1872 to overflowing and the lava had run two miles northward over the crater floor; the central depression was filled some fifty feet from the same source. In August of the same year the pit was emptied of lava but still very hot and full of dense vapors, but within a year (August, 1872) it was again overflowing into the great central depression.

March 1, 1872. Clarence King and Arnold Hague.—King reports: "A fluid stream of basalt overflowed from the molten lake at the south end of the crater and flowed northward along the level basaltic floor of the pit. Numerous little branchlets spurted from the sides of the flow......and then congealed. I repeatedly broke these small branch streams and examined their section. In every case the bottom of the flow was thickly crowded with triclinic feldspars and augites; while the whole upper flow was nearly pure isotropic and acid glass."

October 21, 1872. D. H. Hitchcock.—"Halemaumau is like what it was from 1845 to 1868, an immense dome six hundred feet higher than the centre of the pit, equalling in altitude the bordering black ledges. On its summit are two lakes from which lava streams down in various directions. Nothing is left of the high banks surrounding the old south lake."

On March 3, 1873, Halemaumau was reported occupied by two lakes nearly circular.[91] But in January, 1874, the surface of the great lake was thirty-five to forty feet below the rim and the two parts had become oblong, according to a visitor.[92] In

1873 June a more careful observer was at the crater, Mr. J. M. Lydgate, who made a map of the place in which the pools were again distinctly circular as is shown in the reproduction of Mr. Lydgate's map now among the archives of the Government Survey (Fig. 70). The central depression of 1868 is still distinct, although partially filled.

The Volcano House record, while containing much trash, certainly has also on its pages much that should be preserved; much that is not elsewhere recorded.

[90] American Journal, 1879, ii, 454. Letter of August 30, 1871.
[91] Chas. Nordhoff: Northern California, Oregon and the Sandwich Islands.
[92] Miss I. L. Bird: The Hawaiian Archipelago, 55, 253.

I have endeavored to cull what I believe to be authentic. The period we are now considering is covered as follows (I have quoted the record as written; not merely as I think it should have been written):

January 7, 1873. Between 11 and 12 o'clock last night Mokuaweoweo started active again. The wind has been from the southward, and the whole day a dense body of smoke has been passing over Kilauea and across Puna off to sea. Weather hazy and top of the mountain seldom visible. Kilauea quite active, but no lava flowing.

January 31, 1873. Miss Isabella L. Bird.—There was considerable activity, eleven fountains of fire and waves of fire perpetually breaking into fiery spray.

March 2, 1873. C. H. Williams.—The lake is at present divided into about two equal parts by a wall of lava. [Plate XLIV, lower view.]

March 13, 1873. J. N. Gilman.—The south lake is divided by a partition which forms two lakes.

March 22, 1873. Godfrey Brown.—South lake was very active, the jets of lava reaching to about fifty feet of the top of the bank.

June 5, 1873. W. L. Green.—The surface of the molten lake appearing to be fifty or sixty feet below the edge·····The level of the molten lava in the lake is some two or three hundred feet above the general level of the depression (a mile or so long), over which you walk to the lake. Mauna Loa is now active.

July 2, 1873. S. W. Pogue.—Very little action.

July 5, 1873. Luther Severance.—Crater active; lakes

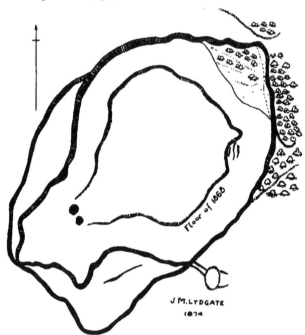

FIG. 70. SURVEY OF KILAUEA BY J. M. LYDGATE.

full to the brim. [See Fig. 71, which seems to represent this phase of Halemaumau (South Lake). Unfortunately the present owner of the photographic negative cannot assure me of its date.]

July 8, 1873. G. Jones.—At 9 A.M. the lava with which the south lake has been filled for some time broke through on the eastern slope facing the Volcano House, and has been running towards and into the basin [central depression of 1868]. On the 12th the south lake was very active and still full, although the new flow of over half a mile in width still continued. The crater on the summit [Mokuaweoweo] was also active.

July 28, 1873. H. Birgham found both lakes and the cones tolerably active, and saw the brook of lava flowing down the side of the south lake.

August 11, 1873. Dr. O. B. Adams.—The outflow from the south lake still flows and is visible through a large crack. It appears to be about twenty feet wide and flows like a mountain torrent.

FIG. 71. CRATER OF KILAUEA.

August 29, 1873. Luther Severance.—Crater very active.

September 22, 1873. W. W. Hall.—I have just returned from a very interesting trip to the crater of Mokuaweoweo on Mauna Loa. Started from Kapapala with my guide John B. Kitu, a half-caste, at about 10 o'clock on the 18th, and stayed at Ainapo, the upper ranch, until half-past one. From there a man with pack mule and tent with food and blankets accompanied us and we all kept on our way up through the koa woods until four o'clock when we reached the usual camping ground. As it was so early, and as I was anxious to get as far as possible on the first day, we pressed on for three miles farther up the mountain where we found a very good camping ground where we pitched our tent and made a large fire, and spent a comfortable night. I had intended to start by five in the morning, but in the night a horse and a mule got away and went down the mountain. John started at three in the dark for them and reached camp again at six o'clock. We left "Hall's camp" at 6:30, and after passing or climbing over the most awful road I ever saw for four hours, we reached the crater at 10:30 o'clock. From the place where we left our horses we went along the bank towards the north....We went to the northeast point, and looking down the precipice, say about eight hundred feet, over the shelving mass of loose rocks and debris, I thought we might possibly venture to go down. I asked John if he would be willing to go with me, and he said "yes." So we started down, crawling carefully over the loose boulders, and letting ourselves down over huge rocks, until after half an hour's awful labor we reached the bottom.....

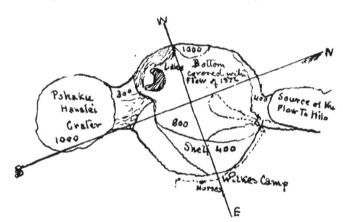

FIG. 72. W. W. HALL'S SKETCH PLAN OF MOKUAWEOWEO.

which is now entirely covered with the flow of last year. From where we stood the awful walls of rock arose on every side, and it looked as though no human being could ever ascend from that vast depth. We had not time to go to the active south lake where the molten lava was heaving and surging with loud reports and hissing noises, so we took a turn over a third of the field of burning-hot pahoehoe and returned to the point where we entered. There are many blowholes in this field, and from some of them I collected specimens of lava too hot to be held in the naked hand. At night fires can be seen in these holes, and at all times the hot steam and gases rising with a hissing sound. The heat of the black pahoehoe was so great as to blister my feet through a thick pair of boots. We returned by the same way by which we had descended, and when we were again on the bank I felt that God had indeed protected us in a most singular way from every harm, and thanked Him for His goodness......It was a most fortunate thing for me that I had no bad feelings whatever, and could make as much exertion there as down here. Had it been otherwise I should never have attempted such a descent......About a mile from where our horses were we came across stone walls that.must have been built for the sides of a house or camp. I found an iron eye-bolt and a piece of soft pine, both of which must have been there thirty years. I think this was Wilkes' camp of 1841, and I brought these away as relics. The crack containing water and ice seems to continue nearly round to the point where we descended, and in some places the openings are large enough to bathe in. We reached the horses, ate some lunch, and started down at 2 P.M., well paid for our great exertion.

September 27, 1873. T. Spencer.—Crater active, flowing all night toward the Volcano House.

January 17, 1874. J. E. Chamberlain.—Visited the crater fourteen years ago. The crater has filled up one-half. The two craters, 1859 and 1874, are almost totally unlike.

March 24, 1874. L. M. C.—The south lake has been gradually filling up until last night, when it overflowed. At eight o'clock the whole of the edge of the lake facing this house was alight with the flowing lava. A sudden change in the weather has accompanied this outbreak—cold wind without rain; thermometer 42°.

June 9, 1874. Frank Thompson.—The lava has been flowing from the open lake all day.

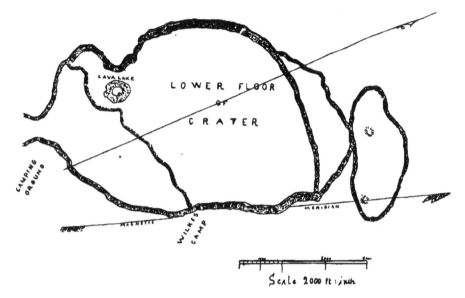

FIG. 73. SURVEY OF MOKUAWEOWEO BY J. M. LYDGATE.

June 24, 1874. John M. Lydgate.—The plan of the crater of Mokuaweoweo [Fig. 73] is from actual survey by triangulation. A base of 1876 feet was measured on the eastern side and from this, using a seven inch Queen transit, some twenty points were fixed indicative of the shape, topography, etc., of the crater. Its greatest length including the basin at the north end is 17,000 feet, or about, 3.2 miles; excluding this it is 15,000 feet; its greatest breadth is 8600 feet or about 1.7 miles; its greatest depth 1050 feet. The floor, however, is continually rising owing to repeated overflows, and the lake is about 500 feet in diameter, and at the time of our visit was quite active, more so than I have ever seen Kilauea.

July 8, 1874. D. H. Hitchcock.—Volcano is very active. Crater filling up with new lava, but evidently sinking more and more as a whole. Halemaumau half the height of the lower or southern bank. Mokuaweoweo brilliant last evening.

July 10, 1874. G.[Gilman]—At 7.30 this evening, two sharp, quick shocks of earthquake were felt here,—an interval of about three minutes between them. The new flow begun last night seems to be gaining, a large portion of the central basin being alight with the flowing lava.

August 29, 1874. F. A. Schaefer.—Although at my previous visits ('61, '64, '66, '67, '74) I have seen more lakes in Kilauea in action, I have never seen any one lake in a greater state of commotion than this time. We found the south lake divided into two lakes of similar size by a bank about forty feet high, and the approach to either of them rather more difficult than in years past, on account of recent overflows of lava. Approaching the left-hand lake we had to pass through a great deal of sulphuric smoke which necessarily shortened our stay there, and prevented us from going as near to the brink of the lake as we would have wished, but still allowed an impressive glance at the surging and spouting liquid fire. The right-hand lake seen from a bank eighty feet high pre-

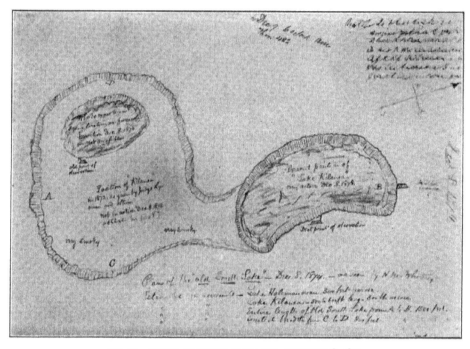

FIG. 74. SKETCH OF ACTION IN KILAUEA DECEMBER 8, 1874.

sented a magnificent spectacle. The bed of the lake was in constant commotion. Along its banks the waves of liquid fire dashed into spray like the waves of the ocean on the rockbound coast, and at times the molten lava was thrown high into the air......Returning we visited several openings which afforded us a view into a living stream of lava flowing from the south lake in an easterly direction, with a rapidity difficult to estimate. A river of liquid fire rushing along with extreme rapidity and with the characteristics of a mountain stream losing itself in the lower bed of the crater......Thermometer 54°–68°; once it went to 51°.

September 9, 1874. B. F. Dillingham.—Have to report the crater of Mokuaweoweo in the same condition topographically as reported by last party and illustrated by J. M. Lydgate......The burning lake itself was less active than reported by the last party, still the action was very satisfactory at both ends of the lake, that nearest the camp the most active, throwing up jets varying in size and height, occasionally throwing up some hundred feet or more, the color of the lava appeared to us very peculiar being a bright vermilion and sometimes blood-red.

September 20, 1874. C. E. Stackpole.—At one o'clock last night the lava broke through the crust in the eastern edge of the basin, near the trail, and flowed rapidly westward. The liquid lava spread over several acres of the basin in a few moments, flowing very rapidly. The outbreak was accompanied by a dull, sullen, roaring sound, apparently far below the surface. In spite of a heavy fog, the fire lighted up the crater and surroundings; every part of this house was filled with the glare, making it as light as day. By three o'clock the lava had cooled and the flow had ceased. A steady rain all night, no wind, thermometer 64°.

October 21, 1874. Rev. Titus Coan.—Found the crater quite active.

December 8, 1874, H. M. Whitney.—Found the crater in about the same state of activity as at former visits; but the area of the lakes has increased and changed very much since my last previous visit in 1864. Then there was but one lake, now there are two, both much larger than Halemaumau formerly was......Halemaumau is located in the southern part and not easily accessible. The new and larger lake at the right is called Kilauea and our party stood within six feet of the edge of the bank on the windward side from which position a fine view was obtained of the whole of this boiling cauldron, and at a hundred feet above the liquid mass. [See Fig. 74.]

December 29, 1874. F. S. Lyman and W. H. Reed.—The two lakes, Kilauea and Halemaumau are both very active, and the large flow of lava from Halemaumau into the basin of the crater, which we were told occurred on the 27th inst., is still aglow, occasionally bursting forth on the surface and at the lower edge. The roar from the lakes was very loud at times during the night.

While Kilauea went on in much her usual way during the ten years from 1864 to 1874, Mauna Loa seemed to be adopting the chronic state of activity long a characteristic of her lower neighbor. In 1868 the activity began as we have seen, and while the size of the rent (some three miles long), allowed the surplus lava to escape rapidly, that outflow seems to have for a time closed that escape valve, and the activities were transferred to the summit crater, Mokuaweoweo. In December, 1869, visitors to the summit found much steam but no visible fires. During the first few weeks in 1870 steam and smoke arose from the crater in such quantities as to to be visible at Hilo. This did not last long and later in the year Mr. Luther Severance found Mokuaweoweo quiet. On the tenth of August, 1872, Mr. Coan saw from Hilo[93] "a lofty pillar of light two thousand feet high". No fire was seen from below, only its reflection on the column of vapors. It should be borne in mind that when "a bright light like a star" is seen from the coast level at Hilo it means, if from the summit crater, a fountain playing at least twelve hundred feet high, so flat is the summit plain of Loa in the midst of which the crater is situated. All through August and into September the activity of Mokuaweoweo continued. On August 23d a tidal wave was observed at Hilo in calm weather and without earthquakes. The first wave rose four feet, then at an interval of six minutes a second three feet high, and so diminishing for a dozen waves. There is no evidence of connection with the island volcanoes. Certainly the summit

[93] American Journal, 1872, iv, 406; 1873, v, 476.

crater of Loa was not emptied as Mr. J. M. Lydgate found a fountain still playing the latter part of August, and Mr. H. M. Whitney, also a careful and experienced observer, found in September a fountain of lava seventy-five feet in diameter and five hundred feet high in the southwest corner of the crater; the pool around it covered about a third of the bottom, and certainly did not indicate any tapping of the supply at any lower or submarine level. In January, 1873, the action as seen from Hilo was "marvellously brilliant,"[94] the illuminated vapors rising thousands of feet. The herdsmen at Ainapo reported the mountain as constantly quivering like a boiling pot. The light was suddenly quenched, but in April the activity was fully renewed. On the sixth of June Mr. W. L. Green was at the summit and from him we learn that—

The fountain generally played to a height of from three hundred to four hundred feet, as estimated from the known depth of the crater, although some spires or shoots would now and then rise to a greater altitude. The form of the fountain would constantly vary, sometimes being in the shape of a low rounded dome, then perhaps forming a sort of spire in centre, with a fountain in the form of a wheat sheaf on each side. Sometimes it would look like one great wheat sheaf. On this day the visible vapors or gases connected with this fountain were quite insignificant; by daylight we could see none, but at night-time the bright reflection from the molten lava made visible a light blue haze which quietly left it. Some observers of this same fountain, a few months before, and when it was much higher, reported that they heard the sound of escaping steam or gases. Some of them even believed that they heard the roar of escaping steam or vapors, some time before they arrived at the edge of the crater. We enquired very particularly, however, from one of the most intelligent of the party, and he assured us that there was no proof that the noise they heard was that of escaping steam or gases. I have sketches drawn by two of the party, which show little or no steam or gases. There were two noises, however, which were very easily distinguishable: one was the dull roar of the fall of this fountain of heavy liquid, and the other was the metallic clink of the fall of the solidified lavas which were constantly taken up by the fountain and thrown onto the solid rocks at a little distance from it. Indeed, these solid pieces and separate portions of the molten lava, which cooled in the air, formed a light falling veil over the dazzling lava fountain, and as it fell close round the sides, it formed a black level scum which floated on the lava lake, out of which the fountain rose. Whenever a more than usually solid mass of lava fell within the area of this lake, it seemed to force itself through the black, floating scoriaceous mass and make a golden splash of the white-hot lava beneath it. From different parts of the crater, and away from the fountain, white fumes arose like those which often appear in Kilauea crater.

This night and for two nights previously, there was so little cloud, or condensed vapor above the edge of the crater, that it was not sufficient to reflect the light of the great molten fountain below. For weeks previously we had seen this reflected light, which indeed, was the only possible means by which a light in the bottom of the crater can be made visible to an eye situated outside of it, but below the level of its edge. The night before we left Kilauea, however, the light on the top of Mauna Loa was not to be seen, although the night was clear, and it was only when we got close to the crater, that a light smoke could be seen drifting away from it, whilst the great fountain of molten rock was playing below.

There was indeed, nothing about this fountain that gave the impression of its having been produced by steam, incandescent or otherwise, or elastic vapors of any kind, but everything seemed

[94] Coan, American Journal, 1873, v, 476; 1874, vii, 516; 1877, xiv, 68.

to favor the idea of its being a simple hydrostatic effect, and as though a great artesian bore had been made to a stratum of molten rock, which had only been awaiting an opportunity to overflow.[95]

Miss Bird, who accompanied Mr. Green in this ascent, writes of it in her usual fluent style, and Dana is inclined to quote her as authority; but from a knowledge of her inaccurate and slipshod relations of other doings on these islands, I must look with suspicion on her testimony, and this is not needed, as Mr. Green was with her. We have seen in the Volcano House records of Messrs. Adams and the brothers Hitchcock that the action continued for eighteen months, most of the time with force enough to sustain jets of lava. Mr. Coan remarks that there were but few earthquakes during this period, and these of no importance.

In January of 1875 Mr. W. L. Green reports action in Mokuaweoweo lasting several weeks, and on August 11th Mr. Coan reports:[96] "The summit crater was again in brilliant action. The action continued, as appeared in the view from Hilo, for one week, and without any observed evidence of an eruption." In the Narrative of the Voyage of the Challenger[97] it is stated that parties from the vessel during the stay at Hilo, visited Kilauea, and "during the ascent a globular cloud was seen hanging in the air in the distance, which, as the guide explained, hung over the summit of Mauna Loa itself....As night fell this cloud perpetually reformed by condensation, and was lighted up by a brilliant orange glow reflected from the molten lava in the great terminal crater, and the general effect was just as if a fire were raging in the forest in the distance."

February 13, 1876, Mr. Coan reports a brilliant but short eruption on the summit, but no other outbreak noted.[98] On February 14, 1877, occurred another short but brilliant eruption from the summit. All the afternoon the mountain top had been covered with cloud or smoke as some considered it, but at half-past nine in the evening the

1877 curtain rolled away, showing a bright red reflection on the dark cloud banks above. As seen from Hilo by Mr. Coan, "the display of light was most glorious," columns of what Dana claims were illuminated steam, rose "with fearful speed to a height of fourteen to seventeen thousand feet, and then spread out into a vast fiery cloud, looking at night as if the heavens were on fire."[99] From Waimea Mr. Curtis J. Lyons of the Government Survey writes that the smoke masses were

---

[95] Vestiges of the Molten Globe, ii, 166. On page 168 of the same work he remarks: "With regard to incandescent steam, which Captain Dutton suggests as possibly representing to the eye a portion of these fountains, we may say, that we have never seen, on Hawaii, at any of the eruptions of molten lava, anything like incandescent steam. The *illuminated* smoke, gases, or vapors, which reflected the white-hot lava below them, we saw in abundance at the crater of 1859, and they are quite common at Kilauea and elsewhere; but incandescent steam we have never recognized at any of them." Captain Dutton had never, I believe, seen a lava fountain of any size, and found it hard to believe in their entire solidity.
[96] American Journal, 1877, xiv, 68.
[97] Vol. i, pt. 2, p. 766. The ship anchored in Hilo Bay August 14, and left on the 19th.
[98] American Journal, 1877, xiv, 68.
[99] American Journal, 1877, xiv, 68. Letter of March 17, 1877.

ejected to a height of not less than sixteen thousand feet above the top of the mountain, where they hung forming a dense stratum of smoke. The velocity with which they ascended was such that the first five thousand feet were passed inside of a minute.[100] From the deck of the "Kilauea" at anchor off Kawaihae, "five distinct columns of fire could be seen belching forth from the mountain." This lasted but six hours, and on Thursday night no light was seen, although the summit was covered with smoke. Four slight earthquake shocks were felt at Waimea and one at Kohala. Those who hastened to Hawaii to see this outbreak were disappointed, but in Kealakeakua Bay they found the runaway eruption. As the steamer approached the bay columns of steam or smoke were seen rising from the sea, much like the spouting of a school of whales, and numerous pieces of lava were floating about.

According to the natives, the eruption was first seen at three o'clock on the morning of the 24th about a mile from shore, and it appeared like innumerable red, blue and green lights. Some thought these were the steamer's lights, only they were so numerous as to excite consternation. Keei Point forms the southern boundary of Kealakeakua Bay, and the steam and lava rose as far as a mile beyond the point apparently from a submarine fissure running about N.N.W. by E.S.E., and where the water has been from twenty to sixty fathoms deep.

Boats from the steamer put off to the scene of the greatest commotion, rowing directly over the most disturbed part where the boat was repeatedly hit by the rising masses of lava, nearly all of which on reaching the surface were red-hot, emitting gases strongly sulphurous. In cooling the lava cakes sank as rapidly as they rose to the surface. Specimens were obtained[101] which are very porous, and from the accounts much of it was the froth called *limu*. A severe earthquake shock was felt on the western side of the bay during the night of the eruption. Eleven years after this, while camping on the shore of this beautiful bay, near the site of Cook's and Vancouver's observatories, I paddled my canoe over the region where this "submarine volcano" broke out and found that it had left no sign. The newspaper accounts were illustrated by most grotesque and impossible pictures of four black columns like trunks of trees and five pillars of fire,—papers of respectability in the United States and Europe. We must now return to Kilauea.

February 2, 1875. Frank J. Scott.—Visited the crater with Mr. J. W. Moore and George P. Castle. Got to southwest side of Halemaumau and stood over the brink of the crater in which the lava stood about forty feet below, and was boiling violently on the edges only. The smoke was towards Kilauea and we could not get to see it, but craters marked C and D were not in action. February 4th, went to the craters again via little sulphur crater marked E, looking down which we

[100] Hawaiian Gazette, February 21, 1877. Further account of this eruption is from the same source published by Mr. H. M. Whitney who went to Hawaii.
[101] A specimen is in the Bishop Museum. It is very cellular lava; not at all *limu*.

saw lava rushing swiftly at a depth of not more than ten feet below where we stood, and in the direction of the hotel. Proceeding to a point of observation marked X we had a fair view of all the craters. The small one marked C was playing with most force spurting its lava in spray ten to twenty feet above its banks. Halemaumau was almost as lively, and the main crater Kilauea was boiling at the base of its cliffs on all sides with vigor. It was about eleven o'clock when we arrived at X. The little crater D was then without signs of fire. After we had been standing about half an hour, this little basin showed fire, heaving and then bursting its scum of gray lava and boiling fiercely. About the same time the lava in the great crater Kilauea was rising fast. Presently it gushed up and with a surge toward the northeast side, appeared to be rushing toward a vent and in a few minutes it subsided to its first level, and all the craters seemed in about an equal state of activity.

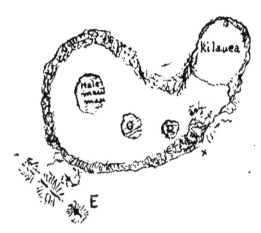

FIG. 75. CRATER IN FEBRUARY, 1875.

None of them were near full as we are told they sometimes are. The lava in Halemaumau was about twenty feet below the lava floor right about it; crater C about the same; D not more than ten to twelve feet, and Kilauea perhaps from thirty to forty or fifty feet. As soon as the great gush from Kilauea found vent we anticipated a good flow of lava on the great lava sink between these craters and the hotel. We returned to dinner at two o'clock via the cave of stalactites on the northeast terrace of the great sink. When we came out from dinner the anticipated lava flow had already submerged an acre or two of the sink on the route of our morning walk and was creeping over the great sink in four different places.

August 7, 1875. C. E. Gilman.—Two severe earthquake shocks were felt here today: one at 4:30 P.M., and one at 6:45 P.M. Motion north to south.

August 15, 1875. Challenger Expedition.—A few of our party visited the crater this evening and found both Kilauea and Halemaumau more than usually active. We left Volcano House at 5 P.M., thus arriving at the scene of action a few minutes before sunset. By this means we got a good idea of the whole volcano by daylight and a grand view of the furnaces by night. Kilauea had five jets playing, Halemaumau having the same number but on a much finer scale. Even as we sat there gazing down, Halemaumau rose in a few minutes to within a few feet of the top of its banks, and I have no doubt that an overflow took place at some point that was hidden from us. The lake then subsided to its former level. Between these two craters, high up on the dividing bank of hard lava, a small cone was blowing every two or three minutes, the jets reaching an altitude of twenty or forty feet.—Spectroscopic observations of the furnaces with a small direct vision spectroscope gave a continuous spectrum, the red showing brightest, an occasional flare in the green. Magnetic observations were made with the dip needle in front of hotel, then the dip circle was carried down to the first plateau and a difference of two degrees in reading was found, thus indicating the powerful influence of the iron in the crater. Photographs were taken of the whole crater, of the craters of Kilauea and Halemaumau, and of the lava cascades.—Mauna Loa is quiet now.[102]

August 21, 1875. J. W. Gilman.—A faint light was seen from here at 9:15 P.M. on Mauna Loa.

---

[102] The photographs of the whole crater and of the cascades are given in the second part of the first volume of the Narrative of the Expedition, but the two views of the smaller craters mentioned do not appear.

September 7, 1875. Walter M. Gibson.—I descended into the crater in company with Mr. Schaefer and Mr. Gilman of the Volcano House, and arriving at the brink of the Kilauea lake I was disappointed in not finding any show of activity. A small jet of lava apparently not larger than a wheat sheaf, to which some lava jets are compared, was all the outer evidence of activity near the edge of the black surface of cooled lava, at a depth of about a hundred and twenty feet from where we stood. However, after a short stay, several jets broke forth, and before we left Kilauea showed considerable signs of activity. I descended again at 10 P.M. on the 10th September, when I observed a wonderful increase of activity. The Kilauea lake had risen to within thirty feet of the top of its highest bluff, or about ninety feet, whilst the Halemaumau lake and the Kilauea iki[103] pit were full and boiling over, and pouring forth streams of lava, some flowing into Kilauea lake and others flowing in a southeast direction towards the basin of the main crater. I observed a new boiling pool about three hundred yards southeast of Halemaumau and outside of the high embankment that incloses the two principal lakes. After my return to the Volcano House, at a later hour after night had set in, I rode with Mr. Schaefer to a point in the west bank of the great crater, and we observed the two lakes in a high state of activity and illuminating the sky above in a most brilliant manner. During the night we could observe from our beds the jets of lava leaping above the embankments of Kilauea and Halemaumau, so that the lava had risen over a hundred feet in these lakes since our first observation on the 7th.

November 23, 1875. C. S. Gilman.—On this date there was at 11:15 o'clock A.M. quite a hard earthquake shock felt in Kau; Kona and Hilo, and another of two shocks, nearly as hard at 7 P.M. The one in the morning threw down several fathoms of good stone wall at Kapapala and also stopped our horses on the road, for the moment, by the motion of the earth.

January 14, 1876. C. S. Gilman.—Last night the lake Kilauea overflowed; a broad stream of lava flowing down into the centre of the crater for some four hours. This morning the summits of Loa and Kea are covered with snow to an unusual extent. Weather clear and very cold.

February 13, 1876. C. S. Gilman.—At 7:45 this evening a very bright light was visible on the summit of Mauna Loa, the first seen since August 11, 1875. It appears to be farther south than the last outbreak. Kilauea very active.

February 22, 1876. Rev. George L. Chaney.—About a mile and a half from the hotel on our way to Kilauea [lake?], we came to an opening in the lava about eight feet wide. Through this opening, in spite of the fierce heat arising from it, we saw a full, rushing torrent of liquid lava, of the brightest flame color, apparently making its way immediately beneath our feet. Both lakes were in fine activity today throwing jets of intense orange-red color from both lateral and medial fountains.

May 2, 1876. D. H. Hitchcock.—Find that Halemaumau has built up about two hundred feet in about one year, and that the lava from the south lake has almost filled up the great central basin. Fires very active; a stream running down the Halemaumau slope the greater part of the night.

June 8, 1876. J. S. Emerson. Visited the South lake approaching it on the north side of the lake; recent lava flows and a tendency to constant changes on the east side rendering the old path from the east unsafe. The lake is quite active and gradually filling up; the surface of the lake has an apparent current or motion in a southwest direction. Weather fine with occasional showers.

June 22, 1876. Herbert C. Austin.—At 9:30 A.M. we were on the edge of the cone looking into the north lake. There seemed to be two boiling cauldrons from which the lava was rolling in great masses of scum to make one complete surging sea.

January 1, 1877. W. P. Toler.—Having made two previous visits, one in 1843, and the other in 1845, I will mention the material differences between now and then. At my two previous visits the entire bottom of the crater was depressed from eight hundred to a thousand feet below the tops of the cliffs surrounding it, whilst now the entire bottom has risen to within four hundred or six hundred feet of the top of the cliffs. At my previous visits the southwest or principal lake of liquid

---

[103] By Kilauea iki Mr. Gibson means the pool within the Halemaumau area called, unfortunately, Kilauea.

lava was only from ten to fifteen feet below the surface of the surrounding plain of hard lava forming the bottom of the crater, whilst now I find a cone about one hundred and eighty feet high with the lake of lava in centre of cone and depressed about two hundred feet below the top of said cone. Again, on my previous visits there was no flowing lava in sight except in the lake, which, however, was boiling actively all over its surface; and now lava is flowing over the surface of the hard lava in many places. On my previous visits only one lake existed, now I find a depression of about two hundred feet where another has since existed though now extinct. I find also that a large portion of the north cliff has fallen in since former visits. My impression is that taken altogether, the sight is not so grand now as at my former visits, because then the entire bottom of the crater was much deeper

FIG. 76. CRACK IN FLOOR OF KILAUEA NEAR EAST WALL, MAY 4, 1877.

than now, and the lake more brilliant in its action, and being nearer the surface was in full view from the point where the hotel now stands, so that our party were all able to read a newspaper by the light from the lake.

May 5, 1877. A party skirted the edge of the late flow of lava, visited the south lake, then crossed back to the house; saw plenty of subterranean fire and found some red-hot flowing lava.

May 6, 1877. S. B. Dole.—On the day and evening before we came, there was a vigorous outbreak on the southeast side of the main crater, a fissure extending from the crater floor through the bank and into the woods beyond. The lava spouted up from this crack to a height of from fifty to a hundred and fifty feet. This action which drained Halemaumau as dry as an ash heap, ceased before our arrival. We gazed into the empty goblet-shaped cavity called Halemaumau, with feelings wherein terror was mixed with our disappointment. The ledge on which we stood was separated from the main rock by a deep crack so that it appeared to be tilted over the hole and ready to tumble in. Avalanches of stone were thundering down the sides of the hole which appeared to be about two hundred and fifty feet deep. The bottom was covered with boulders.

May 8, 1877. H. M. Whitney.—Found the old south lake dead, inactive, closed to public exhibition. In place of it the fires are active in a large cavern, a thousand feet this way [towards the Volcano House] and near the usual track to the old lake.

May 21, 1877. Thomas E. Cook.—The locality of the outbreak [of May 4] is a mile and a half on a straight line about southeast from the Volcano House, and is from a narrow crevice, narrow that is compared with the quantity of lava ejected. The crevice from which the flow took place commences at the foot of the crater wall and extends up to within twenty or thirty feet of the top, say two or three hundred feet, the lava ejected covering several acres of the floor of the crater.

May 22, 1877. Luther Severance.—No fire in the crater.

June [no date]. H. M. Whitney.—Found the action in and around the south lake commencing, and occasionally the light was very brilliant during the night. Thermometer 56° at 5:30 A.M.

August 2, 1877. B. H. Austin.—Since Wednesday of last week the lake has risen, in our judgment, quite thirty-five feet. We found its fires were very active.

August 12, 1877. Luther Severance.—Crater very active last night.

September 8, 1877. W. H. Lentz.[104]—Bottom of the south lake fell about fifty feet last night.

October 9, 1877. Rev. W. P. Alexander.—I visited this volcano forty-five years ago. It was much more active then than now.

December 24, 1877. Rufus A. Lyman.—Grand flow from north base of hill on the north side of Halemaumau. Two fountains at the source of stream. Some time during this year Wilkes Pea and his father, the latter guide of the Wilkes Expedition found Keanakakoi occupied by boiling lava.

January 18, 1878. Curtis J. Lyons.—Halemaumau is now about four hundred feet long by a hundred in width. Lake Kilauea is to the west of it and not approachable. There is an extensive flow of lava from the north side of the latter, about three-quarters of a mile in length. Present height of cone, estimated, one hundred and seventy-five feet.

September 20, 1878. Dr. J. Mott-Smith.—Halemaumau very active. Kilauea could not be approached, but it, too, is in great activity. A flow from this lake extends more than a mile across the great crater. At night from this house I counted twenty-two spots of fire glowing on the line of this flow. In my former visits, in 1851, '56 and '62, I saw no display of fire to compare with that now seen. The floor of the crater is much changed and elevated since my last visit; all the old landmarks have been obliterated.

October 28, 1878. W. H. Lentz.—The largest flow of the season took place this morning. A solid river of fire three-quarters of a mile long by a quarter wide.

January 7, 1879. H. M. Whitney.—The crater is now and has been for three weeks (or since the heavy rains set in) very active. There are now as formerly two lakes connected [separated] by an isthmus, the old south lake being much larger, and the lava in both rising nearly to the rim around them. But it has not run over the rim, the lava bursting out on one side or the other every few days, making streams which are gradually filling up the central basin. There was an unusual occurrence a few days since,—a stream flowed out on the south side of the south lake, lighting up the whole southern part of the crater. Last night fires were seen in every part of the crater, and it was very brilliant. The hill surrounding the south lake is now higher than I have ever seen it, and parts of it are nearly on a level with the top of the south wall of the large crater. Mauna Loa has presented a splendid sight for ten days past, having been covered with snow down to the forests. The snow fell on the night of December 26th and remained till yesterday, January 6th, when the heavy rain washed it away. Thermometer stood at 50° this morning.

March 18, 1879. A party attempted to ride around the main crater but gave it up after going half way. South lake said to be inaccessible from below.

April 21, 1879. W. H. Lentz.—Bottom dropped out of crater.

April 23, 1879. G. Groeper.—Found the ———— thing extinct.

[104] Keeper of the Volcano House.

April 28, 1879. Rev. A. O. Forbes.—Crater almost extinct. Much more steam than usual on the sulphur flat beyond this house. The two lakes of fire have disappeared in the depths of an immense pit from which only a few puffs of smoke and steam arise.

June 24, 1879. W. H. Lentz.—Both lakes very active, Halemaumau throwing jets of lava up at least fifty feet above the rim of lake so often that the lake looks like a fountain of fire from the verandah.

July 2, 1879. W. Tregloan.—One great lake very active.

July 14, 1879. W. H. Lentz.—Eight in the morning a large column of black smoke rising from south lake. 8:10 A.M. large flow of lava from the lake extending over at least one-eighth of the entire floor of the crater. 8:30 A.M. sulphur banks on south side of crater on fire; at 10:30 a large portion of the bank of south lake fell in.

July 15, 1879. Rev. Chas. M. Hyde.—Was greatly interested in watching last night the glow of the burning lava flow extending from the hill straight across to the sulphur bank; it had the appearance of a burning city.

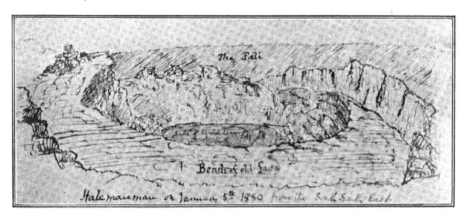

FIG. 77. SKETCH OF HALEMAUMAU, JANUARY 5, 1880.

August 25, 1879. G. H. Luce.—One lake or river quite active.

January 5, 1880. T. J. Kinnear gives a sketch of Halemaumau from the south-southeast.

April 8, 1880. A party ascended Mauna Loa and found much snow; could not look down into the extinct crater.

May 1, 1880. W. H. Lentz.—9:30 P.M. Mokuaweoweo burst out in a large lurid light, with a roar resembling thunder. 10:05 P.M. a second eruption, this time from the crater to the north of Mokuaweoweo, apparently as large as the first. 11 P.M. still another, this time southwest from the first, making in all three active fires on top and slope of Mauna Loa. Kilauea very active, both lakes booming, a third forming, several large flows on floor of crater.

May 5, 1880. A party ascended Mauna Loa and found snow on summit and considerable action in the south lake with high jets of lava.

May 18, 1880. J. M. Alexander.—Halemaumau about four hundred feet broad throwing molten lava over seventy feet high......a new lake forming on the east.

June 20, 1880. W. H. Lentz.—5 A.M. quite a heavy shock of an earthquake; no damage, no change in volcano.

July 24, 1880. W. T. Brigham.—Photographed crater and ascended Mauna Loa from this side.

(PAGES ARE TORN FROM THE BOOK HERE.)

I shall interrupt the Volcano House record to give more fully my observations at this visit, although they have been published,[105] as there are some omissions and additions to be made to avoid repetition and supply lacunæ.

On May 1, 1880, an outbreak from the summit crater of Mauna Loa was

1880   reported. Some persons made the ascent and found a fire-fountain from the

floor of the small crater adjoining Mokuaweoweo, but this soon ceased and no lava escaped from the crater or from any visible rent on the mountain side. This was unusual, and thinking the slight summit eruption was probably a prelude to a more

FIG. 78. AN IMPROVED VOLCANO HOUSE.

extensive outbreak, I started in June from Boston for the Hawaiian Islands, taking with me Mr. Charles Furneaux, a well-known artist, that I might be able to preserve for scientific study, should we be so fortunate as to see an eruption, those appearances that the camera does not retain and which are so difficult to describe.

As soon as possible after our arrival in Honolulu we sailed for Hilo and made the ascent to Kilauea. The road had certainly not improved during the fifteen years since I had last traveled over it, but on the evening of July 24, 1880, with Mr. R. Forbes Carpenter and Mr. Furneaux, I arrived at the northeast bank of the crater where we found a very comfortable hotel replacing the grass shanty I had occupied

[105]American Journal of Science, July, 1887, p. 19.   [512]

in 1865, while surveying Kilauea. The scene was familiar. Five times had I come to the crater at night on my way from Hilo, and almost as many times when journeying from Kau, but the wonder of the view never dulled, and tonight the fires far away to the southwest were very brilliant, brighter, perhaps, than I had seen them before.

On the morning of the 25th, we descended into the crater by the usual path leading under Waldron's Ledge. The temperature on the upper bank was 58° Fahr., and the steam from the many cracks parallel with the crater-walls seemed more

FIG. 79. KILAUEA IN 1880. CHAS. FURNEAUX.

abundant than usual. The massive walls had been much broken, and huge fragments of ancient lava had been tumbled down in the path, making the descent much easier, and also indicating more clearly than I had ever seen before, the way in which this vast crater has attained its present proportions. The original walls may have been of small extent, but the jar of earthquakes cracks the not firmly united layers of lava which compose the bounding walls, and finally throws down to the floor blocks of lava in size proportioned to the strength or frequency of the shocks; then the next period of activity in the lava-supply sends over the floor streams of lava which float or melt these blocks, thus clearing away the talus. It is difficult to understand how the lavas raise and float the much more compact old lava, but I have seen it done more than once, and the impression the sight conveyed was of a black hand gently passing under the heavy block and raising it or carrying it along. In the same way lava has insinuated itself beneath stone walls built to bar its progress and lifted and overthrown the futile barrier. So extensively has this process been at work in Kilauea that my survey of the crater, made with great care in 1865, and six years later adopted by the Trigonometrical Survey of the Hawaiian Government and republished on their official map, is already antiquated except in a few points, ascertained by my monuments still standing; the whole boundary has perceptibly changed, and I consider Kilauea nearly five per cent. larger than it was eighteen years ago. The change visible on the bottom of the crater was even greater. I was provided with an excellent barometer, by the kindness of my friend Mr. Carpenter, and found by it that while the bottom of the crater, at the base of the outer wall where first reached in our descent, was 650 feet below the Volcano House, the central portion was only 300 feet, or, in other words, the floor was raised in the general shape of a flat dome 350 feet high. Nor was this hill of lava simply the overflow of the lakes whence the lava runs in frequent outbreaks; the mass was partly composed of these numberless little overflows, but the great mass was evidently elevated in the centre, and the cracks everywhere indicated that this elevation was not a slow cumulative action, but had been, at intervals, greatly and irregularly accelerated.

In 1865 the floor of the crater was very irregular, full of caves and intersected by great cracks, but its general surface was nearly horizontal. A few years later the floor fell in over about a third of its area (see Fig. 69, p. 107) and the caves and cracks were alike obliterated, a funnel-like depression with but slight signs of fire at the bottom. The action, however, continued until the tunnel was not only filled up but the overflow from it reached the outer walls of Kilauea, and then, for a while, the action decreased and the lava cooled. A renewal of activity floated this crust as is indicated by occasional outflows at the edges, and so the intermittent action had in 1880 formed a tolerably regular dome surrounded by four lakes (the latest on the southeast began to form on May 15th) of an average diameter of a thousand feet each. The walls of these lakes of fire were much broken and changing daily. They were elevated in places far above the contour of the dome, and from the action of heated vapors, were decomposed until their layered structure was plainly visible at a distance by the bands of brilliant colors not unlike those of the clay cliffs at Gay Head on Martha's Vineyard. Emerald-green, vermilion, blue and Indian-yellow, irregularly distributed, indicated either very little homogeneity of the masses or uncertain action of the sulphurous and acid vapors. · [514]

It was very easy to see what toppled down these fantastic cliffs, for the molten mass within the lake was most active near the edges and under the banks which were generally undermined horizontally to the extent of fifteen or twenty feet by the white-hot, restless waves. From the under surface of these over-hanging shelves depended long and flexible skeins of what seemed to be volcanic spun-glass, or Pele's hair, lapped by the white waves, and seeming, in the glare in which they swung, to be hot to transparency. These pendents were very numerous, often a foot in diameter and six to ten feet long, fibrous as asbestos, and very flexible. Although they were one of the most remarkable appearances at the southeast lake, it was nearly half an hour before I had any direct evidence of the process of their formation. Occasionally surface ex-

From South East Lake—toward North.

FIG. 80. FROM SOUTHEAST LAKE, LOOKING NORTHWARD.

plosions took place and the viscous fragments, thrown violently against the roof above, spun out in falling back a glass thread, sometimes several from each lump, the fragment being sometimes as large as a man's head. An attraction, probably electrical, as the compass needle is strongly agitated in the vicinity of the currents from the lakes, drew together these isolated threads until the hank was formed which floated like seaweed in a falling tide. Although I watched several hours I did not see any of these hanks fall into the lake beneath.

The brittle nature of the banks which were formed by overflows and ejected matter loosely cemented by subsequent overflows or spatters, would admit of any amount of degradation, but how is the elevation to be explained? A prolonged stay at the crater suggested the following explanation. The action in these fire-lakes or pools, as has often been mentioned, is very irregular and intermittent, often apparently ceasing on one side until the crust there is cool and hard; it then breaks out again from beneath this new crust, turning it back like the lid of a box against the bank to which it may be soldered by the molten spatters, or, as is more frequently the case, the crust is raised *en masse* and where it touches the superincumbent cliff, carries this up with it and sometimes topples it over onto the outer part of the wall. In this way, I believe, the cliffs seen in the sketch, and the whole bottom of Kilauea, nearly three miles in diameter, have been floated up by degrees. If the action was constant the lava would break out along the edges of the swelling plain, as indeed it does when the inflow of lava is long continued, and the surface would become a general level by the accumulation of the running lava in the lowest places. But in fact, after a certain amount of lava has flowed up through the throats, whose position is marked by the surface lakes just mentioned,—enough, it may be, to raise the cool but somewhat flexible crust a few feet in the middle,—the supply ceases; the liquid which has permeated all the cracks and fissures in the overlying crust as the lava on a larger scale injects dikes in the earth's crust, cools and becomes solid, to be in turn raised by a new influx of lava from beneath. Each layer will be thicker near the source and will thin out as the distance therefrom increases, and this is what the cracks and chasms in the dome show so far as one can get into them. The successive layers are very unequal; one not far, perhaps two hundred

FIG. 81. DIAGRAM OF ELEVATION.

feet from the outer lake, was six feet thick and contained on a rough estimate ten thousand cubic yards of vesicular lava; next to it was a layer not quite two feet thick and diminishing at a distance of two hundred yards to less than half a foot.

After examining Kilauea by daylight, I procured lanterns and returned to the lakes about nightfall, traversing the bed of the crater while the daylight lasted. A guide (so called) who was at the Volcano House, and who went with us that morning, refused to descend after dark, and the hotel keeper (Lentz) put every obstacle in our way;[106] but I had often been there by night before, and my familiarity with the external action of this volcano made it quite safe to pass over any part of the terrible waste in the flickering, lurid light of the earth-fires, as it is only at night that the Halemaumau can be seen in all its splendor. In some respects also it is a safer journey by night than by day; for example, on our way down we crossed a low dome which gave no signs of fire except a clinking sound and a silent bluish vapor common enough in the vicinity of the lakes; the ground was so hot, however, that we crossed it rapidly to save our shoes; on our return about midnight we found that our path had led over a mound wholly

---

[106] *I mention this because it is the only occasion in my many visits to the Volcano House under many different hosts, that I have not met with the utmost courtesy and assistance.*

injected with a network of molten lava filling the cracks not two inches from the surface, and which, now plainly visible in the darkness, was a startling as well as a beautiful sight. In daylight the hot lava looks like black tar, and I have several times had to pull my companions from the spot where they might be standing unconscious of the silent black monster which was almost biting their feet, for it was nearly invisible on the equally black floor.

In all of my previous visits the bank of the active pool had been at least twenty feet above the lava surface, but now we were able to approach the southeast lake nearly on a level, and the effect was much grander than usual. I have spent at various times as many as ten nights in the crater on the banks of this and other similar lakes, and have noticed blue and green flames playing over the cracks in the surface, but these seldom lasted longer than a few moments, and were not confined to any locality. Now, on the contrary, on the top of a huge hummock which seemed to have broken from the bank, was a cluster of blow-holes from which escaped constantly a large volume of gas which burned with a bluish-green flame well shown in Mr. Furneaux's painting of the lake made on this visit. (See frontispiece.) These jets were burning in the morning, and twelve hours after their volume was apparently unaltered. The pressure evidently varied but slightly, and any increase in pressure did not seem to correspond to greater activity in the molten lava. With suitable apparatus it would have been possible to have collected the gas before it was consumed. Its escape caused a noise similar to that of a steamboat blowing off steam. The mention of steam leads me to express a wish that those geologists who see in steam the prime cause of volcanic action, could have been here, and have studied an eruption of the Hawaiian volcanoes. A pailfull of water thrown into the southeast lake would have made more steam than was present all the time we stayed in the crater. It is difficult to mistake a steamy atmosphere for a very dry one; and then if steam was present in any quantity in the gaseous exhalations of Kilauea, the cold winds from Mauna Loa would soon precipitate it as rain, when in fact this is the dryest part of the island.

The ancient Halemaumau or Everlasting House, where fires have been seen, or whence vapors have escaped from time immemorial, was now replaced, I believe, by the four lakes which occupy the position of that single source. The guide and others insisted that the northeastern of the lakes was the Halemaumau, and without renewing my survey, for which I did not have with me the necessary instruments, I could not positively declare that they were wrong, but I sighted from two of my monuments left from 1865, and comparing with my notes of that survey on my return to Boston, I found that the Halemaumau of that day occupied a position nearly southwest of the present so-called Halemaumau, or in the midst of the present four lakes, so that no one of them is entitled exclusively to that name sacred to the ancient worshippers of Pele.

Among other changes the southern sulphur bank had wholly disappeared, having been consumed by a local outbreak of lava which occurred a few months before our visit (July 14, 1879). The other deposit of sulphur on the north side near the hotel seemed smaller, and the impression conveyed was of a much smaller amount of sulphur in and around the crater than was found fifteen years before. None of the fine crystals so common then could be found now.

West of the crater on the Kau road, in the region called Uwekahuna, are many small cracks which indicate plainly a general and extensive subsidence. Farther to

FIG. 82. HALEMAUMAU FROM KAU BANK IN 1880.

the southwest was a long line of smoke or vapor extending, it may be, to Ponahohoa, where Rev. William Ellis found marks of a recent outflow in 1823. I could not then follow the fissure, nor do I know of any one who has done so, but this is the track of many an eruption, and should be thoroughly surveyed, as it is little visited, being barren and of rough surface. (This has since been done to some extent by the Government Survey.)

As the moon rose about midnight we started for the upper bank and the Volcano House. The brilliant moonlight of the tropics glittered on the metallic lava in cold contrast to the hot fire-light we had just left, and as the shadow of the high ledge fell across our path we had to walk warily and in single file to avoid the cracks our feeble lantern hardly indicated. Once on the path up the wall, we separated, and the most active got home half an hour before the rest of the party.

On the twenty-ninth of July, having in the meantime made the ascent of Mauna Loa, I returned to Kilauea. In the afternoon I went to the Kau bank, and while Mr. Furneaux sketched Kilauea from the west, I photographed the cliffs of Halemaumau, and then descending two of the gravelly terraces which form the border of the crater on this side, found myself on the brink of a perpendicular cliff beneath which the lava was escaping from several openings situated on the lower edge of the dome. The action was curious, and although the heat was very great at this height of nearly a hundred feet, I managed to watch and sketch it for nearly an hour. The noise here was peculiar; for in addition to the clinking as of shivering glass, usually heard when this black and glassy lava cools, there was a dull subterranean rumbling as of heavy machinery moving beneath the crater. It was the same noise I had heard during an earthquake two days before at Stone's ranch many miles from Kilauea, and it was not unlike the sound of many looms in a cotton factory. Here there was no earthquake tremor, although there is always in and about Kilauea a vibration of the ground very clearly seen when using a compass needle, but seldom noticed otherwise. The cliff where I watched was not over the lowest part of the crater, but was where the active pools approached nearest

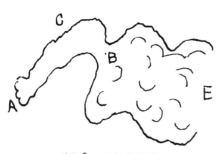

FIG. 83. LAVA SPRING.

to the outer walls, for the dome has a very excentric apex. The fluidity of the lava as it came to the surface was about that of cream. There is, so far as I know, no definite scale to which we may refer various degrees of viscidity, and I am compelled to use homely comparisons, which have the further disadvantage of being a variable standard. It was white-hot cream when it came out from under the crust, but in the distance of perhaps a foot had changed to a cherry-red molasses, while a few feet more transformed the stream into full red tar. By daylight the color ranges from that of arterial to venous blood, and thence to a slaty blue, marking the loss of temperature by chromatic changes. At night all the moving portion is a bright red. A single outlet of small dimensions made much noise blowing, although the gas expelled was invisible. The lava (A in the diagram) issued white-hot, ran a few feet rapidly, then crusted over, retaining its red glow along the edges of the narrow conduit, c. At B there was a contraction and the flow stopped for a while; then the fountain at A renewed the supply and the lava ran rapidly from the narrow outlet B, spreading in a broad, thin sheet which did not lose its color until it reached the point E, while the original narrower and thicker stream had formed a crust and become black in less than a quarter of the distance. In places the lava met upward inclines, then the cooling, but still flexible, crust, made a dam and carried the fluid part up and over a rise of some feet. The little lava spring was an epitome of a full lava flow, and was more instructive than the immense fiery floods that from time to time break out from these volcanoes and flow for many miles. Later in the evening this insignificant flow became more active, covering twenty acres and giving more light than the lakes themselves.

FIG. 84. BATH HOUSE ON THE SULPHUR BANK, 1880.

Over one of the steam cracks near the Volcano House, on the northeastern bank, and in close proximity to what remained of the sulphur bank, had been built a very rude steam bath. A hut of ample dimensions, a box with a stool in it, and loose boards to fit around the neck of the bather, with a wooden sluice from the steam crack to the box and a slide to regulate the admission of steam, constitute the entire apparatus. Seated in the box late that evening, in utter darkness, while the attendant had gone outside with the lantern to get a pail of cold water, I heard, in the stillness, sounds deep down in the steam crack, rumbling and hard noises totally unlike the soft hissing or sputtering of the steam. Fearing that my imagination lent strength if not being to these sounds, I went to a crack outside and, at the risk of pitching in head-first, listened carefully. The same noise was heard distinctly, not unlike that of an earthquake, but feebler.   [520]

NOTES ON AN ASCENT OF MAUNA LOA IN 1880, ABOUT THREE MONTHS BEFORE THE GREAT ERUPTION OF THAT YEAR. BY W. T. BRIGHAM.

From the American Journal of Science, July, 1888, p. 33.

On the first of May, 1880, fire was seen in the crater of Pohaku Hanalei[107] (B in Fig. 85), on the summit of Mauna Loa. Persons who made the ascent saw a fire-fountain much like that observed in 1872, but no overflow followed, and the fires soon disappeared. On the morning of July 26, I left Kilauea for Kapapala. The next morning, while waiting at Stone's ranch for a guide over the trackless beds of aa and clinker on the great mountain, an earthquake occurred at 8:30 A.M. local time. It lasted three seconds, and was accompanied by a loud subterranean noise resembling that of the looms in a cotton mill. The vibration was by no means so noticeable as the noise. Journeying over a grazing land covered with coarse grass, and dotted here and there with blighted koa trees, we reached Ainapo at 1:45 P.M. Although at an elevation of at least 5000 feet, the temperature was at 75°. Late in the afternoon I mounted a fine mule that had been loaned me by a friend, and, with Ahuai for guide, left the ranch. In 1864, with Mr. Horace Mann, I climbed the mighty dome on foot on the opposite side; but this path was, if possible, worse. The forest had been burned, and the blackened stems of the trees were dismal objects unless covered with the *akalá*, a gigantic raspberry vine. The soil in these lower regions seems good, but the ground is much broken, and so full of holes that it would be very dangerous to ride out of the trail after dark. Even in the afternoon, vapors ascended from these holes, which often, if not always, communicated with caverns in the ancient lava streams, and as the day waned the vapors became more distinct. I found as the average of several trials, that the temperature was only two or three degrees higher than the outer air. As we ascended, the actual temperature of the vapor in these holes increased, and of course the relative temperature was much higher. I inferred from this that the inner mountain mass was hotter than usual, as I had never observed so great a difference before, and that an eruption was at hand.

At the upper limit of vegetation we camped, giving our animals the little bundles of hay we had brought for the purpose. The night was cold and on the morning of July 28th, at sunrise, the thermometer marked 52°. We broke camp at five

---

[107] This name was applied by my guide to the south pit crater of Mokuaweoweo, and I still believe it the correct name. This name was also used by Wilkes in 1841 with the concurrence of Dr. Judd and others. Much juggling has taken place with the names of Hawaiian origin in later times, and this name has been applied to at least three craters on this mountain. The one selected by the survey (on what grounds I do not know) to bear the name on the official map is a cone on the summit some distance from Mokuaweoweo in a northeasterly direction. I may add that in the Journal of the Royal Geographical Society, xxv, 194, in a paper by J. G. Sawkins, read June 25, 1855, there occurs this passage: "The crater of Pohakuhanalie is connected with that of Mokuaweoweo, which is much deeper, its walls being nearly perpendicular, and exhibiting 92 layers or beds, uninterrupted by dykes. South of the last named crater there is another, the lava of which was so hot at the time of my visit that we could not walk over it."

o'clock and reached the summit at half-past ten.   A rougher mass of lava I have seldom seen and never before ridden over.   Beds of aa were succeeded by piles of jagg ed scoria in fragments from one to twenty cubic feet in bulk, and over these my mule jumped like a chamois.   At last we came upon a level plain from which had poured the lava that had hindered our ascent.

Although we were on the summit, the crater, Mokuaweoweo, did not at first appear, but on every side were rough piles of lava, some recent, and abundant deposits of the vesicular lava called *limu*.   This limu is of a pale green color presenting at a distance the appearance of vegetation.   Some fragments of it were a foot in diameter, the exterior glazed and of a much darker green, the whole very vesicular and so full of air as to float on water.   In appearance it was frozen froth.   In the midst of this waste plain we found the crater.   Since I saw it fifteen years before great changes had occurred.   Then no change but the gradual decay of time seemed imminent; all was the repose of the dead.   There were some concentric cracks in the outer walls, but the lava between these cracks and the crater itself was so solid as to retain snow and ice all the summer, and the descent into the crater could be made only where the smaller craters broke into the outer wall.   On both the east and west sides the precipices of gray, scarred

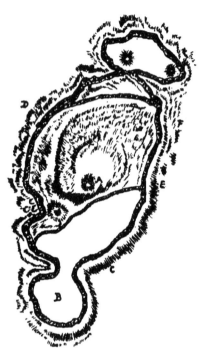

FIG. 85.   MOKUAWEWOEO.

and compact lava rose to the height of nearly a thousand feet, and seemed coeval with the mountain.   At the present time these ancient walls were cracked and tottering to their fall; in some places they much resembled a wall of loose stones artificially laid.   It was dangerous to approach the brink (of the south crater) so loose were the lava blocks, and the vibrations caused by my approach seemed to extend downward several hundred feet towards the talus which had been the result of a tremor more severe than usual.   By lying down I was able to look over and test the height by timing the fall of stones.   The bottom of this lateral pit, as of the main crater, was comparatively level, without cones, and gave no indications of the source whence the fresh black lava had issued. At my former visit in 1864 there were two cones in Mokuaweoweo about two hundred feet high near the eastern wall. In 1870, when Mr. Luther Severance ascended the mountain, there were no cones, although the bottom was much broken and sloped from west to east. From his sketch we learn that at f[108] the wall was very steep; at e the height was estimated at 1200 feet; at h were sulphur banks smoking, but not violently; c marks the point where the trail from Kapapala ends; d the point where Mr. Mann and I came to the crater in 1864; D is the small southern crater, and a is where I found the wall tottering in 1880.

In 1874 the crater was surveyed by Mr. John M. Lydgate, of the Government Survey, and the cones had again formed, two being in the northern lateral crater, and two in the main pit. In 1880 with this survey before me,[109] the changes seemed to be mostly in the outer walls which had crumbled extensively, changing the outline, but not enough to be indicated on a plan so small. In addition, the cross walls E and F were obliterated, and the bottom of the crater was covered with fresh lava. On this, along the edges, was a talus of old lava from the walls, showing plainly that an earthquake had occurred since the eruption of May 1. No sulphur banks or steam jets were seen from either c or a and the deposit of limu, added to the roughness of the lava, deterred me from making the circuit of the south pit to examine a very extensive break on the farther side which looked fresh. Near the break was a black and glistening stream of lava, like that at the bottom of Mokuaweoweo, which extended from the opposite bank as far to the westward as could be seen over the undulating surface. Whence this issued was not easily determined. If it was, as first appeared to be the the case, an overflow from the crater, how could this have been full and yet have left no fresh lava on the broken walls? Usually when a pit crater fills up and is emptied from beneath, the sinking lava leaves a rim or "Black Ledge;" but there is nothing of the sort here. If the stream flowed *into* the crater then the wall over which it came has tumbled down and so removed all traces. I finally concluded that it owed its origin to some of the inclined lava jets that spouted out clear of the crater.[110]

My guide had seen the fountain of May 1, and he assured me that it came up level with the outer walls of the south crater, so that the top was visible as he was lying down some distance from the brink. This would indicate a height of nearly a thousand feet,—not an insignificant jet!

I was convinced that the eruption of May 1 was but the *avant courier* of a greater one, and as the termination of my visit was near, I asked those who were interested

---

[108] For these references see Survey of Mokuaweoweo, p. 159.

[109] See Survey of Mokuaweoweo by J. M. Lydgate, Fig. 73.

[110] In that I was mistaken, as a subsequent survey found an eruption had taken place from fissures near the brow of the cliff, and a later eruption had flowed into this pit. See Survey of 1886.

in these matters to watch for events and report to me. The new eruption began on the fifth of November, and it proved the beginning of the most extensive lava flow that has been recorded from the Hawaiian volcanoes.

We will return to Mauna Loa, for my expectations, aroused by the news of an outbreak in May, although unfulfilled so far as my participation was concerned, still materialized in a most definite manner about six weeks after my return to Boston. Here is the story from Mr. Coan about as it came to me:

Hilo is in a haze of sulphur smoke, and we see the sun as through smoked glass. We have a grand volcanic eruption. On the first inst., a little before daylight, a herdsman who lives about two miles out of town, reported that he had seen a light on Mauna Loa. At 8 P.M. of the same day, my wife called my attention to an unusual light in the direction of the mountain. At first it was partly obscured by clouds, so that we hesitated to pronounce it volcanic. In a few minutes, however, the revelation was clear. The clouds dispersed and the spectacle of a burning mountain opened to our sight. The action was intense. The appearance was as if a vast column of melted rock, a mile in diameter, was being poured out of the mountain with amazing force and vehement heat. Brilliant corruscations shot out in all directions, lighting up the clouds to the apparent height of 30° and spreading out for many miles along the summit of the eastern side of the mountain. The outbreak was in full view from the west side of our house, which was brilliantly lighted up by the fires, while the front part was in a deep shade, rendering the contrast striking.

This eruption occurring in the night, we were unable to determine at once the exact locality. Some thought it was in the deep summit crater, Mokuaweoweo [as it was]: and others that it was at a point a few miles north of it. Since that night the mountain has been so veiled in clouds and smoke that we have not been able to see the fire. Yesterday flocks of Pele's hair, and light particles of volcanic dust and sand were dropped upon our houses and in our streets, having been borne upon the winds for this great distance.

Since my former letter, dated June 20, 1879, Kilauea has resumed great activity. Rarely in its recorded history have the fires been more intense or the filling up more rapid. Lateral streams of liquid rock are bursting through the scoriaceous sides of Halemaumau and flowing down the declivities into the central depression, adding stratum to stratum, while the great lake boils, and dashes its waves against its walls, and sends its burning spray high into the air. The debris around the high walls of the lake is so hot and brittle that most parties who visit the crater do not venture near the burning cauldron, but mount some quiet eminence about one-quarter of a mile from its margin, where they can witness its ragings, and listen to its splashings and mutterings with safety.[111]

October 27, 1880. L. P. Tenney.—Halemaumau is quite active, as is also Kilauea or South Lake.

November 4, 1880. W. B. Oleson.—The lava is flowing on the west side of the crater [main], and quite perceptibly changing the level. There are three distinct lakes without any other than underground connection. Kilauea is crowded into very small dimensions, while Halemaumau remains in outline about as it was a year and a half ago, but not being accessible, no definite idea of its condition could be learned. Apparently the lava has sunken to a great depth, as no sounds could be heard. The special seat of activity was in a new lake toward the southeast, not far removed from Halemaumau. Here there was a vigorous activity, though nothing violent......I have seen two of these lakes when there was a rapid flow of lava alternately from one to the other, and at a time when there seemed to be less activity than at this visit.

November 12, 1880. W. H. Lentz.—About 9 P.M., November 5th, a flow of lava started from the northern slope of Mauna Loa apparently towards Waimea or Hilo, and is still running.

---

[111]American Journal of Science, xx (July, 1880), 71.   [524]

On November 9th, about 8 P.M., the above flow started a branch along the slope and face of the mountain towards Kapapala ranch, Kau, and is still on its journey, making, I should judge, eight to ten miles a day.

December 7, 1880. J. M. Lydgate.—Result of one day's half-hourly observations with two mercurial syphon barometers, one being observed here, the other at Hilo: 4021 feet above sea at Volcano House.

The flow from Mauna Loa which was observed from the Volcano House on November 5th, proved to be the expected eruption which had brought me to Hawaii, and from the duration of its flow, the distance reached by its several streams and the amount of lava poured out it is to be reckoned one of the most important on record.

FIG. 86. VIEW OF HALEMAUMAU IN 1880. FURNEAUX.

On the evening of the 5th, the light was first seen from Waimea, north of Mauna Loa, and a few hours later from Hilo on the northeast. In both cases the lava fountains were distinct, leaping high into the air. This was quite like all former recorded eruptions, but in one way this differed from them all, and that was in the diffuse way in which the streams were poured out; the length of time the lava poured forth was also a noteworthy fact, over nine months. From below the first stream seemed to run north by east towards Mauna Kea, but this stopped after a course of twelve miles, not far from the sheep station of Kalaieha on the high plateau between the great mountains of Hawaii. I have seen the end of that stream and it presents no

[525]

marked peculiarities; the supply at the fountain was evidently diverted,—Rev. E. P.
Baker visited the source several times, and gives us the result of his observations seven
years after. The diagram (Fig. 87) will render his explanation clearer. At the end of
a large crack about eleven thousand feet above the sea, where is now a pit crater (s) of
considerable size called Pukauahi, the flow came to the surface. The crack was on a
"divide," and while the Kea stream started first it probably blocked in some measure
the discharge, and another stream, called the Kau flow, started in the direction of
Kilauea a little higher up the crack. This Kau flow was well seen from the Volcano
House at Kilauea, and for a time it looked as if the lava would reach and flow into the
latter crater. Numerous branches flowed down the crest on
its southeastern slope, and they are quite easily traced from
the House, in suitable conditions of light, to the present day.
The crack ran by the north of a red cone which in July, 1888,
was still smoking, and also a smaller cone (marked v on the
diagram) which was also smoking seven years after the eruption ceased. Dana seems to follow Baker in considering these
cones the obstacle that turned the main stream toward Hilo,
but while the matter is unimportant, it seems from the continued activity that they were a part and parcel of the

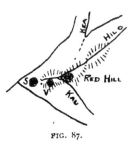

FIG. 87.

eruption, and did not exist before."[112]   Mr. Furneaux' sketch (Fig. 88) shows the red
hill in the centre of the view. In the original sketch the hill is of a brick-red color,
and the curious ribbon of lava in the foreground is of a greenish tinge, and the pinnacle
and ridges of various shades of red and brown contrasting well with the patch of
snow on the left. Steam was still issuing from the cone and other parts of the flow
when the sketch was made.

After four months the flowing lava was about seven miles from Hilo; on June
28th, within five miles; on July 18th, two miles, and on August 10th, it finally stopped
three-quarters of a mile from Hilo. Great was the anxiety as the stream approached
the apparently devoted town, not only in Hilo but all over the group, for the beauty
of the town and the hospitality of its inhabitants were known to all. I am tempted to
quote at some length from letters which show the nature of the flow as well as the
state of mind, for so wonderful are these flows, so spectacular as well as scientifically
interesting, that the words of no one man, however eloquent, can picture the whole scene.
I give extracts from the letters sent to me, and others published in the daily papers,
but all from those well known to me and whose knowledge of the phenomena was not

[112] Characteristics of Volcanoes, 205, and American Journal, xxxvii, 53, already quoted.

that of mere transient visitors seeing such wonders for the first time. The first is from my friend of long time, the late Judge David H. Hitchcock. It is dated from Hilo, Thursday, June 30, 1881:

About Wednesday of last week, the old mountain was observed to be more than usually active, the whole summit crevasse pouring forth immense volumes of smoke. By Friday noon the three southern arms had all joined into one, and rushing into a deep but narrow gulch forced its way down the gulch in a rapid flow. By Saturday noon it had run a mile and was just above John Hall's house on the south side. On Monday morning it was reported to have reached the flats back of Halai

FIG. 88. VIEW OF THE SEAT OF THE ERUPTION OF 1880. FURNEAUX.

Hills. My wife and self started that afternoon with the intention of spending the night alongside the flow. We met crowds of people returning from the flow, and all reported it active and coming rapidly down the gulch. We rode up to it before dark and found that the stream was entirely confined to the gulch and intensely active. It was then about half a mile from the flats spoken of.

The flow was on an average about seventy-five feet wide and from ten to thirty feet in depth as it filled the gulch up level with its banks. The sight was grand. The whole frontage was one mass of liquid lava carrying on its surface huge cakes of partially cooled lava. Soon after we arrived the flow reached a deep hole, some ten or fifteen feet in depth, with perpendicular sides. The sight as it poured over that fall in two cascades was magnificent. The flow was then moving at the rate of about seventy-five feet an hour. About midnight we noticed a diminution in the activity of the gulch flow and soon saw a bright red glare above the tree tops mauka [inland] of us, and were presently startled by the burning *gas bursts*, and the crackling and falling of the trees somewhere

FIG. 89. LAVA STREAM IN A FOREST. FURNEAUX.

above us. The whole sky overhead was lined with the light of burning trees and shrubs. About 2 A.M. we made the attempt to reach the scene of the great activity, and succeeded by going up the south side of the gulch some quarter of a mile. And what a scene lay before us as we ascended a slight elevation! The oncoming overflow had swept over the banks of the narrow gulch and was flowing like water into a dense grove of neneleau [sumac] and guava trees. There they stood in a sea of liquid lava over a space of more than an acre, while the fires were running up their trunks and burning the branches and leaves overhead. The flow was so rapid that the trees were not cut down, for more than two hundred feet from the first of the flow. In one place we saw a huge dome of half melted lava rise up fifteen or twenty feet high and twice that in diameter and apparently remain stationary, while the fiery flood went on.

The reasons of the quick advance of the flow the past two weeks have been the increased activity of the fountain head; the junction of the streams mentioned above, and the fact that this narrow rock bed gulch has formed, as it were, a *flume* to pass the liquid lava along in a solid, narrow stream, without any chance for spreading out laterally.

Extracts from letters of the Rev. Titus Coan:

Hawaii is still on fire, and the smoke and sanguinary glare appear like a line of soldiers in battle. The northern wing of the line is less than six miles from us, and the southeastern is less than five miles distant, while the centre of the line appears the most sanguinary. From the southeast wing the seething fusion has fallen into a rough water channel, twenty to fifty feet wide, which comes down from the main bed of the flow almost direct to Hilo, entering into the Waialama stream, which cuts the beach about midway. In this way the lava at white heat is fast approaching the shore. It is now only two and a half miles from Volcano street and it is very liquid, running much like water. It has, some part of the time, run at the rate of half a mile a day. Our town is greatly moved, and some have suspended all other business to watch the fires. The main body of the fire is moving slowly down upon us in sufficient breadth to sweep our whole town, while the small stream is like advanced pickets on a skirmish line. We are in the hands of our All-wise and Gracious God, and would not be elsewhere. Let Him do according to His pleasure, while it is a comfort to call upon Him in the hour of trouble, and hope in His mercy.

Tuesday, 5 p.m., June 28.—Mrs. Coan and I have been to the lava flow today and returned. We were a little over an hour in reaching the flow, walking our horses slowly all the way. A native with a good horse will reach the fires in forty minutes, and return in thirty. We call the distance three miles. We found two streams of liquid lava coming down in rocky channels which are sometimes filled with roaring waters, but nearly dry at this time. These two gulches are too small to hold the seething fusion, and the fiery flood over-runs the banks, and spreads out on either side. The united width of these streams may vary from fifty to two hundred feet. In going down the steeper parts of these rocky beds the roar is like that of our Wailuku, or our surf, and often like thunder.

The visit to the flow which Father Coan dismisses in so few words, Mrs. Coan describes in a letter written the evening of her return, and I quote portions of this letter:

This has been the darkest day that Hilo has known in connection with the flow of 1881. We knew by the glare of the sky last evening that there was increased activity, and we both said that at no time had the look been more threatening. There was such a broad belt of light, and it looked so near. Before breakfast this morning a native came who had been at the Waiakea flow and told what he had seen—a startling story; but we have become so distrustful of all the native reports that we could not allow ourselves to be much alarmed until we could hear further. Mr. Coan, soon as he could, went down town to get more reliable information, and when he returned, I asked eagerly: "How is it?" and he answered, "Well, *it is all true!*" He had seen several who had been to the

[529]

flow and the reports all agreed. We are feeling sober, for truly we know not but that destruction awaits our beautiful homes—and where shall we go? The people in the Kukuau apana [district] are moving their things and themselves.

June 29.—Ah! How can I tell you the story of yesterday? I look back upon it as a dream of the night, and yet the experiences, the sights, were actual. We had an early breakfast and a little before nine were ready to start for the flow, our Portuguese John accompanying us. When we reached the turn in the road on the Puna side of the cemetery, there burst suddenly upon our view the spot to which the fire had progressed. And it looked alarmingly near, not more than a mile distant; but as we rode on the distance increased and we found we went two miles or more beyond

FIG. 90. WATERSPOUT ON THE FLOW OF 1881. FURNEAUX.

the further one of the three crater-hills. As we followed the trail, others passed us at more rapid rate, and among them the Lymans and Severances with native attendants, and we found many there when we reached the place. A few rods of walking after we dismounted brought us to the margin of the stream, not limpid, sparkling brook, such as one might have looked for in that lovely, emerald oasis, but a red-hot, madly pursuing, death-dealing flow of lava. Years ago, and not so very many either, people lived thereabouts and the land was under much cultivation (Mr. Coan has often been there,—there was formerly a school-house not far from the place), and you can easily imagine what luxuriant growth of grass there would be, and what strong, leafy guava bushes, in what had become almost swampy land since the soil-tillers had abandoned it. But right over this freshness and beauty the flood was coming. More was to be seen beyond, so we pushed eagerly through tall ferns and bushes of neneleau, almost held in our steps by the sticky mud, till we reached a rocky gorge which in times of heavy rains is the channel for the stream that rushes down a perfect torrent to the sea passing under the bridge near the little church at Kalepolepo. This gorge is now nearly dry, except here and there pools of water in its deepest hollows, and here the lava goes plunging on, making falls of its red-hot, gory mass where aforetime cool cascades sparkled and rippled. Here we found crowds of natives and some foreigners watching the wild scene. We were told that Dr. Wetmore and others were still further on where the main branch was; we had seen only overflows from that which was filling up a still larger channel. A native volunteered to guide us through the bushes and over the great rocks in the way, and we soon had sight of the third party on quite an eminence who called us to hasten and join them, but we had progressed only a few yards when word came that the stream in the narrow gorge was moving on so fast that our return was likely to be cut off, and Mr. Coan, marking its advance by the smoke that rose, felt that it was not wise to attempt to go to the further side. John, whom we had sent on, being fleet of foot, to see how it was, hastened back exclaiming: "Like very much, Mrs. Coan see that!" Meantime the gentlemen, who were already

FIG. 91. LAVA FLOW OF 1881 NEAR HILO. FURNEAUX.

there, took note of the warning and retraced their steps: but Mr. W. offered to assist me to a place where I could see it safely; and what I saw was the most awe-inspiring sight of all, for the mass was far heavier and wider spread, and for speed and fury of motion it was like the rapids of Niagara. But it was all tame to Mr. Coan, who had seen so much more, and tame by comparison to what it must be some miles back, for this is only a picket from the army, and Mr. Coan says it sometimes seems as if it were acting just like military tactics,—this skirmishing on the left wing while the right is holding itself in reserve, and coming down when not watched to bring desolation in the rear. What terrific pouring out of fusion there must be to supply these different streams,—their advanced posts, and to make them so lively so far from the fountain. Why, at night it shows an emblazoned front of four or five miles as estimated. When we went back to the middle one of the three tines of the fork, we tarried long to watch its movements so persistent in pushing by obstacles, checked by nothing, heeding nothing, consuming, destroying, bound for the sea.

[531]

THE SCRIPPS INSTITUTION
OF OCEANOGRAPHY
OF THE
UNIVERSITY OF CALIFORNIA
LA JOLLA, CALIF.

Oh! the lovely ferns, one moment waving their fresh fronds in the breeze, the next scorched by the heat, the next a mass of lambent flames, and the next ashes and nothing more. It just makes my heart ache over that. The roar of the lava was something fearful, it was as the roar of a flood. Then the detonations, ten in a minute as timed by the watch, and some of the explosions so heavy we felt the ground tremble under us. John was at one time sitting down in the dry bed of the gorge a little before the lava and nearer it than any one else, when there was a burst of steam through a venthole in the rocks that sent little fragments flying hither and thither, and he was spattered by some of the dirt or mud that came up. Had it been one of the heavier explosions he could hardly have escaped being hurt. While we lingered in the gorge another note of alarm from the natives, to the effect that the flow was approaching the spot where the horses were tied and that soon the road would be cut off, caused us to think well of going ourselves to see how much progress the fire had made in that locality. One of the party called it a false alarm, but then the flow was breaking out here and there so rapidly from over the banks of the channel which it had filled up, no wonder it seemed to some that the danger was everywhere.

It was now noon, and Mr. Coan, wearied, sat to rest on a prostrate trunk, thick green grass under his feet, and verdant boughs of trees above him, but behind him the advancing stream. Here the ground was very level, and of course the flow was not rapid, but foot by foot, yard by yard it rolled forward, and very soon after Mr. Coan had left his seat the burning ruin covered the ground on which his feet had rested and the log was aflame. There was intense fascination in watching all the movements at whatever point we were, and something almost momentarily kept us exclaiming—sometimes it was the quick cooling over the surface forming the corrugated ridges that characterize pahoehoe, and glistening in the sun like perfect bronze—sometimes the puffing of great bubbles that crusted over a moment, then sank back into the fiery bosom from which they had risen —then it rushed down steep places and filling up the hollows from which wreaths of steam curled up, and then its progress through the dense grass, where, for a moment the verdure hung like a canopy over the red serpent gliding under, to melt away and be seen no more. We did not want to come away, and yet how great the mercy that we could come and leave it with the prayer that we might never see it doing greater damage than it was doing. The hours had been full of excitement to me, it was all so much more than I had ever seen before of volcanic displays. I was more weary than I realized when again in the saddle, but the ride home was restful. The air was refreshing after the intense heat, which had burned our faces, and from the point in the road where the view of Hilo, the bay and the greatly indented coast line breaks upon the eye, the prospect before us was perfectly enchanting in its glowing beauty. I have always thought it a view of surpassing loveliness, but now that there is so much more cultivation, and the waste places are emerald rice fields or taro patches, and the Waiakea mill and plantation are seen on the right, the beauty is enhanced. Must the fiery flood leave a line of black desolation through it all? How great the mercy that the track it is now on is one so apart from human habitations, and that there is no danger to human life. Our homes are not to be overwhelmed from this side: that seems plain, and we will still trust that the "hitherto" command has been spoken to the threatener on the right. One breath can quench it as quickly as it kindled it and all our fears abate. A prayer and conference meeting was held that evening at Mr. David Lyman's, and there was comfort in singing the sweet hymns "Father, whate'er of earthly bliss," "How firm a foundation ye saints of the Lord," and "Saviour, like a shepherd lead us;" and I think there was some truth in the saying from the heart "The will of the Lord be done." I wish you could have been there as we were thus carrying this care to the Lord and shared with us the quieting influences of the hour.

I have quoted this letter so fully that my readers, who have not known these people as I have, may recognize the noble souls, trusting and undaunted in the hour of so great peril, who made Hilo what it was, a town of homes.

From the western shore of Hawaii, at Kawaihae, the view of this eruption was very grand. Even in the quietest geological times the early morning approach to Kawaihae on the steamer is very fine with the three mountains of Hawaii lighted by the rising sun. If it be in winter and the snow caps are on Kea and Loa, the rosy glow is worth the journey to see. On the beach the little village is still in shadow of the departing night, and the great temple of Puukohola stands gloomily just beyond the town, but from Kea to Hualalai the glow of the coming day is fast spreading, and the light canoes of the fishermen are nearing the shore. Mr. Furneaux caught

FIG. 92. ERUPTION OF MAUNA LOA SEEN FROM KAWAIHAE BAY. FURNEAUX.

all this, and to the grand dome of Loa was added the two fire fountains and the canopy of lurid cloud of this eruption. The photograph cannot give the colors of the original painting which is in the gallery of the Bishop Museum.

January 17, 1881. Charles Burnham.—After an absence of forty-five years I find the crater [of Kilauea] much changed since 1835. It was then estimated to be eight hundred feet deep over the whole surface. One hundred and ten cones over fifty to seventy-five feet high. There was then a very large lake plainly visible night and day from the volcano shanty.

October 5, 1881. Theo. H. Davies.—The new lake was very active; the bottom edges of the surrounding rock were red-hot and the surface of the lake was always in commotion in some places. I counted nine cauldrons at once where the lava was boiling and splashing, a perfect blood-red, throwing great flakes perhaps twenty feet high. We then went to Halemaumau, but that was not accessible; it seemed to have more jets than the new lake. We went farther to the right and came to a pit of fire; this was hard on the surface but red at the edges.

[533]

December 21, 1881. An immense cave of the pali on the west side took place this day at 9 A.M.

July 14, 1882. F. W. Damon.—New Lake and Halemaumau very active. In the former the lava appears to be slowly rising; it was yesterday within thirty or forty feet of the edge where we stood.

July 14, 1882. Capt. C. E. Dutton wrote much in the Register which he probably afterwards revised in his published work on these Islands, so it need not be copied here. He was also here on September 12th of the same year, and found at Mokuaweoweo "no volcanic action whatever, not even a wisp of steam issuing from any part." [113]

September 12, 1882. W. H. Lentz.—The largest flow of lava that has been here at Kilauea for years took place today at 10:20 o'clock A.M. The only effect seemingly on the lakes was to lower their level about ten feet in each.

December 1, 1882. Rev. Titus Coan died at Hilo, aged 81 years.

February 8, 1883. Rev. A. O. Forbes.—Find more action in crater than there was a week ago.

Professor C. H. Hitchcock ascended Mauna Loa in 1883 and found snow all over the summit: no signs of action. [114]

March 30, 1883. H. M. Whitney.—Found Kilauea in its usual condition with occasional overflows of the lakes, and the crater filling up gradually.

August 9, 1883. Prof. Geo. H. Barton [Professor of Geology in Massachusetts Institute of Technology].—Fine display at South Lake. There were three islands in South Lake.

September 1, 1883. Fred H. Allen.—We saw a sight our landlord said he had never seen: the new lake, after a few moments of great quiet, suddenly boiled in nearly every part, and swallowing the black crust glowed fiery red over the entire surface. So hot was it that we had to step back several yards from the spot where people generally sit when looking at the lake, and even then were obliged to screen our faces with our hands. This same evening we noticed one or two large cracks on the surface of the large crater near the lakes that we had not seen the night before.

October 18, 1883. W. E. Shearburn.—During the time that Mr. J. Bryce and myself were here we made three descents into the crater, and on each occasion the two lakes were very active. On the night of the 13th, a large cave took place in Halemaumau, and on the night of the 17th there was a most brilliant break up of the new lake. Mr. Bryce attempted the ascent of Mauna Loa, but was stopped by the mist.

November 1, 1883. Rev. Edw. P. Baker.—Mr. Richardson and party went to the place near the trail from Puna to Kapapala, where, in 1868, the lava appeared on the surface. The lava came out at several points, but the largest space covered by lava is, say, one-eighth of a square mile. The bearing of Kahuku and the land-slide at Kapapala from Kilauea, is to the right (looking from Kilauea) of the direction of the crack and of the lava that came to the surface in 1868 from Kilauea. [On the 2nd Mr. Baker went to the south side of Halemaumau and threw an iron wire (a lava fragment at the end) into the boiling lava. The boiling process continually pulled the wire down, and down, for about three minutes, when the wire was burned off. A south wind compelled Mr. Baker to go round to the south side of Halemaumau.]

March 9, 1884. C. H. Dickey.—We found a new little crater on the route between Halemaumau and the New Lake. The guide says that it began to form last Tuesday, March 3rd. We visited it as we went to Halemaumau and it looked precisely like the furnace of a blacksmith's forge

---

[113] United States Geological Report, iv, p. 139.

[114] The page containing notes of this, as well as of his visit to Kilauea, has been torn out of the register, so that I was not aware of the visit of this distinguished geologist until I saw, long after this account was written, his note in the register complaining of the outrage. I understood that Professor Hitchcock was preparing for the press a work on the geology of the Hawaiian group, and for that reason I have omitted reference to his valuable papers on the subject in the publications of the American Geological Society and elsewhere.

and over two feet across, but while we were watching Halemaumau the little crater burst forth and gave us a distant view of a lava flow several hundred feet in length. We have named it the "Little Beggar," on account of its viciousness.

January 15, 1885. Dr. C. H. Wetmore.—The crater in vicinity of Halemaumau appears to me to have been considerably built up since my visit here, 7/2/84.

April 25, 1885. Rev. E. P. Baker. — I ascended Mauna Loa, reaching Mokuaweoweo about 10 A.M. April 20th. Snow covered the upper portion of the summit plateau in large masses, and in small scattering patches extended nearly a thousand feet below the summit. I left behind all clouds at the height of between seven and eight thousand feet, all clear and cold too above that. The wind (very cold) was continuous and in heavy gusts, blowing all the while from S.E., S. and S.W. The walls of Mokuaweoweo, especially the western, were plentifully bedecked with snow, and there

FIG. 93. LITTLE BEGGAR IN 1889.

was much snow on the floor of the crater. The spot of the Commodore Wilkes encampment was mostly covered with snow, so that I saw as the only relics there, two sticks, a broken bottle and a few nails. To my remark then and there made to J. Ulumahiapua Pea of Panau, Puna, "Wilkes' encampment," his reply was, "My grandfather Ulumahiapua Pea was the guide." We walked up and back from Ainapo. Six full days were spent in travel. The pocket barometer of Mr. Richardson which I carried showed Mauna Loa to be 13,300 feet above sea level. The summit crater was quiescent, just as it has been for several years: however, sulphurous smoke and steam were issuing from cracks in the floor of the crater, the crater being of the shape of the figure 8 written horizontal. I descended into Mokuaweoweo and spent the night by the steam and smoke cracks in the floor, keeping very warm by the issuing heat, although the night before I slept in a cave with icicles over head. Only one who has been there can realize the formidableness of the task of going down and coming up out of the summit crater of Mauna Loa. The angle of descent was 90° in places, and not apparently less than 75° or 80° any of the way. The place where I descended was at a point on the northeast brink, two-thirds of the descent bringing me to the floor of the first bench, and the other third to the lowest bench of the largest part of the crater. The barometer indicated the floor of the crater to be only four hundred feet below the brink (the real depth being, however, rather more). It was during most of the time in clear sky above the clouds, it being nearly all the time the jaunt lasted rainy below. My last day on the mountain gave signs of a heavy storm, the upper and cirrus clouds being driven over by the southwest wind, and meeting the trade wind and lower clouds, and looking very angry at the place of meeting. The storm that followed was one of the heaviest ever known on the island. I was fortunate enough to reach a camp for shelter (6000 feet up) a few hours after the storm struck me. I found myself affected with vertigo after awaking from sleep on the floor of the crater on the morning of April 21st.

May 17, 1885. L. A. Thurston.—The flow from Little Beggar, which has been running since early in March, has nearly reached the east wall of the crater.

May 18, 1885. W. R. Castle.—Kilauea: Flowing lava about half a mile to right of point where road meets crater bed. New Lake about twice the size of April, 1882. The change seems to be from caving away of the westerly bank, and towards Halemaumau. The island is all that remains of that bank. South Lake changed by caving away of banks with loss of the crest of high ridge to the northwest......Witnessed a break up of the surface which floated to the southeast corner and plunged in. Little Beggar and the flow thence to the northeast are wholly new; so is the break down in the surface between this and the south lake.

In October, 1885, Mokuaweoweo was again surveyed, this time by J. M. Alexander for the Government Survey, and a copy of his survey is given on the opposite page. It is interesting to compare the variations in these plans, which certainly were not wholly due to a changing crater. Alexander found the bottom of the crater covered with fresh lava, but no fires visible. Of the two cones shown on the plan the southwestern one was a hundred and forty feet high and still smoking: steam was rising from "hundreds of cracks." In the northern division of the crater was a circular pit crater a thousand feet in diameter and six hundred feet deep, still smoking from a small cone in its centre. At the junction of this northern division with the north terrace of the main crater an eruption had broken out, like that of 1832 in Kilauea, from the rim, and flowed into both compartments of the crater. In 1864, when on the highest part of the walls, I saw such an eruption that had fallen into the main crater from the rim. Many blocks of a "solid, flinty lava," weighing from fifty pounds to a ton, were noticed on the summit about the crater, sometimes a quarter of a mile from the edge of the crater. These were of the clinkstone used by the old Hawaiians for stone adzes and grindstones, and their position has not been satisfactorily explained. But the account by Mr. Alexander in the American Journal gives more completely his observations:

On the Summit Crater in October, 1885, and its Survey. By J. M. Alexander.
American Journal of Science, July, 1888. p. 35.

During the year 1885 I was engaged for many months in surveying lands on Mauna Hualalai and Mauna Loa in Hawaii, and in that way had an opportunity of making investigations of craters and lava-flows that have some interest connected with the study of volcanic phenomena.

On the first of September, 1885, I set out in company with Mr. J. S. Emerson, of the Hawaiian Government Survey, to ascend the mountain from the table land east of Hualalai, along the south

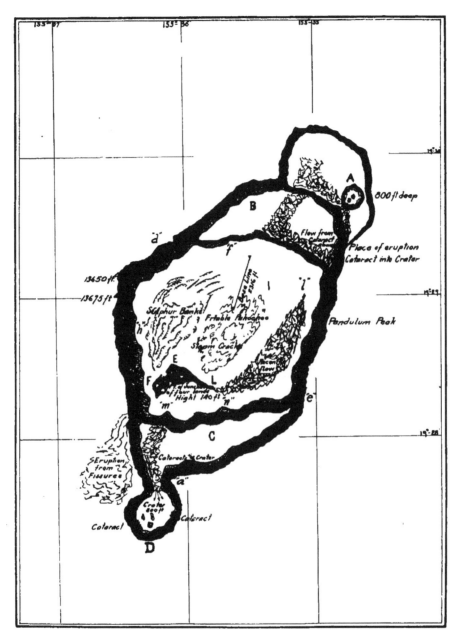

FIG. 94. GOVERNMENT SURVEY OF MOKUAWEOWEO.

side of the lava-flow of 1859. Our route led first through a narrow belt of forest, consisting of mamane, ohia and sandalwood trees; then through a scanty vegetation of ohelos, and the beautiful *Cyathodes Tameiameiæ*, and at last beyond the limits of vegetation, without a vestige of moss or lichen, over a waste of pahoehoe lava, traversed by tracts of aa and deep chasms.

At about two-thirds of the distance towards the summit we passed the rugged crater hill from which the outbreak of 1859 had issued, and here our path was strewed with pumice and "Pele's hair" from that eruption. An enormous quantity of lava was poured forth from the small fissure of this crater, forming a stream from half a mile to two miles wide, and reaching nearly thirty miles to the ocean at Kiholo. Lower down I counted eighteen species of ferns and a dozen kinds of phænogamous plants already growing on this flow.

Reaching the brink of this vast crater, we found that along it were numerous deep fissures filled with ice and water, making ready for avalanches into the crater. Here, and for a quarter of a mile below, we observed many rocks of different kind from the surface lavas, solid, flinty fragments of apparently the foundation walls, weighing from fifty pounds to a ton, which had formerly been hurled out during eruptions. I noticed similar rocks around the summit craters of Hualalai.

At evening the fog lifted and gave us a glimpse into the craters. The central crater [see the plan] was surrounded by almost perpendicular walls, and had a pahoehoe floor streaked with gray sulphur cracks, from hundreds of which there issued columns of steam, and in the south end stood a still smoking cone. South of this central crater there was a high plateau (c), and beyond this high plateau, still farther south, an opening into another crater small and deep (d). In the opposite direction, north of the central crater, appeared another higher crater, like an upper plateau (b) from which a torrent of lava had once poured into the central crater, and north of this again, another crater (a) like a still higher plateau, from which also lava had flowed southward.

Thus it was evident, as appeared more clearly by subsequent investigation, that Mokuaweoweo is not simply one crater, but a series of four or five craters, the walls of which have broken down, so that they have flowed into each other.

We erected a survey signal for determining the location and height of the summit, and also of an important land boundary in the crater, viz: the corner where the four lands of Keauhou, Kahuku, Kapapala and Kaohe met, which is at the cone in the central crater.

During the next month I ascended the mountain again, this time carrying an excellent engineer's transit. In the clear frosty air of the summit station I was able to take the bearings of a dozen survey signals on the slopes and summit of Hualalai. The new spherical signal which I had erected was afterwards accurately determined by observations from more than twenty stations on Mauna Kea, Hualalai and in South Kona, and thus a trigonometrical station was at last located on the very summit of Mauna Loa.

On the second day I descended into the central crater, and found much of the bottom to consist of the most solid kind of pahoehoe; but in some large tracts the pahoehoe was covered with pumice, indicating the violence of the former surging and tossing of the lava. Just before reaching the cone we came to a deeper basin (e) twenty or more feet below the rest of the crater bottom and about 400 feet wide, covered with the most friable lava, swollen upward as if raised by air bubbles, and this basin extended into a lava flow (ll) northeastward along the side of the crater. Probably this was the place of the last eruption and of most of the eruptions of this central crater.[115] The cone, 140 feet high, was composed of pumice and friable lava still hot and smoking. We ascended it and set up a flag there for the boundary corner.

I returned to the second plateau to the north (b), and thence clambered out to the east of Mokuaweoweo by the route of a former cataract of lava from the summit into the crater, the black, shining spray of which lay spattered on the surrounding rocks. Farther south there were the courses

---

[115] Mr. Alexander seems to have put too much faith in the permanent character of this cone as a boundary of lands or a source of eruptions. In 1870 it did not exist, and has been succeeded by others, as will be seen later.

of two other cataracts, which had poured directly into the central crater. At the summit I found the deep fissure from which these cataracts had been supplied with lava, and ascertained that it had also poured an immense stream north upon the first plateau and thence into the central crater. Crossing from this place to the north over the first plateau I suddenly came to a circular crater in the bed of the plateau (A), apparently 600 feet deep and a thousand feet wide, with a cone in its centre still smoking. The next day we took the transit to the stations in the crater, and the following surveyed along the western brink to the extreme south end where we looked into the south crater (D), which is about 800 feet deep and 2,500 feet wide. The length of the whole chasm I ascertained to be about 19,000 feet, the greatest breadth 9,000 feet, and the greatest depth 800 feet, and the area three and six-tenths square miles.

On the southwest side, near the junction of the central crater with the south plateau (C), I found that there had been another eruption from fissures that were still smoking, and that this eruption had sent an immense stream southward toward Kahuku, and had also poured cataracts into the south crater from all sides.

I had everywhere observed that there had been great flows from the summit brink down the mountain, and questioned whether the chasm had filled up and overflowed its brim. This, however, turned out to be an incorrect view. The flows have not been from the lowest parts of the brim, but from some of the highest, which could not have been the case in an overflow. The walls of the craters largely consist of loose, old weather-beaten rocks, and large tracts of the plateau are composed of old pahoehoe, that has not been overflowed for ages, which would not be the case if the craters had filled and overflowed.

These outbreaks from fissures around the rim indicate that the lava has rather poured *into* the crater than *out of it;* and that it has flowed from such fissures in vast streams down the mountain side. The question arises, how has the lava risen high enough to pour in extensive eruptions through these fissures, almost a thousand feet above the bottom of the crater, without rising in the crater and overflowing it? The same question has often been asked in respect to the rise of liquid lava to the summit of Mauna Loa without overflowing the open crater of Kilauea, 10,000 feet below.

While surveying the region, I was extremely interested in the arrangement of the craters; and now, having determined the situation of more than fifty of them on Mauna Loa, Hualalai and Mauna Kea, I have ascertained that there is a method in their arrangement. They are not arranged relatively to the mountain on which they are situated, but relatively to the points of the compass. There seems to have been a series of nearly parallel fissures through which these craters have risen in lines running from S. 40° E. to S. 60° E. There are a few arranged in lines running N. 50° E.

It has been remarked by Mr. W. T. Brigham, in his memoir of 1868 on the volcanoes of the Hawaiian Islands, that while the general trend of the Hawaiian group and of the major axis of each island is N. 60° W., there is no crater on the islands whose major axis is parallel to this line. "On the contrary," he continues, "a very interesting parallelism is observed among all the craters, and invariably the longest diameter is north and south." It would be more correct to say that the major axes of the great craters are usually at right angles to the general axes of the group, *i. e.,* about N. 30° E. Haleakala and the ancient Kipahulu crater appear to take the other direction, but the statement is certainly true of the great craters of Kilauea and Mokuaweoweo, which have other points of resemblance. Thus in both the highest walls are on the western side, and in both the action is working toward the southwest, as is indicated by the fact that the northeast craters are nearly filled up, while the deepest and most active craters are in the southwest end of the depression.

To return to Kilauea. There had been little change since 1882; the islands noticed soon after the formation of the New Lake, in 1881, proved to be floating islands (see Plate LXII). On the sixth of March both Halemaumau and its overflow, the New Lake, were running over and on about the same level.   On the morning of the seventh, between two and three o'clock, the lava of Halemaumau sank out of sight, taking with it the contents of the shallow New Lake.   The preceding activity

1886   seems to have extended northward, as the sulphur banks near the house had become much hotter, and the hotel bath house over one of the cracks was, on the afternoon of March 6th, too hot to be used.   At half-past nine of that evening there was a slight earthquake, and it was followed at an interval of fifteen minutes by three other shocks which made sounds "like the fall of a meal-bag on the floor."   During the night there were forty-one slight earthquakes counted at the hotel, but no damage was done, and they were not felt outside the crater region. It was thought at first that the fall of the walls of Halemaumau, that is, the cone surrounding it, had caused the vibration, but deep fissures were opened at the same time for a mile along the road to Hilo which certainly could not be attributed to this cause. A notable occurrence was the cessation of the discharge of steam from the cracks in the sulphur bank near the hotel two days after (not at the time of the fall of the lava and walls), but the steam gradually returned after two more days.   There is no report as to the temperature of the aqueous vapors at the time of return.   No outlet, or rather outflow, of the lava was noticed.   The main floating island was stranded in the shallow basin, and from photographs taken in 1887 it would seem to have been a portion of crust, but no sufficient examination was made.

Mr. J. S. Emerson, of the Government Survey, reached the crater on March 24th and remained until April 14th.   All this while, he says "no molten lava was anywhere visible in the entire crater.   At certain points of easy access a stick could be lighted by thrusting it down a crack so as to bring it in contact with the red-hot rocks beneath; but in general there was scarcely a place from which I was prevented access on account of the heat."   I quote from Dana the abstract of his report given on page 101:[116]

The total depth below the datum at the Volcano House to the bottom of the basin of Halema'auma'u was found to be nine hundred feet, and below the rim of the basin about five hundred and ninety feet.

On the twenty-ninth of March he descended into the pit: only Rev. E. P. Baker had preceded him.   The sides were covered, not by small fragments of lava, or gravel, or scoria, but by great irregular slabs of the smooth-surfaced lava (pahoehoe), six to eight or more feet long, five or six feet wide, and about a foot thick, and mostly so placed as to slope downward, though many were tilted in all directions; they looked as if ready to slip to the bottom.   But at a depth of about three hundred and twenty-five feet, or two hundred and seventy-five feet from the bottom, where the diameter was about six hundred feet, this rough flooring of pahoehoe slabs came abruptly to an end, and a nearly circular pit began, which had the form nearly of an inverted cone......The lower

---

[116] Characteristics of Volcanoes.   [540]

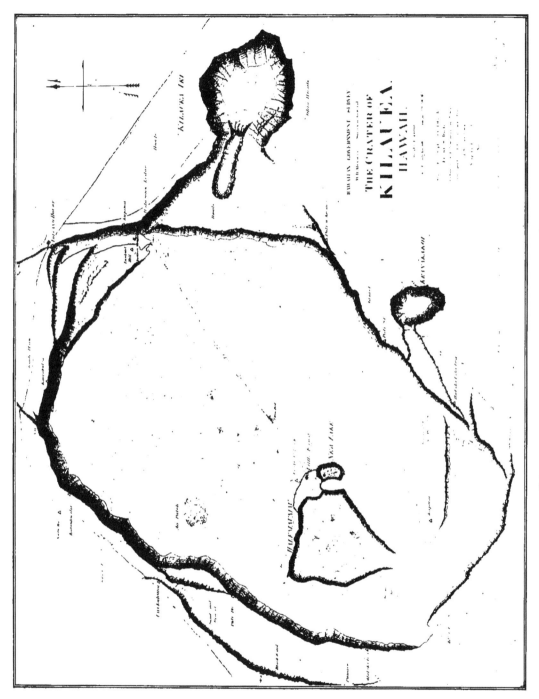

FIG. 95. HALEMAUMAU AFTER THE ERUPTION OF MARCH, 1886.

basin had an even, lustreless surface, free from large blocks and notable fissures, and consisted chiefly of coarse gravel or fragments of lava, but at bottom of smooth black pahoehoe, free from debris, and of somewhat triangular shape, with sides of twenty-five feet. From a small fissure issued a faintly bluish vapor.

In the upper part of the basin, on the northwest side, about three hundred and sixty-four feet above the bottom and two hundred and twenty-five feet below the top, there was a continuous jet of steam from an oval aperture of five to ten feet. This continued to increase, and on the twelfth of April deposits of sulphur were found about it.

Within the basins of New Lake and Little Beggar there were hillocks of smooth-fissured lava, without debris. The huge bulk of the "Floating Island"......on measurement proved to be sixty feet high and fully a hundred feet in length. The walls of the emptied basin of New Lake were for the most part nearly vertical, and were everywhere covered with a black, vitreous enamel [similar to that covering the interior of the tunnels in the flow of 1881, Little Beggar, etc.].

Professor L. L. Van Slyke of Oahu College was at the crater on July 19th, and found great change in Halemaumau. Not only had the lava returned, but the midst of the depression was occupied by a steep cone of loose blocks of lava rising about a hundred and forty feet high, and from four hundred to a thousand feet from the precipitous wall of the pit on the north side, and this cone was surrounded by a lake of lava covering some five acres. This must have been covered with hardened crust, for Professor Van Slyke ascended the cone and he says:

I came to the edge of a deep hole or well, of rather irregular outline, four-sided, perhaps thirty or forty feet wide, and from sixty to seventy-five feet long, and not less than a hundred feet deep. The mouth was surrounded by masses of loose rocks, rendering approach to the edge impossible or very dangerous, except at one point; from this point I could see the bottom of the well, and that it was covered with hardened fresh pahoehoe. At one side the liquid lava could be seen as it was puffed out of a small hole every few seconds and thrown up a few feet. The puffing noise accompanying the ejection of the lava was quite like that of a railway locomotive, though louder. The aperture through which the lava was thrown out might have been three feet long and two feet wide. Immediately below the point where I was standing there seemed to be a constant and tremendous commotion, attended by a peculiar swashing noise, but I could not lean sufficiently far over with safety to see anything. Fumes of sulphur dioxide were coming up in abundance, but being on the windward side I was not greatly annoyed by them.

He again went up the cone, but now from the southeastern side: he continues:

This led to a second well or deep hole, where molten lava was visible. This well was nearly round, with a diameter of perhaps twenty or thirty feet, and a depth of about a hundred feet. At one point the edge could be safely approached; but as it was on the leeward side the fumes of sulphur dioxide could be endured only for a few seconds at a time. Like the other well, the sides were perpendicular. At the bottom was a cone having an opening at the top perhaps ten feet across; and inside liquid lava was boiling with intense violence, every few seconds throwing up a jet of lava, the spray of which came to the mouth of the well almost into my face. The drops of lava thrown to the mouth of the well had cooled enough to become hardened and black when they reached the level on which I was standing. This place was quite noisy, the noise resembling that of violently swashing waters.   [542]

Mauna Loa in Eruption.—As in the eruption of 1867 this eruption, coming twenty years later, was ushered in with seismic disturbances. It was not the usual "beacon light" on the summit that was the sole precursor of the outpouring of lava. All through the previous December earthquakes had shaken all the southwestern portion of Hawaii without doing any damage of importance. They, however, **1887** constantly increased in frequency and force and averaged three a day by the twelfth of January. At Kahuku Mr. George Jones counted three hundred and fourteen shocks between 2:12 A.M. of January 17th and 4 A.M. of the 18th; sixty-

FIG. 96. SOURCE OF THE ERUPTION OF 1887. FURNEAUX.

seven between that time and midnight, and three the following day, or three hundred and eighty-three in all. In Hilea, ten miles west of Kahuku, Mr. Charles N. Spencer reported six hundred and eighteen shocks between 2 A.M. of the 16th and 7 A.M. of the 18th.

With this great number of earthquakes, lava at last broke out on the summit of Mauna Loa, three or four miles northeast from Mokuaweoweo, near the lateral cone Pohaku o Hanalei (see note on p. 143), on the night of the 16th, but this discharge ceased after a few hours. It is noteworthy that this outbreak was on the side of the great summit crater most distant from the region of seismic disturbance and where the eruption finally broke out. [543]

FIG. 97. COURSE OF THE FLOW OF 1887. FURNEAUX.

FIG. 98. WHERE THE FLOW OF 1887 ENTERED THE SEA. FURNEAUX.

There is some contradiction as to the exact time that the lava came to the surface in Kau from a fissure about six thousand five hundred feet above the sea, but it was observed early in the morning of the 18th. Mr. Spencer, who visited the most active source on the 20th, says that there were fifteen fountains of molten lava, the highest estimated at two hundred feet. Rocks weighing tons were thrown up or borne along the stream, and while the flow was slow the first twenty-four hours, the formation being mostly aa and clinkers, and explosions occurred at intervals sending up columns of smoke five hundred feet high. Fortunately Mr. Furneaux was on hand and painted the scene from which the illustration is made. Many photographs were taken, two of which are given by Dana, but they fail to give an impression of the outflow at all satisfactory. They might represent a dead lava bed as well. I feel that the three views made by Furneaux show more completely than any pictures I have seen, the beginning, course and end of an Hawaiian lava flow: even without the color, as we have them here, they show better the sublimity of the scene. While the rate of progress at first was only a mile and a half an hour, when the lava moved as pahoehoe its course was rapid, and on the 29th it reached the sea, after a course of twenty miles, nearly four miles west of the flow of 1868, adding another very disagreeable interruption to the many that cross the government road west of the south cape Ka Lae.

Mr. Furneaux again caught the stream as it flowed rapidly between the walls it made for itself where the slope was considerable and the ground fairly clear. The beauty of the green herbage in the foreground contrasting with the black walls within which this Phlegethon rushed with almost the liquidity of water, canopied by the murky pall above, removes the terror a volcanic eruption awakes in many minds when impressions are caught from those spasmodic outbursts in thickly peopled lands where the loss of life and property adds horror to the thought. Here little damage was done, the beauty and variety of the display will never be forgotten by those fortunate enough to see the flow of 1887.

By noon of the 24th the flow had nearly stopped, after extending the shores from three to five hundred feet, according to Dr. S. E. Bishop, who was in this region on the second of February. As the shore was not abrupt the flow built up no mounds of black sand or ash, and the scene as viewed from a steamer off shore was simply a clear struggle between fire and water for possession of the shore line.

Earthquakes were renewed on the 23rd, the day before the flow ceased, and continued on the 24th. These threw down walls that had a northeast and southwest direction—the walls falling to the southeast—and moved light wooden houses eight or ten inches on a slope in the same direction. Slight damage was done in Kahuku, and even in Hilo, where there was a heavy shock felt near noon on the 23rd. The oscillations are reported as from south-southeast to north-northwest. A heavy cloud of smoke was resting on Mauna Loa all Sunday and Monday, January 23rd and 24th, and on the 25th the sun was almost obscured by the smoky atmosphere; on the afternoon of that day a heavy storm of thunder and rain set in. On February 20th Judge D. H. Hitchcock was on the summit and found the crater quiet, but vapors arising from large fissures.[117] According to Rev. E. P. Baker,[118] the fissure about four hundred feet above the point of outflow was still giving out vapors in July, 1888. No deep crater marked the place of discharge.

February 1, 1887. Rev. Sereno E. Bishop, D.D., in describing (Hawaiian Gazette) the lava ridges left when the flow had nearly ceased, says: "The whole seemed like a colossal embankment, as if ten thousand cyclopean trains of mastodon cars had been dumping the rocks of Mauna Loa for a century towards the sea."

December 29, 1887. Mr. J. S. Emerson writes from Kohala, Hawaii, that the view from that place indicates activity in Mokuaweoweo. "Volumes of smoke and steam have been pouring out of the summit crater, but no glow or reflection of fire has been observed......The summit is heavily coated with snow." On March 29, 1888, signs of activity had disappeared. To return to Kilauea:

August 18, 1887. S. D. Fuller.—"A whitish flame visible about edge at five different points." On the 22nd he adds: "Since my last visit the lake had overflowed a space 250×300 feet. Lava in lake had fallen about six feet. Great activity at two points. A bluish flame observed at four points, two being in middle of lake for a short time. A river of lava flowed into the lake from under high central cone."

January 11, 1888. Rev. E. P. Baker.—"Dana Lake quite active." Fell several feet in a short time.

April 8, 1888. Dr. C. H. Wetmore.—"A beautiful fiery fountain."

July, 1888. W. C. Merritt.—From an abstract of the letter of Mr. Merritt, then President of Oahu College, to Prof. Dana[119] (the original not having been published) we find that Mr. Merritt reached the summit of Mauna Loa at noon of the eighteenth of last July, and encamped near the southeast angle of the crater. The spot was considerably lower than the highest point on the west side of the crater, and probably about 13,400 feet above tide-level. Water boiled at 185° F. between 7 and 8 in the morning, when the temperature was at 56° F. The thermometer was at 62° F. at noon, 40° F. at 7 P.M., 30° F. at 11 P.M., and 26° F. at daybreak, so that during the night water froze in a large crack, ten feet below the surface. About half a mile south by

[117] American Journal of Science, 1887, xxxiii, 310.   [119] Ibid, 1889, xxxvii, 51.
[118] Ibid, 1889, xxxvii, 53.

west from the southern end of the crater of Mokuaweoweo there was a small but deep pit-crater. Having descended the east wall of the central pit of Mokuaweoweo to its bottom, a small cinder cone was found not far from the eastern wall; and just southwest, a pumice [limu] cone in the midst of an aa flow, the summit of which was very hot and reddish from the action of vapors. In the southwest corner of the pit, there was a cone at F [see map on p. 159], from which vapors were escaping, and south of it, at *m*, a circular pit between 300 and 400 feet in diameter, by estimate, and 150 to 175 feet deep. The walls of the pit consisted of the edges of layers of basaltic rock, one of which was 40 to 50 feet thick, and vertically columnar in structure. The floor of the central pit had, as a whole, a slope from the southwest to the northeast, confirming the view that the southwest part of the pit had been the seat of greatest activity, as it is in Kilauea. Southwest of *m*, the outer wall of the central pit was cut through from top to bottom by two parallel fissures, which had a S.S.W. direction, and thence pointed nearly toward the place of chief eruption of 1887. East of *m* and near the wall in the direction of L, there were great numbers of small fumaroles, from which sulphur vapors were escaping freely, and large deposits of sulphur had been made about them. Near *h* two dikes, 2 to 2½ feet thick, intersected the walls, crossing one another at a small angle, the rock of which had a feldspathic aspect.

From a rough measurement, the depth of the crater on the east side was made not over 350 feet. If this small depth is sustained by careful observations, a great change of level had taken place since the survey of Mr. Alexander in 1885. Such a change might have been among the effects of the eruption of February, 1887.

President Merritt also visited Kilauea on July 14th. His letter speaks of the walls of "Halema'uma'u" as, in part, wholly obliterated, as represented by Mr. Dodge: it was fifteen to twenty feet high in some places. The nearly circular lake on the west side of the cone [see plan on p. 170], which he calls "Dana Lake", was in ebullition, but not more active than in August, 1887. The enclosing walls of this small lake were ten to fifteen feet high above the liquid lava within, and fifteen to twenty feet above the floor outside.

Mr. Merritt accompanied the Rev. E. P. Baker, whose notes are of value from his frequent visits to these scenes; they are published in the Journal containing the preceding account; from that source we gather the following: "A descent was made into the southern crater of Mokuaweoweo—probably the first ever made—and the depth found to be seventy-five feet greater than that of the central crater. A fresh-looking lava stream descended into it down the northern wall, which may have been made in 1887."   [547]

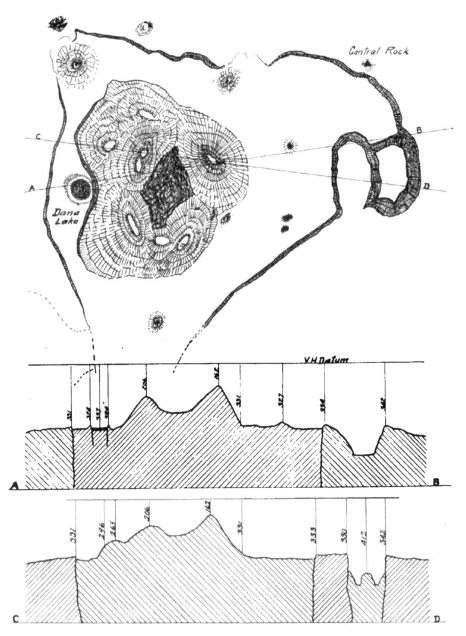

Central Rock

Dana Lake

V.H Datum

FIG. 99. HALEMAUMAU. SURVEY OF JULY, 1888.

Mr. Baker, speaking of the source of the lava streams of the great eruption of 1880–1881, states that:

The two streams from the source, the Kau or southern, and the Hilo or eastern, originated together at the extremity of a long fissure. This fissure follows the course of a "divide," so that a small obstacle was sufficient to turn the flow to one side or the other. The outflow took place on this divide; a northern stream flowed first, then the Kau stream, and then the Hilo. The fissure ran by the north side of Red Hill, a cone with a deep crater which is still giving out vapors, and this hill was apparently the occasion of the turn off southward of the Kau stream, it standing at the point of their divergence.[120] Water boiled near this hill at 196° F. This Kau stream is in general aa, but near the source it is pahoehoe. At the upper extremity of the fissure there is a pit crater, Pukauahi, which is described as the source of the lavas and is still smoking. At this place also water boiled at 196° F.

On the route from Ainapo to the source of the outflow of 1852, the lavas of the 1852 stream, where they were first reached, were of the aa kind; but after a while there was a change to pahoehoe, and soon after this the source was reached—a red cone in the midst of an extensive bed of pumice. Long ditches or trenches occur in the surface of the region which were evidently the beds of lava streams, their sides having been the banks.[121] The flow appears to have had a single outlet. Water boiled at the source at 200° F.

Going from Ainapo to the source of the eruption of 1887, in Kahuku, about 6000 feet above the sea-level, Mr. Baker passed through regions of woods and grass and saw seven running streams and three or four ponds of water. There had been heavy rains. No deep crater marked the place of discharge.

Over the wide region between Mt. Loa and Mt. Hualalai it is hard to tell where the slope of one ends and that of the other begins. [I have already made the same statement regarding the appearance from the other side.] The 1859 flow of Mt. Loa as it came down heading northwestward, turned just enough northward to fetch by the northeastern flank of Hualalai.

The *Kau Desert*, lying to the south and southwest of Kilauea, has a surface of whitish or light colored sand with areas of pahoehoe lava, which is decomposing in places into a reddish soil. It is about eight miles by six in area. It is destitute of vegetation and owes its dryness to its being under the lee of Kilauea.

To return to the Volcano House record:

August 20, 1888. Earthquake at 7:30 A.M.

November 8, 1888. Earthquake at 5:50 P.M. Quite a sharp shock felt all over Hawaii and to Honolulu, according to Mr. H. M. Whitney.

December 1, 1888. H. M. Whitney.—Found Dana Lake and Little Elephant cone which is three hundred yards north of the lake, very active. The South Lake has disappeared altogether, the crater is filled up with rocks and no signs of a pit or of fire remain in it. A flow of aa ran for four days in Kilauea, according to L. A. Thurston.

December 22, 1888. L. A. Thurston.—There are now two sluggish pahoehoe flows running across the path to the Elephant; and on the south and west there are several flows still very hot. There are about a dozen blow-holes in action besides the lake. There is very intense action in the lake, the surface of which is twenty-five to thirty feet above the general surface of the crater south of it, with a confining wall built by itself of only about five feet in thickness at the level of the liquid lava on the southwest side; and a thickness of not more than ten feet at a point ten feet below

---

[120] It seems rather to have been formed by the flow.

[121] See Furneaux' painting of the eruption of 1887, Fig. 97.

FIG. 100. SPATTER CONE IN KILAUEA, 1889.

FIG. 101. LAVA FALL IN DEPRESSION NORTH OF HALEMAUMAU.

FIG. 102. DEBRIS AND TALUS UNDER EAST WALL OF KILAUEA.

FIG. 103. PILE OF CRUSTS NORTH OF HALEMAUMAU, 1890.

the surface. The surface of the lava rose and fell several times a distance of three to four feet. The Pele's hair on the cliffs and adjacent flat south of the lake is about four inches deep, forming a perfect carpet which entirely conceals the rocks.

March 18, 1889. J. Austin.—Saw "Little Elephant" boiling, and "Dana Lake" spouting in fountains.

January 2, 1890. Rev. E. P. Baker.—The volcano is much as it has been since about the 4th November, '89, when a huge crack was formed in the floor of the crater (northwest-southeast)...The formation of this crack was accompanied with a slight sinking of a portion of the central area near the lake.

January 28, 1890. A c l a n d .Wansey and W. T. Brigham were at the crater p h o t o g r a p h i n g and taking notes.

July 18, 1890. Acland Wansey, W. B. Clark and W. T. Brigham were again at the crater, and many of the illustrations of this paper were then made. Of this party Mr. Clark joined a party for the ascent of Mauna Loa, an expedition which Mr. L. A. Thurston thus describes in the register:

Memo of an ascent of Mauna Loa by W. B. C l a r k, of Boston, Julian Monsarrat, W. Gates and L. A. Thurston, under the guidance of Kanae of Ainapo. The time which was occupied in proceeding from one point to another is given for the in-formation of those who may desire

FIG. 104. CRACK IN BED OF KILAUEA.

to ascend the mountain hereafter as a basis of estimate. Left Kapapala ranch at 5:45 A.M., July 26; arrived at Ainapo 8:30; left at 9 A.M.; arrived at upper water-hole 11 A.M.; at Camp Kakina, at the upper edge of vegetation, 1:30 P.M. Temperature at this camp, where the night was spent, was as follows, in the shade:

1:30 P.M., 58° F.	6:46 P.M., 48° F.
5: P.M., 54°	6:56 P.M., 47°
6:15 P.M., 52°	7:25 P.M., 46° Ditto up to 10 P.M.
6:40 P.M., 49°	4:30 A.M., 43°

July 27 left camp at 6:30 A.M. and arrived at the crater at 11:30. Temperature at noon in the shade, 49°; in the sun, 54°; at 5 A.M. on the 28th, 24° out of doors and 28° in the tent. The entire party, except Mr. Clark, were affected with mountain sickness. Descent into the crater was made by Mr. Clark and myself at the highest point of the cliff on this side, near the old Wilkes camp, where there is a breakdown and a debris pile.

[552]

There was very good walking on the floor of the crater, the pahoehoe being unusually smooth. There was evidence of recent eruption from a blow-hole about the centre of the crater which was still uncomfortably warm. The eruption was mostly of a dark pumice stone and a very thin black pahoehoe.

There was steam and some smoke from a spot several hundred yards out into the crater from the western bank. At the southwestern corner of the crater a dense column of steam was rising which did not become dissipated for several hundred feet above the rim of the crater. The spot from which the steam issued was covered with very bright yellow sulphur extending nearly all the way up the crater, and about two hundred feet wide. Immediately at the base of this sulphur bank there was a break down in the floor of the crater some one hundred feet deep and several hundred feet across.

FIG. 105. THE FLOOR OF KILAUEA, 1890.

To return to Kilauea.

September 11, 1890. E. O. White.—We found two blowholes about six hundred feet apart, and a flow from each of them had covered several hundred square feet. The one furtherest to the south looks as if it would soon form a lake about the size of Dana Lake. We next went to Dana Lake and found it quite dead except for a little steam and smoke; walked well on to the lake but found it very hot toward the middle and could see fire in many cracks.

October 11, 1890. S. S. Peck and others.—Dana Lake was boiling violently and throwing up spouts and bombs of fire [see Pl. LX].

December 18, 1890. A. Gartenberg. (As seen from the Volcano House) 10 P.M.: a long ridge of fire is flowing from Dana Lake [?]. The new lake is spouting magnificently. 11 P.M.: There are now two fountains spouting alternately in front of Halemaumau. The new lake is in a great state of ebullition, several fountains can be seen playing high above the horizon.

January 2, 1891. L. A. Thurston.—Dana Lake and the new lake are in a continuous boiling condition throwing up lava from forty to sixty feet. Dana Lake has built up a wall around itself of from six to ten feet high, and the surface of the liquid lava is about ten feet above the surrounding country. I paced Dana Lake off along the base of the wall, making it eighty paces long. It is about one-half as wide. There are nine active blowholes within a radius of twelve hundred feet, this side of Dana about a quarter of a mile. [The debris cone of Halemaumau is a circular crater with a level fresh lava floor about a hundred yards across.]

[553]

February 23-25, 1891. G. Creswell Delamain and W. T. Brigham.—Brunner, by levels from Hilo, found the elevation of the Hotel verandah 3971.64.

March 6, 1891. J. H. Maby of the Volcano House.—At 9:30 P.M. one slight earthquake. At the time of shaking the cones of Halemaumau settled down. From February 10th to March 6th all the fires in the crater were very active and flows of lava were plainly seen over the floor of the crater from the house. At 9:10 P.M. on the 7th a slight shake was felt at the house. On the morning of the 8th on looking over the crater we saw that the cones of Halemaumau, the Dana Lake and Maby Lake had sunk out of sight. The cones of Halemaumau loomed up above the bed of the

FIG. 106. REGION ABOUT HALEMAUMAU IN 1890.

crater some two hundred or more feet before the earthquake of March 6th. Five years to a day since the last drop out in 1886.

March 15, 1891. W. W. Brunner.—Survey of Volcano road [from Hilo] finished. No fire in the crater.

March 18, 1891. Rev. E. P. Baker.—Went round the Halemaumau chasm; the brink is a sheer precipice, but the descent becomes tunnel-shaped a third or half the way down. It is smoking at the bottom.

April 3, 1891. Having seen the cone in the midst of the Halemaumau region a short time before its disappearance, I went to Kilauea hoping the empty pit might give some clue to the how or where of the vanished mass. It was no light bit of crust, that could be melted by the molten lava in a few moments, but a hill of crust, spatters and hardened lava of various form towering at least two hundred feet above the brink of the lake of molten lava which it nearly filled with its mass two thousand feet in diameter at the visible base. This had either stood or been constantly or intermittently rising with its base certainly in contact with the molten lava apparently in its hottest condition, and it had not melted, but, as it seems, had grown in size. I have been on similar cones, as well as this and found the material much like the crust of the crater floor, but here and there perforated with tunnels of irregular form and various size. From the orifices thus formed came at all times hot vapor and often molten lava, even at an elevation of half the height of the cone. It was unpleasant exploration,

FIG. 107. HALEMAUMAU AFTER THE DOWNFALL. NOTE THE WONDERFUL NATURAL ARCH IN FOREGROUND.

for the stifling sulphurous vapors had to be avoided as much as possible by keeping on the windward side, and the things I wanted to examine were often on the lee side. The foothold was of course insecure, but custom makes that tolerably easy to manage, and the heat was generally not unbearable. My examination convinced me that the substance of the cones was the crust of the lake from which the cone rose. It was the most refractory portion of the lava, and just here I must call attention to the need of a laboratory right on the spot to determine the relative fusibility of the lavas found in Kilauea; we know little enough of this problem, and more knowledge in this line would not only explain beyond cavil the aa formation, but why these layers of cooled crust should rise to such heights and not be melted again at the base.

The floating islands often seen on the Kilauea pools (see Pl. LXII) are, in my belief, the incipient central cones; their structure is identical, and so far as can be learned, without following the process through long months on the spot, the formative process is identical also. Is it necessary to imagine some mysterious "accensive force" pushing the crust up from below? Until we know the relative specific gravity of the cooled and hardened cellular crust and that of the compact molten mass of the lake beneath we cannot answer. It is hard, often very hard, for a scientific student to admit that he does not *know*, for his conscience tells him that he has not yet exhausted all the means at his disposal to complete the analysis, but surely, if anywhere, here in this mighty laboratory where God seems to be showing us His most wonderful ways, man must confess without shame to his own ignorance and failure to comprehend. He can well give up the attempt to conceal his ignorance in obscure phrases and pompous names. Giving a thing or a force a name does not explain what it is. This does not mean that we are to quit trying to learn, in our despair at our present failure. I have believed, and the belief is greatly strengthened at each succeeding visit to this volcano, that here is the place for a scientific exploration of world-making ways, far more important than the belated explorations of the life of the Pacific Islanders, either animal or vegetable, that nine scientific expeditions are now conducting from a European base.

I had seen the little mountain of lava that might have extended its edges until the lake was sealed, a condition that might have been followed by another explosive eruption like that of 1789. That would have been a simple result that could have been easily understood, for the remains of the mountain would have been scattered with noise and commotion about the neighborhood. Nothing of the kind was here; only a clean hole half a mile across and five hundred feet deep left on the site of a hill two hundred feet high surrounded by a lake of molten lava. The hill had gone almost without notice, only a slight jar—called by Mr. Maby, who, from his residence on the brink of Kilauea, was familiar with such things, a slight earthquake.

The pit was as Mr. Baker describes it in shape, but there was no smoke; clear hot air was rising from the bottom, but no part was obscured, only the shimmer showed the presence of air above the normal temperature. In one small place not far below the top, a little steam, not more than from one of the cracks near the Volcano House, was visible. I looked for caves, tunnels, some sort or other of subterranean machinery, but there was nothing but a clean hole closed at the bottom and without any suggestion that it led anywhere. As I sat on the brink I noticed what must have escaped Mr. Baker, the still red-hot lava in patches doubtless the overflows left when the rest of the lava descended. The color of the interior seemed strange, for there was not a sign of

black lava of which the cone had been composed, but all was a light reddish gray.
The funnel-like portion was composed of angular fragments of the same color, lying
apparently at the steepest angle they could hold. There was great uniformity of size
in these fragments, and the pile was absolutely clean from dust or gravel. When a
portion of the wall of this empty pit falls in, a black cloud of dust rises like smoke for
some time, as the fragments are ground by mutual attrition. I have noticed this, when

FIG. 108. CRACKS ON THE NORTHWEST BRINK OF HALEMAUMAU, 1891.

at table in the hotel dining room the southerly wind has brought the black sand into
the windows and made our food gritty so as to compel the closing of the windows for
some time. Nothing of this kind was here. The cone disappeared during a night,
and its mass was vastly greater than any fall of portions of the walls ever has been
known. I looked about the crater for signs of this dust but found none. Can we
believe the cone melted and ran out of the comparatively small hole at the bottom
when it had for many months resisted the melting moods of the lake around it? The
only indication that the lava was hotter than usual was this: as I left the Volcano just
before the downfall, I was mounting my horse at eight o'clock in the morning and
noticed a spatter cone on the edge of the lake so brilliant that it looked like an arc

electric lamp in the full sunlight, a phenomenon I had never observed before; the brightest lavas look dull red by daylight.

It is hard to believe that the great cone dropped like a plummet into the lava sea below; it is almost as hard to think of its being ground up in this mill, and the only other way out of the difficulty, or the pit, is to melt the whole down as in a vast electric furnace. The tempter Radium stands by with suggestions for many a theory, but when our greatest chemists and physicists know so little of the part this powerful

FIG. 109. NEW PORTION OF VOLCANO HOUSE.

substance plays in terrestrial dynamics, we may well resist the temptation, although we know that radium abounds more in the Earth's crust than was at first supposed, and it has already been found in many lavas, and in the mineral springs of volcanic regions.

Another thought came to me as I looked upon that great pit. There are at times many lakes of molten lava scattered over the bed of the main crater at Kilauea, but although while active, they spout lava fountains and show the ebullition of Halemaumau, when they go out of commission they leave no pit like this. Not one of them has done so. There is only a shallow depression with a floor as solid as any other part of Kilauea's bottom. We walk over these and, unless their history is known to us, might class them with the other subsidence phenomena which have at times involved, more than half of the crater area. In all these cases, Dana Lake, the New Lakes, etc., Halemaumau seems to be not only the source but also the sinkhole.

The lava in these side pockets, shallow as they are, seldom exceeding fifty feet in depth, contains within itself all the forces needed to throw up fountains, open cracks, remelt crust, etc., that the main Halemaumau possesses. These surface pools ·act as relieving reservoirs, and suggest that there must be others beneath the crust to account for the sudden changes in level in the main lake observed by so many visitors. A fall of four feet in a pool a thousand feet in diameter means the transfer of a very large amount

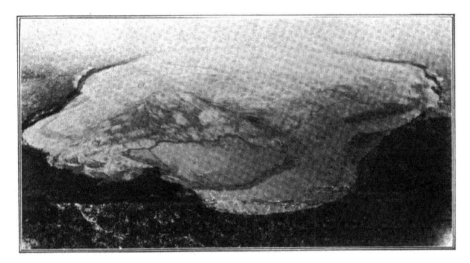

FIG. 110. HALEMAUMAU IN OCTOBER, 1891.

of matter and the exertion of a corresponding force. I have seen such a fall take place within three minutes time, and there was no sensible change in sound or motion, so far as the banks were concerned; the return in the case noted was slower, but it has been observed by others to come back as quickly as it went, indicating that the relieving reservoirs were not far away. From this excursus we must now return to the record.

April 10, 1891. H. M. Whitney.—About 11 P.M. this day the fire returned in the sunken pit of Halemaumau after having been extinguished thirty-five days. When first inspected on the 11th April the fire was very small, occupying or puffing out of a small hole at the bottom not more than four or five feet in diameter.

May 19, 1891. W. R. Castle.—The pit is now 2000–2500 feet long and nearly as wide, greater axis N.E.-S.W. The inverted apex has now filled up with fresh lava to a depth in the centre of about 75 to 100 feet. [Reports intermittent explosions at intervals of five or ten minutes.]

June 29, 1891. Work completed on the new house. [See Fig. 109 on opposite page.]

August 8, 1891. Telephone line from Hilo completed.

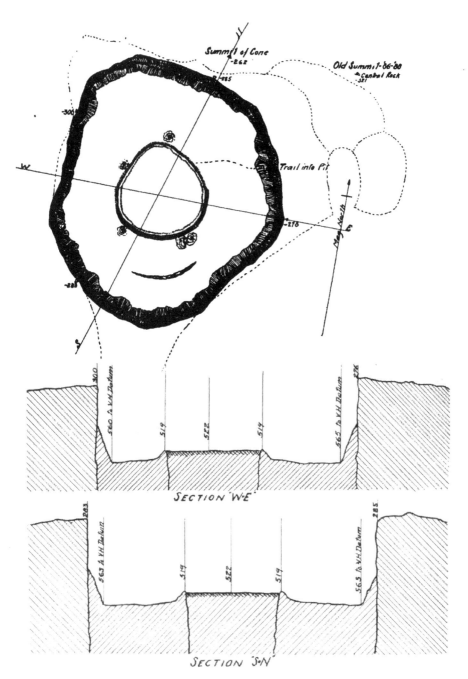

FIG. 111. DODGE'S SURVEY OF HALEMAUMAU, AUGUST, 1892.

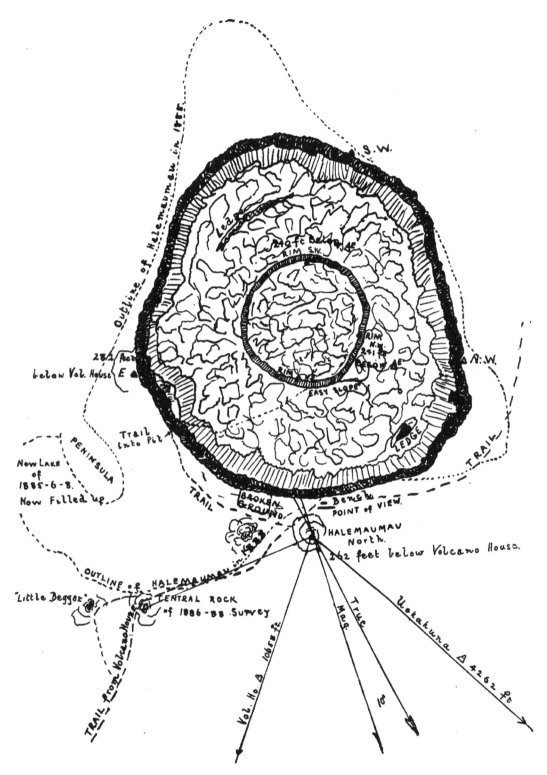

FIG. 112. DODGE'S SURVEY AS COPIED IN THE VOLCANO HOUSE REGISTER.

September 14, 1891. Rev. E. P. Baker.—The molten lava has greatly risen within four months. In May last the liquid fire was 400 or 500 feet below the surface: it is now about 200 feet below.

September 23, 1891. E. L. Baldwin.—Lava about two hundred and fifty feet below floor of crater; lake very active.

October 3, 1891. W. T. Brigham (seventeenth visit).—The lava surface presented the usual appearance when not very active. A few cones lazily discharging small amounts of lava, but not easy to watch so far below the projecting edge of the pit.

November 30, 1891. H. M. Whitney.—The crater floor has been upheaved, and present lake of Halemaumau formed......at least 1000 to 1200 feet across, in full action, throwing up immense jets of lava. [I do not fully understand what Mr. Whitney means by the upheaval of the crater floor. On the same day Dr. Adolph Marcuse, of Berlin, was at the crater and records the following elevations as observed by aneroid: Volcano House, o; lava floor, 480 feet; Half-way House, 420 feet; Little Beggar, 310; edge of Halemaumau, 260 feet.]

December 10, 1891. The surface of the molten lava sank about a hundred and fifty feet, remaining at that level for a month and then gradually rising.

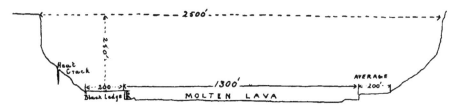

FIG. 113. SECTION OF HALEMAUMAU, 1892.

February 12, 1892. L. A. Thurston.—The lava is now within twenty-five feet of its former level. The entire surface is in a boiling condition, with bursts of spray averaging twenty-five feet, occasionally being thrown to a height of fifty feet. About half-way up the debris slope on the east side where the descent is made, heat comes up a crack.

April 11, 1892. Rev. S. E. Bishop.—In 1887 [July] an area somewhat larger than that of the smooth black floor in the sketch on the opposite page [Fig. 114], was occupied by an irregular mound of debris which had been pushed up by the hydrostatic lifting of the lava column below.[122] Around the base of this mound was a narrow surface of comparatively smooth lava about a hundred and fifty feet below the upper floor around Halemaumau. On this floor, between the mound and the narrow pile of talus on the west side, lay "Dana Lake," so named by our party, small, but in quite active ebullition. [See Pl. LX.] Another lake lay immediately south, apparently smaller, but impossible to properly inspect on account of smoke. In the collapse of March 5, 1891, the whole of the above features disappeared, leaving a pit say five hundred feet deep. The lava soon reappeared, having left its cumbersome and unsightly mound somewhere down below. For one year it has been gradually rising in extremely regular form. The degree of activity in ebullition seems about as great as in Dana Lake in 1887 relatively to the surface occupied......On the main floor of Kilauea extensive overflows have occurred.

July 11, 1892. A. B. Lyons.—Almost daily overflows have taken place. The pit at top is about 2400 feet across; at base of cliff it is about 1900 feet. Lava lake 900 to 950 feet in diameter; black ledge 300 to 500 feet wide.

---

[122] Dr. Bishop accompanied Prof. Dana at the time he here refers to, and has perhaps in mind the "accensive force" of that distinguished geologist.

December 1, 1892. Peter Lee.—The crater of Mokuaweoweo again active after a quiet rest of nearly six years, since February, 1887. The fire appeared last night between ten and eleven o'clock, quickly rising from the summit of Mauna Loa, without any earthquakes or previous signs of disturbance, and continued all night. This morning great columns of smoke are belching forth. [The fire only lasted three days.] The crater of Kilauea continues in its usual activity not seeming in the least affected by the eruption on Mauna Loa.

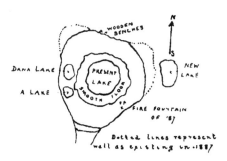

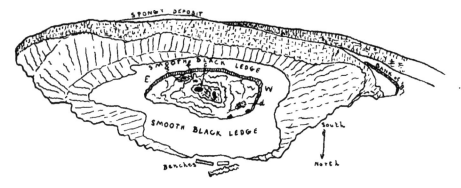

FIG. 114. SKETCH PLAN OF THE LAKES. BISHOP.

July 19, 1893. W. R. Castle.—The lake named "Thurston Lake" has built up for itself a wall about thirty feet high; an even slope gives it the appearance of a cone......It filled and overflowed Sunday the 9th, falling about fifteen feet. Every outburst of fountain or surface swelling is accompanied by volumes of sulphurous vapor. As it rises from the surface it is red-hot, almost at once turning blue.[123] It is far more pungent than the vapor from sulphur banks near house.

March 26, 1894. W. R. Castle.—March 21, in the afternoon, between half-past one and two......the entire surface of the lake appeared from the hotel to be in a condition of intense agitation, spouting and boiling with lava flowing over the side in several places. Suddenly on the north side

[123] *Was not the red color borrowed from the crack or surface?*

stones, lava and "dust" were thrown high into the air with spouting columns of fire, and in the space of less than four minutes the north bank of the lake was tilted up to the height of one hundred feet or more, leaving an abrupt wall over the lake with a steep and broken slope towards the north. A stream of lava has constantly emerged from the northeast slope ever since.

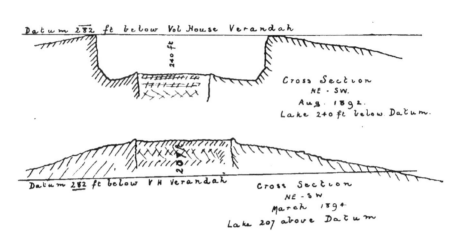

FIG. 115. COMPARATIVE SECTION.

We now come to a most interesting change in the condition of Halemaumau. Fortunately Mr. F. S. Dodge of the Government Survey had surveyed this part of Kilauea in August, 1892 (see plan), and we have also his valuable surveys and measurements during and after the changes we are about to describe. In addition to these we have the observations of L. A. Thurston, Esq., whose frequent visits to the **1894** crater have made him familiar with its physical changes, and from these and other sources we can collect the story scattered in various newspapers, magazines and Volcano House Record. In 1893 the pit had been gradually filling up, mainly by the overflow of its molten contents, which, now here and now there, poured over the circular dam or rim which had in this case been formed more extensively and regularly than usual; but in addition to this elevation by filling, there was evidently a rising of the region around the pit, until in July, 1894, the rim of the lake was but seventy-five feet below the Volcano House level, and the whole surface was visible from the house. This condition is well shown in Mr. Hitchcock's view (Pl. LXVI). In August, 1892, the rim of the pit was 282 feet below the Volcano House datum, and the surface of the lake 240 feet below that. In March, 1894, according to Mr. Dodge's measurements, the lake was 1,200 feet long and 800 feet wide and its surface had risen some 200 feet in nineteen months. In July Mr. Thurston and party saw the remarkable changes that he reports as follows:

Upon arriving at the volcano on July 5, 1894, the principal change since Mr. Dodge's visit was found to be the sudden rising of the north bank of the lake, covering an area of about 800 feet long by 400 wide, which, on the 21st of March last was suddenly and without warning elevated to a height of eighty feet above the other banks and the surface of the lake, the lake being then full. The raised area was much shattered. Two blowholes shortly afterwards made their appearance on the outer line of fracture. April 18th, the hill thus formed began to sink, and on July 5th, was only about thirty feet above the other walls of the lake. On the evening of July 6th, a party of tourists found the lake in a state of moderate activity, the surface of the lava being about twelve feet below the banks.

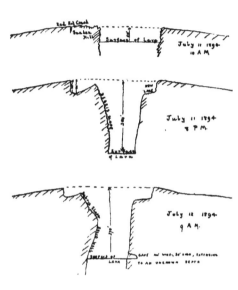

FIG. 116. SECTION OF HALEMAUMAU, JULY 11-12, 1894.

On Saturday, the 7th, the surface was raised so that the entire lake was visible from the Volcano House. That night it overflowed into the main crater, and a blow-hole was thrown up, some 200 yards outside and to the north of the lake, from which a flow issued. There were two other hot cones in the immediate vicinity which were thrown up about three weeks before. On Sunday, Monday and Tuesday following, the surface of the lake rose and fell several times, varying from full to the brim to fifteen feet below the edge of the banks.

On the morning of the 11th, the hill was found to have sunk down to the level of the other banks, and frequent columns of rising dust indicated that the banks were falling in. At 9:45 P.M., at which hour a party reached the lake, a red-hot crack from three to six feet wide was found surrounding the space recently occupied by the hill; the hill was nearly level; the lake had fallen some fifty feet, and the wall of the lake formed by the hill was falling in at intervals.

The lava in the lake continued to fall steadily, at the rate of about twenty feet an hour from ten o'clock in the morning until eight in the evening. At eleven A.M the area formerly occupied by the hill, began to sink bodily, leaving a clean line of fracture; the line of this area was continually leaning over and falling into the lake. From about noon until eight in the evening there was scarcely a moment when the crash of the falling banks was not going on. As the level of the lake sank the greater height of the banks caused a constantly increasing commotion in the lake as the banks struck the molten lava in their fall. A number of times a section of the bank from 200 to 500 feet long, 150 to 200 feet high, and twenty to thirty feet thick would split off from the adjoining rocks, and with a tremendous roar, amid a blinding cloud of steam, smoke and dust, fall with an appalling down-plunge into the boiling lake, causing great waves and breakers of fire to dash into the air, and a mighty "ground swell" to sweep across the lake dashing against the opposite cliffs like storm waves upon a lee shore. Most of the falling rocks were immediately swallowed up by the lake, but when one of the great downfalls referred to occurred, it would not immediately sink, but would float off across the lake, a great floating island of rock. At about three o'clock an island of this character was formed, estimated to be about 125 feet long, twenty-five feet wide, and rising ten to fifteen feet above the surface of the lake. Shortly after another great fall took place, the rock plunging out of sight beneath the fiery waves. Within a few moments, however, a portion of it, approximately thirty feet in diameter, rose up to an elevation of from five to ten feet above the surface of the lake, the molten lava streaming off its surface, quickly cooling and looking like a great rose-colored robe, changing to black. These two islands, in the course of an hour, floated out to the center and then to the opposite bank. At eight in the evening they had changed their appearance but slightly. By the next morning they had, however, disappeared.

About noon the falling lava disclosed the fact that the small extension [New Lake] at the right of the lake was only about eighty feet deep, and it was soon left high and dry; simply a great shelf in the bank, high above the surface of the lake. As the lava fell, most of the surrounding banks were seen to be slightly overhanging, and as the lateral support of the molten lava was withdrawn, great slices of the overhanging banks on all sides of the lake would suddenly split off and fall into the lake beneath. As these falls took place the exposed surface, sometimes a hundred feet across and upwards, would be left red-hot, the break having evidently taken place on the line of a heat-crack which had extended down into the lake.

About six o'clock the falling bank adjacent to the hill worked back into a territory which, below fifty feet from the surface, was all hot and in a semi-molten condition. From six to eight o'clock the entire face of this bluff some eight hundred feet in length and over two hundred feet in height, was a shifting mass of color, varying from the intense light of molten lava to all the varying shades of rose and red to black, as the different portions were successively exposed by a fall of rock and then cooled by exposure to the air. During this period the crash of the falling banks was incessant. Sometimes a great mass would fall forward like a wall; at others it would simply collapse and slide down making red-hot fiery landslides; and again enormous boulders, as big as a house, singly and in groups, would leap from their fastenings and, all aglow, chase each other down and leap far out into the lake. The awful grandeur and terrible magnificence of the scene at this stage are indescribable. As night came on, and yet hotter recesses were uncovered, the molten lava which remained in the many caverns leading off through the banks to other portions of the crater, began to run back and fall into the lake beneath, making fiery cascades down the sides of the bluff. There were five such lava streams at one time.

The light from the surface of the lake, the red-hot walls and the molten streams lighted up the entire area, bringing out every detail with the utmost distinctness, and lighted up a tall column of dust and smoke which arose straight up. During the entire period of the subsidence the lava fountains upon the surface of the lake continued in action, precisely as though nothing unusual was taking place.

Although the action upon the face of the subsiding area was so terrific, that upon the portion between the falling face and the outer line of fracture was so gradual that an active man could have stood on almost any portion of it without injury. Enormous cracks, twenty to thirty feet deep, and from five to ten feet wide, opened in all directions upon its surface, and the subsidence was more rapid in some spots than in others, but in almost all cases the progress of the action was gradual, although the shattered and chaotic appearance of the rocks made it look as though nothing but a tremendous convulsion could have brought it about. Another noticeable incident was the almost entire absence of sulphurous vapors, no difficulty in breathing being experienced directly to leeward of the lake.

At nine o'clock the next morning the lake was found to have sunk some twenty feet more; the banks at the right and left of the subsiding area, which had been the chief points of observation the day before, had disappeared into the lake for distances varying from twenty-five to one hundred feet back from the former edge, and the lower half of the debris slope had been swallowed up in the lake, disclosing the original smooth black wall of the lake beneath at a considerable overhanging angle. At the level of the lake, and half filled by it, was a great cavern extending in a south-easterly direction from the lake [see Fig. 116]. The dimensions were apparently seventy-five feet across and fifteen feet from the surface of the lake to the roof of the cave. It could be seen into from the opposite bank for about fifty feet. This may have been the duct through which the lava had been drained, although it manifestly was not at the bottom of the lake, for up to July 16th, that had continued to rise and fall from five to ten feet a day, and constantly threw up fountains, somewhat more actively than before its subsidence. The entire area of subsidence is estimated to be a little less than eight acres, about one-half of which fell into the lake. While the breakdown was taking place there were many slight tremors of the banks generally resulting in the precipitate retreat of the observers from the edge, but although the danger was great the spectacle was so grand and fascinating that the party returned again and again to watch it. At the Volcano House two slight earthquakes were felt on the afternoon of the 11th, and one vigorous one at 2 A.M. on the 12th. During the week several slight shocks were felt in the town of Hilo, thirty miles away, yet none were felt at Olaa, half way between, nor at Kapapala, fifteen miles in the opposite direction, although the latter is a place peculiarly susceptible to earthquakes.[124]

Mr. Dodge's survey made on July 30th (Fig. 118) shows the changes wrought in Halemaumau that Mr. Thurston has so graphically described. The figures both on the plan and sections are the distance below the Volcano House datum.

August 7, 1894. Walter F. Frear.—The lake was active, the largest fountain (Old Faithful) playing once or twice a minute, coming up each time as one, two or three bubbles, and then being quiet until the next burst; the other fountains, four to six generally at a time, playing often several minutes before quieting down. Old Faithful always played in the same place, this being the same place in which it played in March, '92, when I saw it on four different days. The guide says it has been in the same place ever since. The other fountains were not confined to any particular locality.

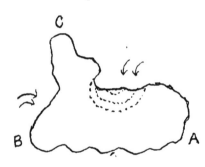

FIG. 117. OUTLINE OF ISLAND IN LAKE.

Aside from the surface appearance of the lake, there were at this time three points of special interest, (1) the change in height of the lake, (2) the falling in of the sides of the pit, and (3) the floating islands. The guide informed me that the height of the lake and the contour of the walls of the pit were substantially the same on July 24 as just after the drop of July 11. This was apparently so......There was no change in the height of the lake and no falling in of the sides from the 24th until after the 27th. On the 28th and 29th there was much falling in of the sides, as shown by frequent clouds of dust, and on the 30th I noticed that the lake had fallen about fifteen feet. On August 2d there was also much falling in, and on August 4th I noticed that the lake had fallen about twenty feet more......

The guide said that two large islands made of pieces of fallen cliff had drifted at the time of the drop and become fastened, one to the north wall, the other to the south wall. These were still large on the 24th, but had mostly melted away by August 4th. There was one large island near the middle of the lake each time I went down. The first three times I could not see the whole of it from any one point from which I looked at it. On the 30th I got a good view from another point. Its shape was as in Fig. 117. Its length, A–B, was perhaps a hundred and thirty feet, its height at B about eight feet, at A about twelve or fifteen feet, and at C eighteen to twenty feet. Its surface

[124] Thrum's Annual, 1895, p. 78.   [567]

was flat, except that there was a depression in the middle shown by the dotted lines in the figure. It was black and smooth as if covered by molten lava thrown over it. The sides were steep, but not all perpendicular. On August 4th its outline had changed slightly; it was nearly flat, the depression having been nearly filled; it was level, the lower portions having been raised to the height of the point c: the sides were for the most part perpendicular or overhanging and there were

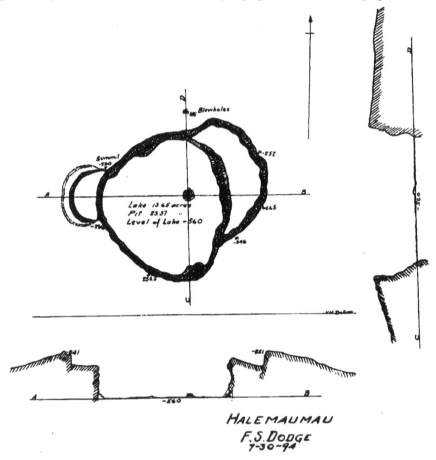

FIG. 118. SURVEY OF HALEMAUMAU BY F. S. DODGE, JULY 30, 1894.

swift currents in the lake near the island in the direction of the arrows in the figure. On August 4th I saw another island to the south of the large one. It was oval in shape, perhaps twenty by thirty feet in its diameters, and about ten or twelve feet high, with perpendicular and overhanging sides. I visited the pit crater Makaopuhi July 31st, and on August 2nd I saw considerable steam issuing from cracks in it mostly at the intersection of the wall with the talus, that is, along the top of the talus.

May 28, 1894. Rev. S. E. Bishop found the lake much as in 1892.

September 13, 1894. Road from Hilo completed.

[568]

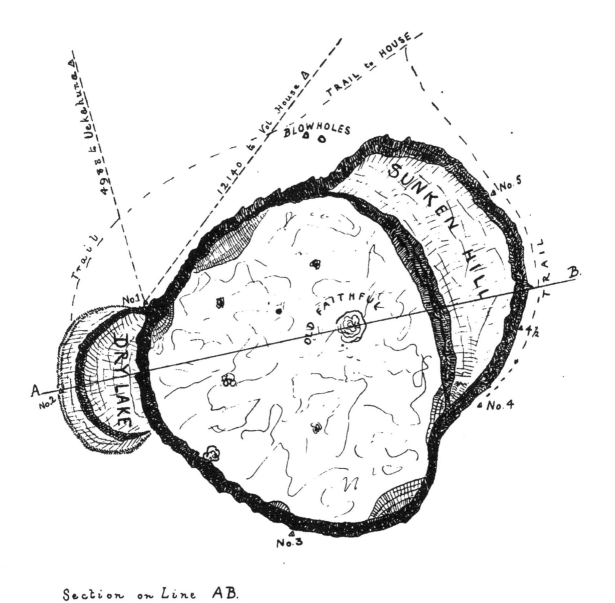

Section on Line AB.

1430 ft

900 ft

319 ft

Scale. 200 ft = 1 inch

FIG. 119. MR. DODGE'S SURVEY: ANOTHER COPY.

December 6, 1894. J. M. Lee.—The fire in the crater disappeared quietly during the past night.

November 6, 1895. Telephone line from Kailua to Volcano House completed this day.

January 3, 1896. The lava returned to the crater at 11:30 P.M. and formed during that night a lake about two hundred by two hundred and fifty feet. There has been no fire in the crater since December 6, 1894.

January 28, 1896. Fire disappeared again.

April 21, 1896. The crater of Mokuaweoweo broke out some time last night, but owing to dense clouds the smoke was not noticed until this morning at 7:25 A.M. With exception of a slight earthquake at 9:50 this evening everything is quiet, and at intervals when the clouds roll by we can see the fire brilliantly reflected in the sky. Kilauea is continually smoking, but otherwise inactive.

April 28, 1896. A party started for Mauna Loa's crater.

I was in Italy at the time of the eruption of Mauna Loa in 1896, in the very midst of the Vesuvian region, and so lost this interesting Hawaiian eruption; but we have most fortunately the record of two most competent men each in their department, Dr. Benedict Friedländer of Naples, a vulcanologist of experience here as well as in other regions, and Mr. D. Howard Hitchcock, whose paintings of Hawaiian volcanic action have not been surpassed. I am fortunately able to present the graphic account and photographs of one, and the painting of the other, although this last is but the ghost of the beautiful original in the Bishop Museum (Pl. LXVII). Dr. Friedländer's ascent was made, it will be seen, from the same side as my own in 1864. I quote his published account more fully than I otherwise should, as it gives so much more than the simple details of the volcanic action.[125]

On the morning of April 21st, 1896, while riding from Waiohinu, Kau, towards Honomalino in Kona, I noticed a large, white cumulus cloud, far above the fogs that frequently cover the slopes of Mauna Loa. The evening of the same day there was a bright fire-reflection visible from Honomalino; and because that glare was exactly in the direction of Mokuaweoweo, there could be no doubt that I had the good fortune to be in the right time in the right spot. Though the usual starting point for Mokuaweoweo be Kapapala ranch, or the Volcano House, and though I was not even sure if Mauna Loa was accessible from any other side—without great difficulty at least—I decided to try it, and had not to repent the attempt. The western slope of Mauna Loa is its shortest; and the condition of the roads or trails, on the upper part of the lava, turned out to be by no means worse than that on the southeastern slope. Succeeding parties probably would find it much easier, as we had to seek for our road from the upper limit of the woods on; none of our party had been up to the summit from this side, not even the guide, who only knew the trail through the forests and how to get up to a certain height......Our party was composed of Mr. John Gasper, Mr. Charley Ka as guide, a native boy, my European assistant and myself.

We left Mr. Gasper's house on the upper Kona road on horseback in the early morning of April the 25th. The trail for some miles leads into a thick and most wonderful forest, in which I saw the largest koa trees and fern trees I met with on the islands. The trail itself was in places rather bad, but not worse than many others. In a height of about 4600 feet, a short distance before Mr. John Paris' dairy is reached, the forest becomes less thick and by degrees is succeeded by the form of vegetation characteristic of most of those districts of Hawaii where the formation of humus is not yet advanced sufficiently for supporting a richer vegetable life. Small shrub-like *metrosideros*

---

[125] Thrum's Hawaiian Annual, 1897, p. 72. Also in *Himmel und Erde*. Berlin.

(lehua), *cyathodes* (puakeawe), *vaccinium* (ohelo), are the most striking plants of that zone. We left our horses at a height of about 7500 feet, where they were able to get some wet grass, from which point we walked; but now after having explored the way, Mr. Gasper thinks he could take parties up to the summit entirely on horseback.

The kind of mist between fog and rain, so well known to many visitors to Kilauea, prevented us from going farther than about 8500 feet the first day. We pitched our tent; made up a large fire from dry lehua wood, and greatly enjoyed the contents of a number of tins of provisions. Towards sunset it cleared up, when a fine view of Hualalai and the green gentle slope below our place as far as the sea was afforded us.

Slowly the clouds dissolved also on the other side, except a large cumulus of the well-known shape of the Italian pine; a large mass of vapor floating to an enormous height and connected with the mountain, or with the crater, only by a narrow trunk of dim bluish smoke. The afternoon sun

FIG. 120. ERUPTION OF MOKUAWEOWEO, 1896. DR. FRIEDLANDER.

illuminated the cloud: its snowy white slowly turned yellowish, then, towards sunset crimson, and soon the volcanic glare became visible; first the narrow pillar, then the whole cloud formation becoming aglow from the incandescent matter beneath. A cool wind blew over the almost barren land and its scanty shrubs. We crept into our tent after having impressed our memory with that wonderful and highly characteristic sight of Mokuaweoweo's threatening volcano cloud in the clear moonlight.

The next morning we started early. Tent, photo outfit, water and provisions were carried on a pack mule, the only animal we took above the forest limit and to within a short distance of the summit......In consequence of the flatness of the top of Mauna Loa you never see the summit until you are right there. Invariably the upper horizon is limited by a lava rim that looks exactly as if it must be the edge of the crater: after you reach that rim, another hill becomes visible, and when you reach it there is another still. More than ten times one or another was convinced that it was the rim of Mokuaweoweo; but my aneroid contradicted them and was right. Unfortunately the native boy and my attendant were not far from being quite used up. We had to stop frequently and so progressed very slowly indeed; but we pushed on and in the afternoon were as high as 13,000 feet. After we reached this altitude we left the mule and the two exhausted men behind, because the upper part of that side of the summit was mostly formed of the aa kind of lava. While the two men pitched the tent, the rest of the party passed on without delay. We heard distinctly a surf-like noise that indicated the presence of lava fountains; the pillar of bluish smoke was quite near; and yet no trace of the immediate vicinity of the crater was discernable······

The upmost top of Mauna Loa is almost level, with only a very slight uphill slope to the rim. At once the opposite side of the crater becomes visible; a few steps more and we were on the brink of a perpendicular precipice and saw the whole crater. What was noticeable in that first moment was the rather considerable amount of snow forming narrow white lines on the opposite crater wall; and two large lava fountains, the bright reddish yellow color of which made a fine contrast to the blackish crater bottom······

The surface of the lake was crusted over, but rent by a very large number of crevices, through which the glow was slightly visible in the daylight and very bright in the night······During my

FIG. 121. ERUPTION OF MAUNA LOA, 1896, AT NIGHT. DR. FRIEDLANDER.

presence there were two large and one small lava fountains, the former of which played with great regularity and without any interruption. We were looking against the longer diameter, which followed the line on which the fountains were playing; apparently they started from a rather straight crack. Their height was difficult to estimate from our place of observation, as the downward look was too steep: but I do not believe that the largest was more than 50 feet high. A succeeding party, three days later, reported far larger figures: 150 to 200 feet. Either one of these estimations is very far from the truth, or, the fountains had increased their height in the lapse of three days; the latter supposition seems to me more probable. The color of the fountains was very bright, more yellow than reddish, even in the daylight; after sunset they were almost dazzling, and also the system of cracks was very striking. I succeeded in obtaining lasting evidence which proves that the fountains were not very far from real white-heat. The full moon and the fountains affected the photograph plate almost alike. As the fountains of Mokuaweoweo came out absolutely black in a five second exposure with an F. 6.3 lens on a 26× Seed's plate, I am convinced that a much shorter exposure would suffice······My picture (Fig. 121) was taken only half an hour after sunset, when the reflected

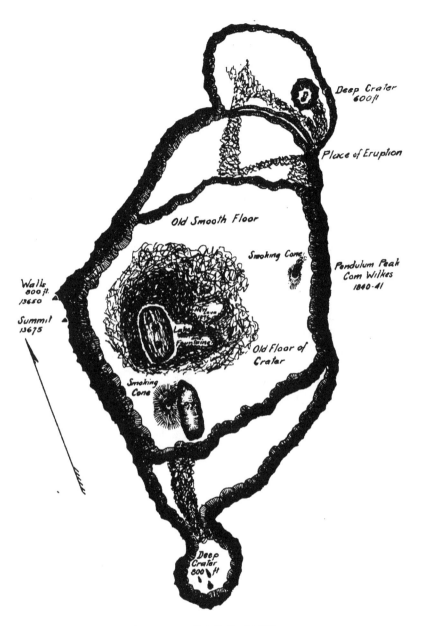

Deep Crater
600 ft

Place of Eruption

Old Smooth Floor

Smoking Cone

Pendulum Peak
Com Wilkes
1840-41

Walls
800 ft.
13650

Summit
13675

Hot Lava
1873

Lake
Fountains

Old Floor of
Crater

Smoking
Cone

Deep
Crater
800 ft

FIG. 122. MOKUAWEOWEO IN 1896.

daylight was still pretty strong. A gentleman of the other party exposed his plate in the very night and obtained not only the fountains but the cracks also......

In closing, the differences between the activity of the Kilauea lake and that of Mokuaweoweo are to be enumerated. From the molten lava of Kilauea there arises only a thin smoke, that in the reflected light is intensely bluish, and if looked at against the bright sky, yellowish brown. A volcano cloud proper does not exist at all as a rule, and only under certain circumstances, mostly in the early morning and again at sunset. The invisible overheated steam will condense to a cloud, but I invariably noticed that the seeming volcano cloud was a free floating mass of condensed steam without any appreciable connection with the lava lake. Mokuaweoweo, on the other hand, as long as it was active, nearly *always had* a cloud; and that cloud *always* had a noticeable trunk or pillar of smoke: the latter, as I could see from the top, arose almost entirely from the fountains. These, though they seemed to me far less high than to the party of April 29th, yet were higher than any I had seen in Kilauea; and furthermore, I almost believe (though I could not affirm it positively) they were somewhat brighter than those of Kilauea.

I may add that the cloud commonly over Kilauea does not have a visible connection with the lava below, but is far from a mere passing cloud (many of these sweep across the crater), but remains stationary a long time, and is at such a height that it is visible from a great distance, especially when illuminated by the molten lava beneath. In Hitchcock's picture the considerable heat of the distant fountains is indicated by the melted snow on the lee side of the crater: on the right, Mauna Kea, snow-capped, is seen above the rim.

May 6, 1896. The eruption on Mauna Loa ceased after fifteen days action.

July 11, 1896. Fire returned to Kilauea at a depth of six hundred feet. This activity continued for three weeks without increasing the lake. After this the lava lake gradually disappeared and the fire was confined to a cone in the bottom, from which lava occasionally poured out. This kept on during August and September, when the last sign of fire disappeared.

June 24, 1897. J. M. Lee.—There was again a little fire visible—lasted three days only—down in a cave. For some months smoke has been abundant and dense.

Kilauea still remained inactive, but on the morning of July 4, 1899, Mauna Loa commenced a short eruption from a crack not far from the point of the eruption of 1880-81. In July, 1899, Professor C. H. Hitchcock saw the eruption from a distance. Prof. Albert S. Bickmore, of the American Museum, New York, was here with his photographer, Mr. C. C. Langill, who made some good views of the eruption.

1899 Of some of these I have colored lantern slides. Three years before the guide Gasper had told Dr. Friedländer that he thought he could take a mounted party to the summit from the west side, and this year he made good with several parties. We have a detailed account from one of those who visited this eruption with Gasper, Mr. A. B. Ingalls, of Oahu College,[126] from whose published account we gather the following facts: Reaching Mokuaweoweo on the western side, after much the same experiences that have been related by Dr. Friedländer, great volumes of steam were

---

[126] Thrum's Annual, 1900, p. 51.   [574]

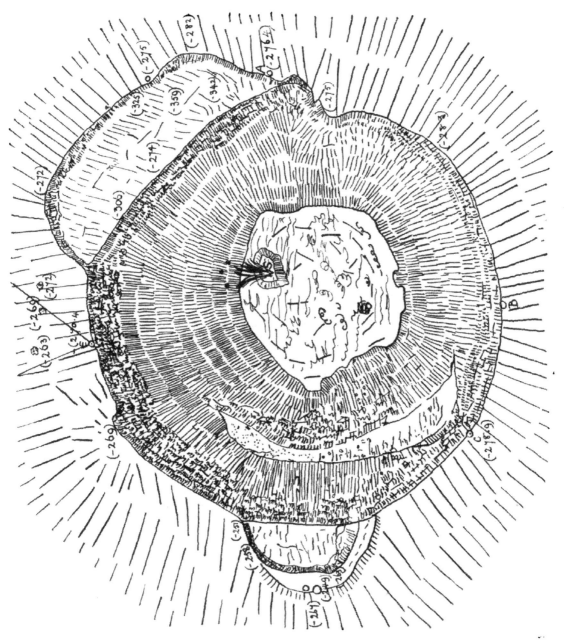

FIG. 123. HALEMAUMAU.

seen to the south of the main crater, probably from the already described cracks common in that region.   There was a crack in the crater floor roughly parallel to the western wall, west of the major axis of the pit, from which steam jets in considerable number, but not of much activity, were the only signs of any eruption.   The floor was much like that of Kilauea, and no traces of the lake of the previous eruption are mentioned. Making their camp where they reached Mokuaweoweo, Mr. Ingalls with a few companions passed around the northern end of the crater, and by a difficult trail descended the mountain slope some three or four thousand feet to the source of the outbreak. The cone from which much of the lava was flowing is shown in Fig. 124.   As near as they could estimate, the fountain was one hundred and fifty feet high.   On the return to camp they met an unexpected danger.   To quote Mr. Ingalls:

Having remained by the crater several hours, we began to retrace our steps to our camping place, ten or twelve miles distant on the summit of the mountain.   We had proceeded but a short distance when we noticed that the wind had shifted around 180°, and that the fumes from the upper pile were drifting down and across our former trail, and also far off to the northwest were hovering down upon the slopes of the mountain.   This caused me a little anxiety as soon as I saw it, but we tramped along until we encountered the fumes.   Then anxiety became acute; the sulphurous fumes were dense and strong.   We attempted to pass through, but could not do so, either close to the base of the cone or farther away to the northwest.   The choking sensation in the lungs, and irritation in the nostrils could not be endured.

The situation looked serious: to cross the hot aa between the lower and upper crater and thus gain the windward side of the upper crater was absolutely impossible.   We tried it.   To attempt retreat down the mountain towards Hilo was out of the question.   The general direction to Hilo was down the slope over the barren lava to the forest, and then a two days trip through the jungle, unless we might accidentally strike a trail, and worse than all that, we had no water for such a trip; every canteen was dry······Just then the wind shifted 10° more, crowding us toward the hot aa.   At this moment we began to utterly depair of ever reaching civilization······Then one of the party, studying the cloud of fumes, saw near the top of the cone a patch of blue sky through a rent in the smoke. This less dense portion was slowly drifting along with the rest.   Brief calculation from its motion indicated about where it would settle down upon the rocks to the north.   "Fellows, there's our chance!   Come on!"   Snatching up packs and canteens we ran with all speed to the spot, made a dash through the vapors, which choked us terribly and irritated both eyes and nostrils.   The boy with the heavy camera plates falls down, overcome.   Grabbing his pack I pushed him up and urged him on a few steps farther.   They closed in behind us, but we were on the upper side of them now, and were safe.   Never again, as we looked back on those vapors during the night, did we see another break in them.   The remainder of that night and part of the next morning were occupied in making the ascent of the slopes and reaching again our summit camp.   Without water, with sore feet and painful steps, with aching muscles, with hands benumbed with the cold, freezing air, up over the shoe-cutting aa we stumbled along, picking our way as best we could by the glare from the volcanic fires and the dim light of a quarter moon.   Someone, exhausted, dropped down; we all rested a little; then up again until another dropped exhausted.   After a time exhaustion became so great that to sit down to rest meant to immediately fall asleep; but the freezing wind piercing our garments chilled us to the bone, and presently we would awake with chattering teeth and quivering limbs.   Thus the night passed.   Morning began to dawn; the sun lighted up the distant clouds below us, and the smoke of the volcano, still drifting off to the north, hung like a claret-colored scarf against the feathery whiteness of the clouds beyond.   A cheerful warmth in the sunbeams was very welcome.

Two streams flowed down the mountain, one toward Kau—this lasted only ten days—while the other and larger ran toward Hilo in the track of so many others, finally ceasing July 23d. Then came severe earthquakes, felt in various parts of the island during that day, but no harm was done; neither did the flow of three weeks do any harm as it passed through a region already blasted by previous streams of comparatively recent occurrence.

FIG. 124. A SOURCE OF ERUPTION, 1899. HITCHCOCK.

January 14, 1898. Frank Godfrey.—Not a sign of life [Kilauea].

March 26, 1898. L. A. Thurston estimates the pit as 800 feet deep and 150 feet in diameter at the bottom. He also notes increased heat in the crack parallel with and four hundred feet distant from the north wall. "It is sizzling hot a foot back from the edge and shows a cherry-red about twenty feet down. This is the first fire seen in the crater since June 24, 1897."

March 2, 1900. L. A. Thurston. — There was a breakdown filling the "bottomless pit," and some fire.

[577]

February 14, 1901. L. A. Thurston.—Very little sulphur vapor arises from two or three spots on the north and east sides.

August 3, 1901. W. T. Brigham.—Found Halemaumau a conical pit clear to the bottom; some sulphur on western wall.

August 25, 1901. Fred Waldron.—At 10 P.M. a lake four hundred feet in diameter has just formed in the bottom of Halemaumau on the Kau side. It has the shape of an irregular quadrilateral.

September 12, 1901. L. A. Thurston.—The new lake has subsided, leaving a black ledge 100–150 feet above the present bottom....No fire is visible in the daytime, but it can be seen at night.

June 12, 1902. L. A. Thurston.—No change in crater rim since February 14th. Pit generally filled with sulphur vapors.

August 25, 1902. F. Waldron.—At 10 P.M. a bright glow was observed over Halemaumau; on going over it was found that a lake had formed at the extreme bottom near the base of the wall on the Kau side. This lake is now about 400 feet in diameter.

September 12, 1902. L. A. Thurston.—The new lake at the bottom of the pit has subsided, leaving a black ledge at an estimated height of 100-150 feet above the present bottom of the pit.

October 13, 1902. W. E. Skinner.—Brilliant display over surface of lake.

October 20-27, 1902. Whitman Cross, of the United States Geological Survey.—On Monday the 20th instant, there were almost no signs of activity. The lava flow produced by earlier action was recognizable. With a tape line parallel tangents to the circular outline of the crater were drawn, which were 1500 feet apart, representing the diameter. The depth to the consolidated lava was estimated to be 825 feet; and the north-south diameter of the same was 575 feet. The vertical wall on the south was deeper than upon the opposite side, while in the first case there was a gradual slope to the lava floor. On the other side the slope was higher up and connected two walls. On the north edge of the lake there was a blow-hole or spatter cone about twelve feet high exhibiting two small glowing spots, and sulphurous fumes arose from the cone without noise. October 23d there was a sound of escaping gas from the blow-hole, like the sharp puffs of a locomotive getting under headway; they were irregular, though often strenuous. At 3 P.M. a part of the top of the cone was blown off, followed by the sound of thrashing and surging lava. At every throb splashes of lava were thrown out of the orifice and the cone grew rapidly. At 3:35 P.M. the whole northwest side of the mound was broken down and a torrent of lava burst out like water from a pipe. The flow was steady, with occasional spurts throwing small masses a few feet into the air.

The lava was liquid, red-hot, changing to dull red and black as the crust formed, and as it spread out the domes and ropy lines so characteristic of the general floor of Kilauea made their appearance. By 5 P.M the flow had covered half of the floor. At 7 P.M. the whole floor was covered and the liquid still continued to gush out; then it decreased and new spatter cones were built up with orifices by 9 P.M., from which jets of lava were occasionally thrown out.

The new lava lake exhibited during the evening the common phenomena so often described. Cracks formed in the dull crust, lava pushed out in sheets or tongues, plates of the crust turned up and sunk in the molten lake beneath. The illumination was often brilliant, and all the conditions combined to make the scene grand and impressive. On October 24th there was no flow; the floor was so solidified that the fracturing and extrusion of lava was rare and of small extent. At the blow hole there was frequently repeated the process of sealing up the orifice by viscous matter, then a bursting out, making a new hole, which would be sealed up again in an hour or two.

On the evening of the 25th the strong glow indicated action, and there was another thin flow over the sheet of the 23d. The spatter cone remained on the north side and no other vent could be seen. The action was that of sealing up and bursting again, without any discharge. On the 27th, just before daylight, a bright glow was noted over Halemaumau, which was occasioned by another thin flow.

November 8, 1902.—Charles R. Frazier.—Lake at bottom of pit very active.

[578]

When Hawaiian Hall of the Bishop Museum was planned I had reserved a suitable space in the centre for a relief plan of Kilauea, and as the place was now ready, I went to the crater with my assistant, W. A. Bryan, to collect the needed data. Both by many photographs of the outer walls, and barometric measurement of all unde-

FIG. 125. ERUPTION OF 1903 BY DAY. C. BALDWIN.

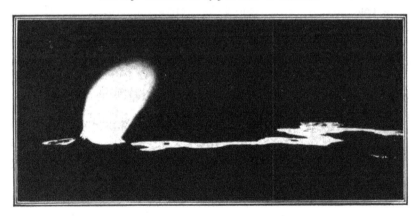

FIG. 126. ERUPTION OF 1903 BY NIGHT. C. BALDWIN.

termined heights, I collected considerable material, while Mr. Bryan made on the spot a small model in clay of the proposed relief, correcting it from many positions. The final plan now on exhibition is on a scale of 130 feet to the inch, and was constructed by Mr. Bryan with great care, and has met the approval of all scientific men who have

seen it. Ten days were spent at the crater in this work, and the volcanic manifesta-
tions were not of special interest, as the pit remained quiet and mostly clear of smoke,
giving us, except on rainy days, good views of the whole area, and permitting exploration around the pit, and on its lee side. In the finished model arrangements were
made to remove the region around Halemaumau if at any time a marked change should
take place, and substitute a remodelled portion in its place. Only the difficulty of
finding place for so large a model has prevented the preparation of a similar model of
Mokuaweoweo. One of Haleakala would also be desirable, but the surveys of that
vast crater are not yet sufficient for the work of model making.

> *March 19, 1903.* Professor J. C. Branner was at crater.
> *June 21, 1903.* W. R. Castle.—The time has come when the United States Government
> might well reserve the whole region of Mokuaweoweo to the sea at Puna, a long, narrow strip to
> include Kilauea and the line of pit craters, a comparatively worthless strip of country commer-
> cially. It should also include the Koa tree moulds at Kuapaawela, where a forest of giant trees was
> surrounded by a deep flow of later age.
> *August 23, 1903.* Clouds of smoke ascending from the pit, indicating a cessation of action.
> *October 6, 1903.* St. Clair Bidgood.—The summit crater Mokuaweoweo broke out today at
> 12:45 P.M. December 8th activity ceased.
> *November 25, 1903.* Halemaumau again in action, and a lake, forty by a hundred and twenty-
> five feet, formed early in the morning and remained active until January 10 of the next year.

Many people visited this eruption, and many reports were published,[127] but
these being generally by inexperienced observers are somewhat in need of pruning.
Still, certain interesting matters may be sifted from the mass, and the camera affords
us (by the kindness of Mr. C. Baldwin) an indisputable testimony to at least one
stage of the outbreak. We may select reports from parties reaching the summit from
both sides of the mountain. Naturally the first party was from Hilo, and it left the
Volcano House by the Kapapala route already described. Starting from Kapapala
ranch in the morning on horses and mules, with pack animals and ample supplies,
they reached the 10,000 feet level at 2 o'clock P.M., and camped until 7 A.M. the
next day. The summit was reached at 2 P.M., and the temperature was reported at
several degrees below zero. All were so affected by mountain sickness that, rolled in
their blankets, they threw themselves on the cold lava at the brink, suffering severe
pains in the head. Those who cared to look saw a small pool towards the northwest end
of the main crater, north of the centre of activity of 1896. Over the rim of this pool,
and, according to Mr. T. C. Ridgway, who left a plan in the Volcano House Record
which is here reproduced (Fig. 127), the stream flowed northeast for more than a mile
with a branch bending southward. The fountains which illumined the high column
of vapor were confined to this lake, and the outpouring lavas made a cone as clearly

---

[127] Thrum's Annual, 1904, p. 163.   [580]

shown in Mr. Baldwin's picture. The party left the crater the next morning at 7 o'clock, and by evening were at the Volcano House. One of the party declares that the roar of the "fire geysers sounded like the smashing of heavy seas against the rocks. The spouting columns of white-hot lava arose......to heights of several hundred feet, and would fall back as blackened boulders and huge chunks of congealed cinder."

A party from Napoopoo were caught in a severe hailstorm and lost their way, reaching the summit after great hardships. "The sight was simply indescribable. Columns of fire from forty to a hundred feet were playing, now here, now there. We counted about thirty fountains [meaning such fountains as are common in Kilauea's pools]: one fully formed cone nearly seventy-five feet high in about the centre of the crater, and one forming a little to the southwest of it. There was smoke or steam everywhere in the crater, but the principal eruption was in a line running through the centre of the crater of Mokuaweoweo from the southeast to northwest."

Several of the party state that the entire crater floor was covered with molten lava, but others limit the lava to the stream already mentioned in the northern half of the crater. This party from Napoopoo had a bad time coming up,

FIG. 127. MR. RIDGEWAY'S PLAN OF THE ERUPTION.

and had left some of their number in camp at the 11,000 feet level; after spending two hours and a half on the summit they returned rapidly to this camp. In the words of one of the party: "On arrival one of the guides who had remained with the sick one at camp had coffee ready for us, and horses saddled and packed; no time was lost, as we wished to make the edge of the woods before dark. We left the 11,000 level at 11:30 A.M. and proceeded downward at a brisk walk, the animals feeling very cold and eager to walk. Hardly had we descended a thousand feet when the sky darkened and a most terrific snow and electrical storm was upon us. The hail was so pelting and heavy that it hurt our hands, although we wore woolen gloves. The mules refused to move, and before many minutes the ground or lava was white with snow. The lightning was vivid and hissed dreadfully, followed almost instantly by tremendous thunder. We found no shelter, and were almost frozen stiff. On and on we rushed, and the lower we got the less of the storm we saw. Dangerous as the roads had become we made all possible speed. After an hour and a half the storm's fierceness was broken, and from there the homeward journey was uneventful. At the 8,000 feet level those affected by mountain sickness recovered. The down trip took exactly fourteen hours;

FIG. 128. CAMP ON THE EAST SIDE OF MOKUAWEOWEO, 1905. W. T. POPE.

no stops were made. We went from where we camped to Napoopoo, arriving in the morning at 1 A.M." This eruption was confined to the main crater and lasted two months, followed by a small flow from Pohaku o Hanalei.

To return to the Kilauea record:

November 25, 1903. St. Clair Bidgood.—Lake about 40×125 feet. Fountains playing continually and surface very active. Remained active until January 10, 1904.

February 13, 1904. J. B. Castle.—Crater inactive.

May 14, 1904. Bishop Restarick.—Crater quiet.

February 23, 1905. Demosthenes Lycurgus.—Fire at bottom of pit.

March 20, 1905. W. Williamson.—Fire at bottom.

May 1, 1905. L. A. Thurston.—Pit has filled up since November.

July 22-23, 1905. Professor W. T. Pope and party were on the summit of Mauna Loa. By his kindness I am enabled to present to my readers some of the good pictures he made on this trip. The view of the camp south of Pendulum Peak, and the one used by many parties from

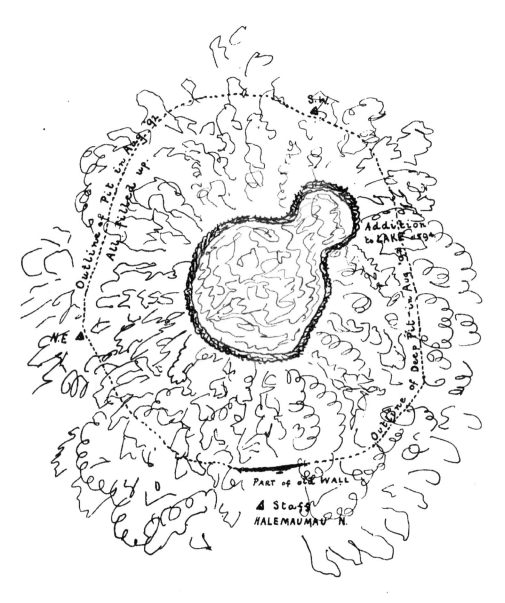

Outline of Pit in Aug. '92. All filled up.

S.W. ▲

Addition to LAKE 1894.

Outline of Deep Pit in Aug. '92.

N.E ▲

PART of old WALL

▲ Staff

HALEMAUMAU N.

FIG. 129. HALEMAUMAU IN DECEMBER, 1906. BALDWIN.

Kapapala, shows well the exceedingly rough nature of the surface.   The outlook from the plateau (Fig. 130) gives some idea of the vast western wall and its nearly perpendicular surface, while the nearer view (Fig 131) of the eastern wall shows the layers and the talus, and also the fresh lava flows on the floor.   The descent can be seen to be far more difficult than that into Kilauea.   One can easily imagine, while looking at these pictures, the disgust of the botanist Douglas, who saw nothing worthy the attention of a naturalist !

September 16, 1905. L. A. Thurston.—Little sulphur in smoke : no noise [in Kilauea].

December 15, 1905. Clifton H. Tracy.—The volcano is more active than for three months, athough the fire is still confined to two cones in the southwest.

January 22, 1906. A. Loebenstein measured the depth of the pit at 576.9 feet.

December 2, 1906. E. D. Baldwin.—Fire visible in pit after nearly a year of inactivity .

FIG. 130. WESTERN WALL FROM PLATEAU. W. T. POPE.

January 9, 1907. Eruption of Mauna Loa. After a few slight earthquakes that were felt, not all over Hawaii, but in a few places only, about midnight on the ninth of January a bright light appeared on the summit of Mauna Loa, as it seemed at first, and it was some time before the true locality of the outbreak was determined. This proved to be far below the summit on the southern slope of the mountain, in the Kahuku region, already the seat of the eruptions of 1867 and 1887. As may be seen on the map, its source was higher up than either of these flows, and about half way down it divided into two nearly equal streams with a small and rather unimportant one between these and nearer the westerly one. Many visited this eruption, but there was little to relate differing from its predecessors. One or two points, however, appear in the summary given[128] that may well be reproduced here :—

So violent was the activity, and so liquid the flow of pahoehoe lava that the stream reached and crossed the Government road on the Kona side of the lava flow of 1887 in two days, advancing in places at the rate of seven miles an hour, destroying the telephone lines and stopping traffic for a

---

[127] Thrum's Annual, 1898, p. 131.   [584]

short time. By the 16th it had extended over thirty-five miles of waste land, and in a moving mass fifteen feet high, and half a mile wide, changed in character to aa, it kept onward at the rate of thirty feet an hour, shortly afterwards subsiding, but only to give way to a new flow which also crossed the road and seemed to have come from the same source, though at a much lower elevation.

The second flow was merely a branch of the first stream, and, like that, was, at its separation at the Kamoalaala hill, pahoehoe; but as it advanced and cooled it assumed the aa form, and this was the nature of both branches as they crossed the road, showing a depth of fifteen to thirty feet, which was increased at the end, which

FIG. 131. AT THE FOOT OF THE WALL. W. T. POPE.

of both streams was some three miles from the sea, to over fifty feet. A lake some 800 feet in diameter formed in the course of the flow, and a party of prominent citizens managed to get a clear view of this lake, and their description is as follows:

[There were] two great holes in the bluff out of which two streams of lava were running. A little way from the shore was a fountain that kept shooting hot lava fifty or sixty feet into the air. Occasionally the lake would cool in spots, making little black islands, and then a wave of molten lava would rush across the surface and bury them. This continually changing scene entranced the observers for some three or four hours. [It is noteworthy that this temporary lake exhibited the motions of the pools in the crater of Halemaumau, indicating the origin of fountains, etc., to subsist in the lava stream itself.] A stream of lava ran between the party and the lake; yet, desiring a closer view, they crossed the flow, which was all aglow underneath, and got right to the base of the lake which had built itself up about sixty feet. Looking up a glowing hill to the rim of the lake did not give assurance of safety, so they retreated; then rested for the night, taking hour watches, lest the walls of the lake give way and rush down the hill, which sight, should it occur, they desired to see. On January 24th the flow ceased, but activity at the source continued for some time.

FIG. 132. MOVING MASS OF AA IN FLOW OF 1907. PERKINS.

FIG. 133. FRONT OF THE AA FLOW, 1907. PERKINS.

This lake finally broke through its encircling walls and followed the rest of the flow down the hill. The lava where the flow crossed the road shows many very brilliant particles of olivine, and at the time of eruption unusual quantities of sulphur were noticed by many visitors. Kilauea, which had been slumbering, again roused into action about the time that this Mauna Loa eruption ceased. We take up the Volcano House Register again.

January 23, 1907. Rev. E. W. Thwing.—The lake was more active, and steadily rising.

April 12, 1907. Immanuel Friedländer found little fire.

May 12, 1907. Demosthenes Lycurgus.—After some days quietness in the crater, fires returned last night; cone on north side of pit quite busy, spurting every few minutes to a height of fifty to sixty feet. A stream of lava from above flowed almost around the whole floor of the pit. May 28: active and the "hole" that sank some weeks ago is rapidly filling up.

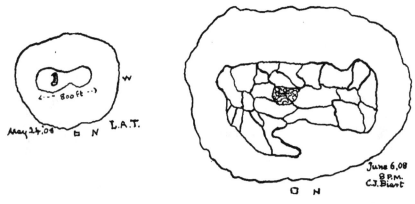

FIG. 134. LAKE, MAY 24, 1908.　　　　FIG. 135. LAKE, JUNE 6, 1908.

July 10. Lycurgus.—A lake of fire seventy-five feet in diameter.

July 25. Lycurgus.—Fire returned, but in small quantity.

November 20. Lycurgus.—The volcano became active again after a quietness of seven months. The whole pit was lighted up. The next day those who went down found only a little cone on the Volcano House side of the pit, with flames of fire, but no lava flows or fountains. In the evening the fires disappeared again.

December 7, 1907. W. A. Wall, Surveyor.—Found the pit 450 feet deep to a contraction only 200 feet in diameter, and this, a little lower down, showed fire about 40 feet across.

December 16, 1907. W. B. Henshall.—Quite active.

May 24, 1908. L. A. Thurston.—I estimate the pit to be 200 feet in depth, and the lake 800×400 feet in the form [shown in diagram, Fig. 134] with an island in the middle of the larger end. There is more activity than at any time since the breakdown, March 11, 1894.

June 6, 1908. C. J. Biart made a sketch of the lake at 8 o'clock P.M. (shown in Fig. 135).

June 21, 1908. L. A. Thurston.—The depth of the pit is about the same as on May 24th last, but the size of the lake has increased about fifty per cent. The diagram by C. J. Biart fairly represents it. [587]

Early in September, 1908, Halemaumau, which now was a single pit on the top, or near it, of the huge dome of lava which forms the floor of Kilauea—about four hundred feet above the general floor of Kilauea in 1864, when the writer first visited and surveyed the crater—had filled with lava to within a convenient point for **1908**   observation from the highest part of the rim, and not a few visitors made photographs of the pit both by day and night, some of which I am privileged to use for the clearer understanding of the condition. Never before perhaps have so many

FIG. 136. HALEMAUMAU IN AUGUST, 1908. PERKINS.

night scenes been secured, and those I shall present will give, so far as black and white can give, some idea of the wierd appearance of the molten lava as seen through the opening cracks, often enough described, but hard to understand from mere words.

The process of filling had been a slow one, for the pit left after the last emptying was a very deep one. For a long time there had been no fire (or molten lava) in the visible crater; walls of cracked and irregularly disposed rock supported a black, uneven, and much cracked rim, which seemed in places ready to fall, and generally projected over the abyss. When the lava again appeared it was like a small spring of tar at the bottom, which was at least six hundred feet below the average rim. So far below the spectator that it seemed of little importance or interest, but it was the sign of returning action, and soon the molten matter accumulated in a little pool whose surface was broken at intervals by the spouting lava in the way familiar to all who

FIG. 137. SURFACE OF HALEMAUMAU BY NIGHT. PERKINS.

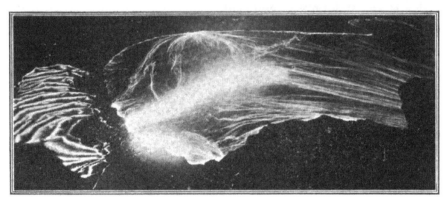

FIG. 138. SURFACE OF HALEMAUMAU BY NIGHT. PERKINS.

have seen Kilauea in action. The spring which supplied the vast reservoir was intermittent, and the surface of the pool rose slowly and irregularly. As it rose, however, the action increased, as is usual, and all through August the height of the lava column, at least fifty feet above the base of the dome, was critical. How much longer could the walls of Kilauea withstand the pressure? Fountains of lava frequently spouted, and as many as fourteen were counted in a single evening, the glow from the pit illuminating the whole crater so that lanterns were hardly needed for the parties who visited the "everlasting house of Pele" by night. While the action was distributed over the whole surface of the pool, some of the fountains seemed to have a definite position which they retained for days; such was a vigorous one in the eastern half of the pool which hardly varied its place during the two weeks of our stay at the crater. It was like the "Old Faithful" of previous years, although not in the same place. Under the east bank the floor was at times at a lower level than the general surface of the pool, which seemed to form a rim or dam there, and thus repeat in a measure the process so often seen in Kilauea, and shown especially in Silva's remarkable photograph (Pl. L). As seen in Perkins' view of the east end (Fig. 136), two falls of molten lava mark the raised wall, and the reader will bear in mind that much of the surface to the right is red-hot and subject to the breaking up and gushing forth of white-hot lava. By night the scene is by no means so tame as it appears in the photograph, where the red-hot lava is no brighter than the black lava of the walls. Mr. Perkins has caught the effect better than any others whose work I have seen (Figs. 137 and 138), and one can see the bright lava drawn out from the cracks, a process which gives the impression of currents flowing in a definite direction. The light, cloud-like effects are from the brightly illuminated gases, and it will be noted how local the escape of these gases is; not a sign of any such emission over most of the exposed surface. In Mr. Thrum's picture (Fig. 140) a long crack is seen from which the lava seems to flow toward the spectator; and this picture also shows how the action was spread over the whole surface of the pool. In Fig. 141 are seen the tiny watch-fires which are so beautiful a feature of the night view. These are often so small and so constant that they are like lanterns placed as danger signals. [128]

A view from the northwest bank of Halemaumau, taken at the same visit (as Fig. 136) by Mr. Perkins, shows the shelter hut whence the best views have been obtained a little to the left of the centre of the picture (Fig. 139), and it also shows the irregular outline of the pit and the varying level of its walls. From this it will be seen that the rim where the outlook is built was not at that time undercut, but seems as solid and safe as any part, while the impression given, especially at night, is of an overhanging shelf. Another curious fact is to be seen in this capital picture: while the structure of the rim in the foreground, where it is lowest, gives the impression (and a correct one) that the pool had overflowed here, yet on the much higher part of the rim farther to the left the same formation is found, and certainly the pool could

---

[128] The walls of Halemaumau may be shown in these night views, when the illumination from the lava is insufficient, by a short exposure by daylight, and, leaving the camera undisturbed, repeating the exposure by night.

not have overflowed all round simultaneously. Has the higher edge been raised or the lower edge been depressed? If so where are the faults in the wall?

On Friday, September 4th, in the early afternoon the fountains ceased to play, and soon the subsidence of the pool began. Parties coming up from the pit at dusk reported the fall at several hundred feet, but the light as seen from the Volcano House and reflected on passing clouds did not seem less than it had been when darkness came

FIG. 139. HALEMAUMAU FROM THE NORTHWEST IN 1908. PERKINS.

on. Mr. C. B. Thompson, Mr. Chas. N. Forbes and myself at once started for the Halemaumau. The earth light was still sufficient to show the path. All over the surface of the pool, which had fallen perhaps a hundred feet generally, but much lower on the northern side under the observation hut, were bright lights, and most of these remained stationary during our visit.

In the centre of the pit was a curious break running east and west, at the edge of which was a vertical slab of lava, semicircular in form, resembling half a mill-stone, and other slabs continued the wall for some distance. Over these fell a cascade of lava in a condition I had never before seen; its particles seemed to be in a state of mutual repulsion, and although white-hot, fell through the central hole of the "mill-stone" as meal. There seemed absolutely no cohesion, no signs of plasticity in the molten lava. There seemed to have come a spirit of disassociation into the pit, and the white hot particles of lava seemed in haste to get as far from each other as possible. They scattered like a flock of frightened birds. Another puzzle added to the lengthening list!

The descending lava had left pockets of molten rock in the walls; these emptied themselves on to the sinking crust with spatters and flashes. Masses of lava had also

FIG. 140. HALEMAUMAU BEFORE THE BREAK. D. F. THRUM.

been left adhering to the loose walls, and one of these, apparently weighing twenty tons, broke from its place, sliding down a path marked by a trail of white-hot lava so brilliant as to light up the clouds above the crater. Before it had fallen fifty feet the huge boulder broke in two, displaying its interior, brilliant as an arc light, and then began the utter disintegration of the mass as it thundered down, the bright particles scattering as did the "meal." All the while the danger signals burned here and there over the black crust. Here and there would come a break, and the old movement of apparently viscid lava was seen for a moment, but it soon broke up. Less fleeting was a huge interrogation mark drawn in fire on the western side. What, indeed, did it all mean? And the question was unanswered when at last the burning mark had faded.

Directly under the cliff on which the observation hut stands was the deepest hole into which all the incandescent meal of this infernal mill was sinking down; even had it been safe to approach the edge to get a good view into the abyss, the heat was prohibitory, and while the mill-stone in the midst still poured its grist down the slope, the danger signals grew dimmer, and here one went out in the darkness, and no lamp-lighter was at hand to renew it; the walls seemed to have shaken down all their loose rocks, the crust was no longer breaking, and the glory of the scene had ended. We could still see light from Halemaumau when we reached the Volcano House, but how dim compared with that which had brightened the whole crater the night before! Saturday night the pit was totally dark, no sign of fire could be seen from the house. All seemed over, but the emptying of the pit had stopped, and that was an indication that soon the action would be renewed, and no such long period of inactivity as had

FIG. 141. NIGHT VIEW OF HALEMAUMAU, AUGUST, 1909. MISS M. REED.

been the rule for many recent years was to be expected, and on the third day the lava rose again with great violence, throwing spatters above the rim of the crater. Nor was this a mere spasmodic action, for the renewed action has continued to the present writing.

March 13, 1909. At Hilo, about 3:30 A.M., two sharp shocks of earthquake, separated by a slight interval. Pictures were swung, and light objects were upset. March 14, three slight shocks in the forenoon, and another in the evening.

Thus far this informal History was approved and ordered printed March 26, 1909, but a visit to the Volcano of Kilauea on October 7th, 1909, undertaken to settle certain doubts in the record, determined me to add to the record herein printed such observations as have been placed in the Volcano House Register during the interval caused by the unexpected delay in the printing. I am the more ready to do this as

[593]

this volcano has developed in the meantime an action to me new and very interesting; and also that the volcano has been visited by the very distinguished English vulcanologist Dr. Tempest Anderson of York, and the well-known professors in the Massachusetts Institute of Technology, T. A. Jaggar, Jr., and R. A. Daly, the last two interested in the establishment of a permanent observatory at Kilauea, a result so ardently hoped for many years and frequently referred to in these pages.

AFTER the breakdown of September 4th, the lava soon returned to Halemaumau, and the Register resumes the notes:—.

December 12, 1908. E. D. Baldwin.—Lava returned September 7th, and in two hours was within 150 feet of the spot whence it fell September 4th. According to the accounts the lake rose and fell spasmodically after the 7th, and during some time in October had reached a place one hundred feet below its elevation on the 4th, only to fall again as evidenced by the present black ledge some forty-five feet higher than the level of the lava as it now stands.

During November and December the lake has assumed again its steady filling action, and at this date [Dec. 21, 1908] is 235 feet below the point of observation. Two nights ago the lake was nearly 250 feet deep.... The small rim of the lake is constantly being built up, and many small flows pour over the sides; last evening within three hours there were some eight overflows, many reaching the walls of the pit. There were three other centres of action at the rim of the lake where the continuous splashes of the fountains have formed spatter cones; one at the southwest corner, another at the north side, and the third, a heavy moving fountain, at the east corner.... Old Faithful was still in its old position, but only bubbling up every few minutes.

Mr. Baldwin also speaks of "traveling fountains" on July 26th, when Old Faithful started traveling in a westerly direction, followed quickly by another great fountain, until there were at one time four or five of these curious fountains. Some of these struck the shore under the observation point with great fury, splashing over the bank. I shall describe these more fully when I come to my own visit.

April 7, 1909. Professor T. A. Jaggar, Jr., records temperature of steam cracks. As his visit to these Islands was to ascertain the desirability of establishing such an observatory as the author has repeatedly advocated, he will doubtless publish his report, which will be more interesting than any such brief quotations of his recorded or spoken results. Soon after his visit, Dr. Tempest Anderson arrived at Kilauea, and after a brief visit joined the author in a hurried trip to the crater of Haleakala on Maui, where we camped in the crater two thousand feet below the rim, which rises some ten thousand feet above the sea. In the bottom are many cinder cones, some a thousand feet high, and of beautiful regularity; the sides often dotted with the beautiful "Silver-

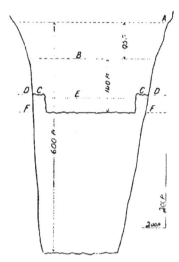

A. Observation point 279 ft. below V. H. floor.
B. Level of lava September 4, 1908.
C. Black ledge formed in October, 1908.
D. Level July 26, 1908.
E. Level October 7, 1909.
F. Level December 21, 1908.

FIG. 142. SECTION OF PIT. BALDWIN.

sword plant" (*Argyroxiphium sandwicense*), and the record of their eruption accentuated by volcanic bombs of beautiful regularity and divergent size, from a few inches to several feet in diameter. These bombs, so abundant here, are rare on the other Hawaiian volcanoes. Dr. Anderson took many photographs which it is to be hoped he will publish, for his great skill in this work was supplemented by very favorable weather. From Maui he went directly back to Kilauea, and has made the following record in the Register:

July 11, 1909. Dr. Tempest Anderson.—I have been here over three weeks at intervals during the last month. The place grows upon me, and the Volcano increases in interest. It is different from anything I have seen in the Old World, the West Indies, or in Central America. There one sees volcanoes building up piles of ashes and lava by explosions and outflow. Here explosion is subordinate, while there goes on also a process of solution and undermining which at present is more active than the building up. This is really the most striking difference noticeable. Beyond this the steadiness and restrained activity of Kilauea is remarkable. In regularity Stromboli in Europe compares; but in its case activity takes the form of frequent small explosions instead of a steady flow. The volcano I have seen most strictly comparable is Matavanu, that broke out in 1905 in Savaii, Samoa; in that case a river of molten lava flows in the bottom of the crater, enters a tunnel and runs underground several miles to the sea, into which it flows visibly by many changing mouths with the formation of vast clouds of steam. Matavanu, therefore, is certainly a river, while Kilauea may be either a river or a boiling pot. Characteristic of this whole region, and unknown to me elsewhere, are the pit craters so frequent here, and of which Kilauea and the crater of Mauna Loa [Mokuaweoweo] are prominent examples.

July 5-14, 1909. Rev. J. M. Lydgate made the plan on the opposite page; it will be noticed that the lava pool was at that time confined to a depression in the floor of the pit. Mr. Lydgate disclaims great accuracy, but his plan is substantially correct.

July 5-14, 1909. Miss M. E. Haskell.—During the first half of July the southeast part of the crater was clear enough of fumes for a descent. For additional data for the map [p. 219] a descent was made by Mr. J. M. Lydgate, with Prof. R. A. Daly, of the Massachusetts Institute of Technology, and Miss M. E. Haskell, of Boston. To the east of the Rest House, at the west end of the "Fallen-in area outlying crater," the descent began. In the external wall of the crater a cave was found five feet high by about eight by four or six, with stalactited roof and walls. The stalactites were of lava a finger-length or less, crusted with delicate white, tasteless crystals, some of which Mr. Daly collected for analysis. On the floor a white crystalline powder, with a soda taste, lay thick in patches; also collected for analysis. At the eastern end of the fallen area a rope was used for thirty feet of the descent to the first bench. Thence the trail is marked on the map. Some of the white stains conspicious on the precipitous walls on the south side from the Rest House and elsewhere were examined and found to consist of crystals similar in appearance to those in the cave. Fallen boulders from these walls were also whitened with the crystals in spots. The floor of the first and second benches is as chaotically upheaved as the roughest part of Kilauea the great. One pile, visible from the crater top, is like a spatter cone. The floor of the last bench, 49 feet above the molten lava, is covered with a crust but a few months old and comparatively smooth. Fumes all along the route were much lighter than their appearance from above led us to expect, and the last bench was quite clear. On July 19th, part of this bench above the southwest cave fell in and closed the cave, and on the first and second benches fumaroles opened near the trail and made descent impossible.

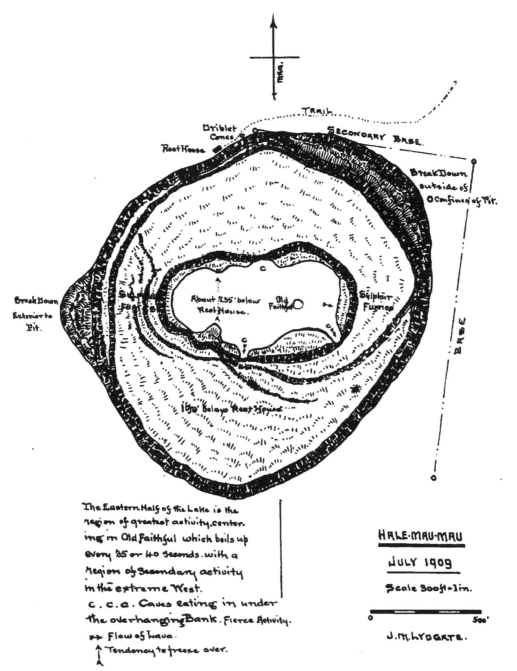

TRAIL

Driblet Cones

SECONDARY BASE.

Rest House

Break Down
outside of
O Confines of Pit.

Break Down
Exterior to
Pit.

About 235' below
Rest House.

c

Old
Faithful

Sulphur
Fumes

c

BASE

150' below Rest House

The Eastern Half of the Lake is the
region of greatest activity, center-
ing in Old Faithful which boils up
every 25 or 40 seconds. with a
region of Secondary activity
in the extreme West.

c. c. c. Caves eating in under
the overhanging Bank. Fierce Activity.

→ Flow of Lava.

↑ Tendency to freeze over.

HALE-MAU-MAU

JULY 1909

Scale 300ft=1in.

0   500'

J. M. LYDGATE.

FIG. 143.   PLAN OF HALEMAUMAU IN JULY, 1909.

Nevertheless some rash people ventured down at a time when the fumes were less abundant, and were there photographed by Mr. Moses, a photographer of Hilo.

In approaching the crater on the evening of October 6th, a bright glow was seen over the tree tops as the gloaming came on, and when we came out on the bank before the Volcano House the *beauty* of Kilauea appealed to me as never before. The whole diameter of Halemaumau was lighted up with a clear and almost uniform light, while from the central third arose an ever-changing and exquisitely graceful column to the height of many hundred feet, then expanding into the usual overhanging cloud. This column was by no means smoke, but a thin vapor only dense enough to reflect the color of the boiling lava below, and this vapor was controlled by constantly changing currents or intermittent supplies to spread and contract, curl and twist into most beautiful and attractive shapes. Not long, however, did the exhibition present itself, for the mists came between us and the pit like an old horn lantern, and we saw only the general glow all that night (October 6th). In the morning there was only the thin smoke coming irregularly from the whole surface of Halemaumau, but thicker and whiter than the abundant steam that arose from many parts of the main crater bottom as well as from the perennial cracks on the upper banks, for it had rained abundantly during the night.

I went early down into the crater to avoid company, for there is to me a solemn feeling of exhilaration in this grand temple of the living God that cannot be shared with strangers. At the very beginning of the descent my old friends the *elepaios* came flying to see, in their curiosity, who was the intruder, and they seemed almost to welcome me in their sweet notes. But once on the crater floor and the stillness was complete, even the breezes were silent, it seemed out of tune to break it with the crunch of one's tread on the lava. I paused on the bridge over the great crack and distinctly heard the dropping, on the deep bottom of the water resulting from last night's rain; the water at this end of the path made more noise than the fire at the other. As I approached the pit I turned to the left and came upon the brink where the downfall of the wall had occurred, so that only two-thirds of the pool could be seen, and little of the heat felt. It was well not to see the whole at once. Strangely it was not the wonderful cauldron of boiling lava that first caught my attention. On the high western wall that faced me was an opening, as the mouth of a tunnel, half way up the almost perpendicular wall. It was very regular and apparently about ten feet high and twelve feet wide. That was on a part of the wall exposed during my previous visit about a year ago, but it was not there then. Its black mouth indicated some depth, but although the sun was behind me I could see but a very little way in, and this was the sort of duct I had always imagined the pit would disclose if emptied; and yet, I had repeatedly seen the empty pit and never a conduit of such size, if indeed any, that could be considered passages for the retreating lava while the pit was emptying itself.

On the outer walls of the pit was the line distinctly marking the surface before the fall of September 4th of last year; below this, on the south side, was a series of dislocated benches like seat rows in an amphitheatre, but inclined at various angles to the horizontal; on the eastern side was the large mass of wall which had sunk perhaps a hundred feet as shown on the survey of Mr. Lydgate, and over this (of which the inner edge is much the higher) was the most comfortable, although not the most extensive, view of the molten pool, the heat at the usual point of observation being altogether unbearable.

This pool, to most visitors the great attraction of Kilauea, was, as we had supposed from the brilliant light reflected from the clouds the night before, in a remarkable state of activity. Not a sign of the alternate crusting over and breaking up so common a phenomenon on former visits to Halemaumau; all was in violent and excessive commotion within the banks of the great pool. At first the current controling the whole surface was strong towards the east bank, moving, as I estimated, at the rate of five miles an hour, but others visiting the pool on the same day at a later hour trebled this estimate. It seemed as if the molten contents were pouring out, and one looked at the opposite rim to note a subsidence, but there was none. Over the entire surface were jets by many score, not like the fountains seen when lava breaks from the mountain side or from the bottom of Mokuaweoweo, but jets more like those shown in Plate LX of Dana Lake. These were of varying diameter, but perhaps averaged twelve feet in height. All were moving in the current, but apparently independent of it in some degree, for frequently those behind would overtake the next in advance, melt into its substance and continue with accelerated speed: this action was repeated until perhaps ten were gathered into one great sheaf, increased in height as well as in diameter until the united mass was fifteen or more feet high and ten feet in diameter, when it dashed violently against the bank, throwing spatters on to the bench above and spinning abundance of Pele's hair from the drops. All the trail shown on Mr. Lydgate's map was covered by the splashes.'[19]

These "traveling fountains," mentioned before by Mr. Baldwin, were new to me in all my observations of the Kilauean pools. Pele had not exhausted her repertoire, and presently some large, almost flat, floating islands appeared on the western margin. Whence they came was not evident, but they were very black, perhaps a hundred feet by fifty and appeared to be launched from the brilliant glow on the west coast. They had not floated a hundred yards from the shore before the jets (which I likened

---

[19] This trail was marked in the copy of the map in the Register, but does not appear on the copy he sent me, which was used for the illustration.

to dogs pursuing and jumping at their prey), seemed to bite mouthfuls from the sides until the mass seemed to writhe in pain, and near the midst of the pool a larger fountain, perhaps "Old Faithful," rose suddenly and swallowed what of the island the side skirmishers had left.   Three other islands of similar size and form met the same fate before I started around the brink to discover the point of origin of these perishing islands, but on the journey round, the pool was not visible, and when, after some delays on the way to photograph the spatter-cones, the west bank was again in sight, the motion had reversed and the current was running as rapidly as before in the opposite direction, and no islands were on the surface.   I looked for flames, but saw none.   The vapors were at times very transparent, then of a bluish tinge, and again opaque and smoky.   There was less noise than usual, for there were no falling crusts, only liquid lava.   I was sorry not to see the reversal of current, but at former visits (when, however, the motion was by no means so rapid) the change was made with very little disturbance and little slackening of speed.   The currents are a more common phenemenon but the speed is usually much less than at present; the apparently causeless change of direction is also familiar.

The pool seemed somewhat larger than when measured by Mr. Lydgate, but still was not filling the bottom of the pit, and did not seem much higher.   I tried to see what changes appeared in the surface of the boiling pool with the changes from clear to smoky fumes emitted, but the change was so gradual that no change was noted.   On my way back to the Volcano House I passed a hot place on the trail about halfway between the pit and the bottom of the path down the bank, which I did not notice in the morning.   From the first level stretch on the rising path there is a good view of the dome-like bottom of the crater.   I had no means of measurement, but I do not feel deceived in thinking that this dome is at least fifty feet higher than it was last year.   I have never seen the dome shape so distinct, and it seemed ready to overtop the western outer wall.   When I first came to the spatter cones near the Rest House, I noticed a large cloud of steam issuing from near the base of Uwekahuna, but on my return two hours later it had disappeared; probably the effect of the rains during the previous night.

As the sunlight faded the beautiful peach blossom tint appeared on the vapor over the fire, and it deepened into red and orange as the night came on, until the wonderful effects of the previous night were surpassed.

[600]

PLATES

PLATE XLI.

Two views taken from nearly the same position on a small stream near Hilo, during the eruption of 1880-81. In the first the lava flow has just reached the brink of what was a small waterfall: this has been boiled up and the molten rock is taking its place for a fall of some twenty-five feet. By daylight the falling lava looked dull red or black, but at night resembled more a flow of blood. During the night the pool was dissipated in steam, and the second view shows the pool utterly obliterated by the lava. This is by no means an uncommon occurrence in the Hilo region where the water courses are often in the path of the descending lava stream.

PLATE XLII.

A descent into Halemaumau when the lava in the foreground was too hot to step upon. Very little vapor was present and no sulphurous fumes.

PLATE XLII.

PLATE XLIII.

The upper figure shows "The Three Sentinels," spent blow-holes on the north edge of Halemaumau. Although taken several years ago, the photograph well represents the present condition of these cones.

The lower view was made by the author a few years ago of the surface over-flow from Halemaumau falling into the break at the east side of "Little Beggar."

PLATE XLIV.

Two views of pools in Halemaumau. The upper shows the self-made embankment formed of crusts and over-flows. Note the absence of steam or other vapor over the active pool. The lower shows the dam separating the pools. The surface of the lava seems smooth as water.

PLATE XLV.

A cone in Halemaumau : note the outer wall of precisely the same material.

The lava pool below the rim of Halemaumau.   The surface near the shore is hard and accessible.   Little vapor rises from the central portion which is active.

PLATE XLVI.

A portion of drawn out cooling lava from lava-fall.

PLATE XLVII.

A small mass of a-a, natural size.

•
PLATE XLVIII.

A cave stalagmite of the slender variety. Broken from the floor of a cave in Kilauea.

PLATE XLIX.

The broader form of cave stalagmite from Kilauea. The drops near the bottom seem to be hollow, and have been broken in extracting the specimen from the cave floor. This form is less common than the last.

PLATE XLIX.

PLATE L.

POOL IN HALEMAUMAU.

The raised lake in March, 1894. Note the extent of escaping steam from the upper edge of the Halemaumau pit, which is more widely diffused owing to previous rain. There is little escape of steam from the lake surface, and that is concentrated in two places. While the overflow of the lava is irregular, the general level of the rim is preserved. The stone blocks in the foreground mark the trail.

PLATE L.

PLATE LI.

VIEW OF POOL IN HALEMAUMAU FROM BELOW.

View taken on March 20, 1894. It shows well the overflows which make the present floor of Kilauea.

CRATER OF KILAUEA.
MARCH 20, 1894.

PLATE LII.

POOL IN HALEMAUMAU.

Showing the pool of the previous plate, but from a slight elevation. The level surface of the pool indicates the curvature of the crater floor in the neighborhood.

PLATE LII.

PLATE LIII.

THE SOUTH LAKE AND ISLAND.

The elevated region around Halemaumau at this time was very irregular, and the lava crust around the rim of the pools was much cracked. The cone on the right was difficult of access. The stranded island is distinctly shown.

PLATE LIV.

CONE IN HALEMAUMAU.

A small pool of lava is seen at the base of the cone. The abundant sulphurous vapors made the ascent of this cone very unpleasant and even dangerous. The rim of Halemaumau is seen in the middle distance.

PLATE LV.

CONE IN HALEMAUMAU.

Note the loose rectangular blocks and apparent layers in the mass of the cone.

PLATE LV.

PLATE LVI.

CONE IN HALEMAUMAU.

At this time five hundred feet high and perhaps two thousand feet in diameter.

PLATE LVI.

PLATE LVII.

THE EMPTY PIT.

The edge of Halemaumau after the descent of the cone. The walls are not perforated by galleries, nor is there any visible exit at the bottom. At times the conical pit was free from smoky vapors for hours, although hot air was continually rising.

PLATE LVII.

PLATE LVIII.

On the brink of the pit.   Note the walls built up by successive overflows.

PLATE LVIII.

PLATE LIX.

The peculiarly cracked condition of the lava in the foreground is probably due to the rise and fall of these banks, of which portions are ready to break off and form islands.

PLATE LX.

DANA LAKE.

This small lake, which was a side issue of the main pool, and of little depth, showed all the phenomena of the main pool, and the lava fountain in the foreground is very characteristic of these outbreaks. The deep red color of the jets appears black in the photograph. Taken by J. J. Williams.

PLATE LXI.

SOUTH LAKE.

Note the great extent of smooth surface.   Accessible as shown in the foreground.

PLATE LXI.

PLATE LXII.

The so-called floating islands—portions of the cooled crust or of the broken banks. These islands lasted for some time, and when the pool was drained grounded on the bottom.

PLATE LXII.

PLATE LXIII.

A FLOW OF AA.

The flow moves slowly onward, tumbling the rough masses of all sizes of which it is composed, and seldom shows any signs of liquid lava except possibly here and there at the lower edges.

PLATE LXIII.

PLATE LXIV.

The source of the flow of 1880–1881 after the violence had ceased. The molten lava is issuing quietly from cracks on the summit of the flow. This well illustrates the outflow from cracks below the initial spatter cone or cones. The cones are shown in the sketch by Furneaux given in the text.

PLATE LXV.

A crack in the floor of Kilauea. This would illustrate the so-called canals spoken of by Rev. T. Coan and others. These cracks, if opening slowly, make little noise; but a sudden crack is accompanied by a sound like the discharge of a great gun.

PLATE LXVI.

D. Howard Hitchcock's painting of Kilauea in 1896, with the raised rim of Halemaumau to the right of the centre. This is in the picture gallery of the Museum.

PLATE LXVI.

PLATE LXVII.

The crater of Mokuaweoweo, on the summit of Mauna Loa, during the eruption of 1896. From a painting by D. Howard Hitchcock, now in the picture gallery of this Museum. The snow cap has melted on the lee side of the crater. Mauna Kea, snow-capped, appears on the right.

PLATE LXVII

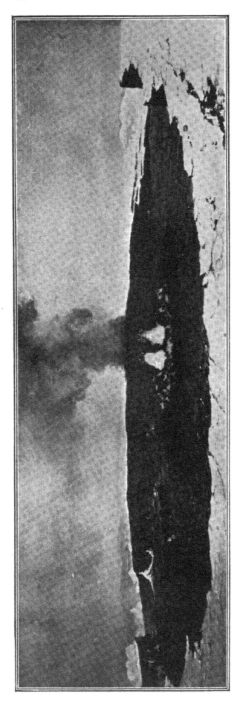

. . . .
. . THE
. OF CALIFORNIA
.LA. C LIF

scripps institution of oceanography
LIBRARY
University of California, San Diego

*Please Note: This item is subject to
RECALL after two weeks if requested
by another borrower.*

DATE DUE

NOV 22 1982	
NOV 7 REC'D	
APR 2 1987	
MAR 13 REC'D	
MAR 16 REC'D	
NOV 30 1988	
NOV 30 REC'D	

SI 23   *UCSD Libr.*

CPSIA information can be obtained
at www.ICGtesting.com
Printed in the USA
LVHW06s1126041018
592271LV00023BA/134/P